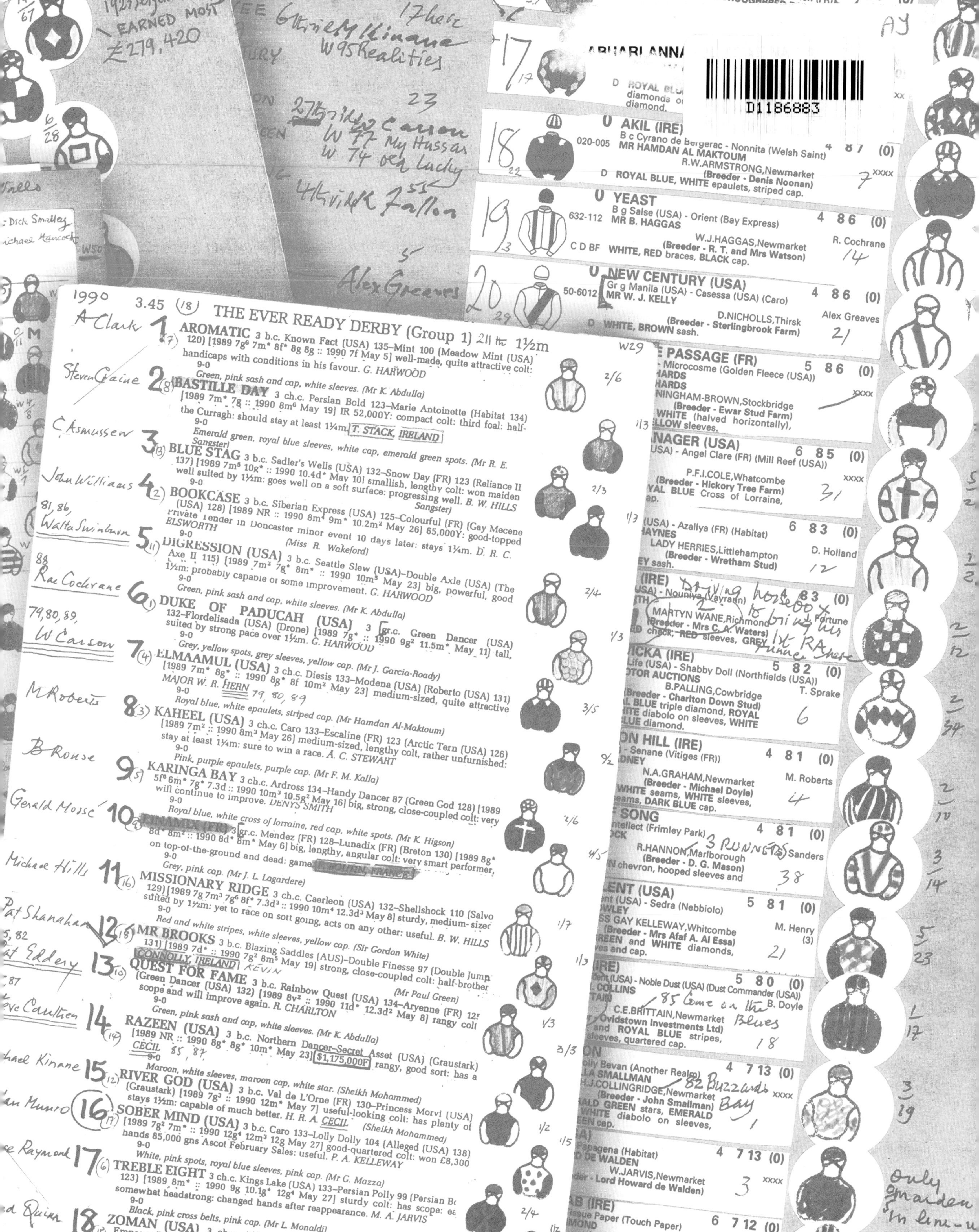

1990 3.45 (18) THE EVER READY DERBY (Group 1) 1½m

1 AROMATIC 3 b.c. Known Fact (USA) 135–Mint 100 (Meadow Mint (USA) 120) [1989 7g⁶ 7m* 8f* 8g 8g :: 1990 7f May 5] well-made, quite attractive colt: handicaps with conditions in his favour. G. HARWOOD
9-0
Green, pink sash and cap, white sleeves. (Mr K. Abdulla)

2 BASTILLE DAY 3 ch.c. Persian Bold 123–Marie Antoinette (Habitat 134) [1989 7m* 7g :: 1990 8m⁶ May 19] IR 52,000Y: compact colt: third foal: half-brother ... the Curragh: should stay at least 1¼m. T. STACK, IRELAND
9-0
Emerald green, royal blue sleeves, white cap, emerald green spots. (Mr R. E. Sangster)

3 BLUE STAG 3 b.c. Sadler's Wells (USA) 132–Snow Day (FR) 123 (Reliance II 137) [1989 7m⁵ 10g* :: 1990 10.4d* May 10] smallish, lengthy colt: won maiden ... well suited by 1½m: goes well on a soft surface: progressing well. B. W. HILLS
9-0
(Mr R. E. Sangster)

4 BOOKCASE 3 b.c. Siberian Express (USA) 125–Colourful (FR) (Gay Mecene (USA) 128) [1989 NR :: 1990 8m⁴ 9m* 10.2m² May 26] 65,000Y: good-topped ... Private Tender in Doncaster minor event 10 days later: stays 1¼m. D. R. C. ELSWORTH
9-0
(Miss R. Wakeford)

5 DIGRESSION (USA) 3 b.c. Seattle Slew (USA)–Double Axle (USA) (The Axe II 115) [1989 7m² 7g* 8m* :: 1990 10m³ May 23] big, powerful, good ... 1½m: probably capable of some improvement. G. HARWOOD
9-0
Green, pink sash and cap, white sleeves. (Mr K. Abdulla)

6 DUKE OF PADUCAH (USA) 3 gr.c. Green Dancer (USA) 132–Flordelisada (USA) (Drone) [1989 7g* :: 1990 9g² 11.5m* May 11] tall, ... suited by strong pace over 1½m. G. HARWOOD
9-0
Grey, yellow spots, grey sleeves, yellow cap. (Mr J. Garcia-Roady)

7 ELMAAMUL (USA) 3 ch.c. Diesis 133–Modena (USA) (Roberto (USA) 131) [1989 7m* 8g* :: 1990 8g* 8f 10m² May 23] medium-sized, quite attractive ... MAJOR W. R. HERN
9-0
Royal blue, white epaulets, striped cap. (Mr Hamdan Al-Maktoum)

8 KAHEEL (USA) 3 ch.c. Caro 133–Escaline (FR) 123 (Arctic Tern (USA) 126) [1989 7m² :: 1990 8m³ May 26] medium-sized, lengthy colt, rather unfurnished: stay at least 1¼m: sure to win a race. A. C. STEWART
9-0
Pink, purple epaulets, purple cap. (Mr F. M. Kalla)

9 KARINGA BAY 3 ch.c. Ardross 134–Handy Dancer 87 (Green God 128) [1989 5f⁶ 6m* 7g* 7.3d :: 1990 10m³ 10.5g² May 16] big, strong, close-coupled colt: very ... will continue to improve. DENYS SMITH
9-0
Royal blue, white cross of lorraine, red cap, white spots. (Mr K. Higson)

10 FINAMIX (FR) 3 gr.c. Mendez (FR) 128–Lunadix (FR) (Breton 130) [1989 8g* 8d* 8m² :: 1990 8d* 8m* May 6] big, lengthy, angular colt: very smart performer, on top-of-the-ground and dead: game. P. BOUTIN, FRANCE
9-0
Grey, pink cap. (Mr J. L. Lagardere)

11 MISSIONARY RIDGE 3 ch.c. Caerleon (USA) 132–Shellshock 110 (Salvo 129) [1989 7g 7m³ 7g⁶ 8f* 7.3d³ :: 1990 10m⁴ 12.3d³ May 8] sturdy, medium-sized ... suited by 1½m: yet to race on soft going, acts on any other: useful. B. W. HILLS
9-0
Red and white stripes, white sleeves, yellow cap. (Sir Gordon White)

12 MR BROOKS 3 b.c. Blazing Saddles (AUS)–Double Finesse 97 (Double Jump 131) [1989 7d* :: 1990 7g² 8m⁵ May 19] strong, close-coupled colt: half-brother ... CONNOLLY, IRELAND
9-0
(Mr Paul Green)

13 QUEST FOR FAME 3 b.c. Rainbow Quest (USA) 134–Aryenne (FR) 125 (Green Dancer (USA) 132) [1989 8v² :: 1990 11d* 12.3d² May 8] rangy colt ... scope and will improve again. R. CHARLTON
9-0
Green, pink sash and cap, white sleeves. (Mr K. Abdulla)

14 RAZEEN (USA) 3 b.c. Northern Dancer–Secret Asset (USA) (Graustark) [1989 NR :: 1990 8g* 8g* 10m* May 23] $1,175,000F rangy, good sort: has a ... CECIL
9-0
Maroon, white sleeves, maroon cap, white star. (Sheikh Mohammed)

15 RIVER GOD (USA) 3 b.c. Val de L'Orne (FR) 130–Princess Morvi (USA) (Graustark) [1989 7g³ :: 1990 12m* May 7] useful-looking colt: has plenty of ... stays 1½m: capable of much better. H. R. A. CECIL
9-0
(Sheikh Mohammed)

16 SOBER MIND (USA) 3 ch.c. Caro 133–Lolly Dolly 104 (Alleged (USA) 138) [1989 7g² 7m* :: 1990 12g⁴ 12m³ 12g May 27] good-quartered colt: won £8,300 ... hands 85,000 gns Ascot February Sales: useful. P. A. KELLEWAY
9-0
White, pink spots, royal blue sleeves, pink cap. (Mr G. Mazza)

17 TREBLE EIGHT 3 ch.c. Kings Lake (USA) 133–Persian Polly 99 (Persian Bold 123) [1989 8m* :: 1990 9g 10.1g* 12g⁴ May 27] sturdy colt: has scope: ... somewhat headstrong: changed hands after reappearance. M. A. JARVIS
9-0
Black, pink cross belts, pink cap. (Mr L. Monaldi)

18 ZOMAN (USA) 3 ch.c. Affirmed (USA) ... Emperor (USA)) [1989 ...

18 0 AKIL (IRE) 020-005 B c Cyrano de Bergerac - Nonnita (Welsh Saint) 4 8 7 (0)
MR HAMDAN AL MAKTOUM
R.W.ARMSTRONG, Newmarket
(Breeder - Denis Noonan)
D ROYAL BLUE, WHITE epaulets, striped cap.

19 0 YEAST 632-112 B g Salse (USA) - Orient (Bay Express) 4 8 6 (0)
MR B. HAGGAS
W.J.HAGGAS, Newmarket R. Cochrane
(Breeder - R. T. and Mrs Watson)
C D BF WHITE, RED braces, BLACK cap.

20 0 NEW CENTURY (USA) 50-6012 Gr g Manila (USA) - Casessa (USA) (Caro) 4 8 6 (0)
MR W. J. KELLY
D.NICHOLLS, Thirsk Alex Greaves
(Breeder - Sterlingbrook Farm)
D WHITE, BROWN sash.

Peter O'Sullevan's

HORSE RACING HEROES

MIXER
3:20

Peter O'Sullevan's

HORSE RACING HEROES

SIR PETER O'SULLEVAN CBE

Published in 2004 by Highdown
an imprint of Raceform Ltd
Compton, Newbury, Berkshire, RG20 6NL
Raceform Ltd is a wholly-owned subsidiary of Trinity Mirror plc

A catalogue record of this book is available from the British Library.

ISBN 1-904317-75-8

Designed by Tracey Scarlett
Printed by Rotolito, Italy

INTRODUCTION

As a longtime compulsive hero-worshipper it is at once a privilege and an indulgence to recall with admiration and affection a dozen of the players, equine and human, who have enriched the life of this devout aficionado throughout more than half a century's involvement in the multicoloured mini-world of horse racing.

I owe a debt of gratitude to many who have responded generously to my queries; sought to repair my typewriter, and offered welcome words of encouragement during the past few months.

However, reluctant to exhaust the patience and stamina of any potential reader before the 'off', so to speak, I am limiting identification to a trio, or three and a bit: Julian Muscat whose skill in raking through the embers of my memory has been invaluable; Pat, my wife, whose forbearance has been matched only by that of our understanding, under-exercised poodle, Topo; and the ubiquitous Seán Magee, with his acute accent and acute eye.

Called upon at the proof-reading stage to fulfil the role of long-stop, Seán immediately became indispensable wicket-keeper.

The errors which, hopefully, are limited, would have been extravagantly multiplied without his intervention.

Peter O'Sullevan

July 23 2004

Contents

ARKLE

Once in a while, among the tens of thousands of potential racehorses born annually worldwide, a tiny foal will rise unsteadily on spindly legs which are destined to carry him/her to celebrity far beyond the normal perimeter of the sport.

When farmer Henry Baker's widow Alison, of Malahow, decided to send her talented mare Bright Cherry to be mated with the impeccably bred, but racewise undistinguished stallion, Archive, whose modest fee was 48 guineas, she did so, like all relatively small-time breeders, more in a spirit of well rehearsed hope than confidence.

Just as well: for when Bright Cherry foaled at Ballymacoll Stud, Co Meath, on 19 April 1957, her son, who was to be named Arkle, offered not the faintest shred of evidence that, within seven years, the Rules of Racing would need to be rewritten to accommodate his talent.

The Arkle statue at Cheltenham racecourse.

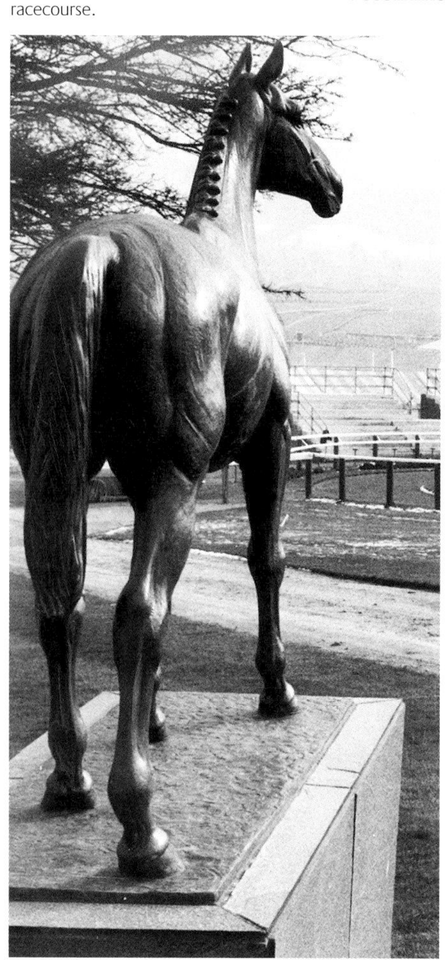

No more impressive in action than he was in repose the bay gelding, now three years old, was sent to the local bloodstock sales on 4 August 1960 with no great reluctance by Alison Baker and with a reserve of 500 guineas.

The charming, urbane, Co Dublin trainer Tom Dreaper, who handled the equine aspirations of a Debrettful of owners on both sides of the Irish Sea, took a passing interest in the gangly gelding for family reasons. He had won a bumper (Flat race run under jumping rules) on Bright Cherry's prolific winner-producing dam, Greenogue Princess, in an era when these races served as a pleasant introduction for young stock rather than the cut-throat events they were to become before the turn of the century.

He mentioned to one of his patrons, Anne, Duchess of Westminster, that she might care to have a look at him. Meanwhile a renowned English horse-fancier Captain Charles Radclyffe – like the Duchess, a good friend of Queen Elizabeth the Queen Mother – was trying to determine what it was that instinctively appealed to him about this clearly unexceptional individual. Standing at opposite ends of the sales ring, both Tom and Charles bid discreetly.

A final barely perceptible inclination of Tom's trademark pipe and the lot was his at 1,150 guineas.

Anne, Duchess of Westminster, formerly Miss Nancy Sullivan of Co Cork, picked up the tab, introduced the young horse to the mints with a hole in the middle and packed him off to her Cheshire estate and a private tutor.

Arkle (named after a Sutherland mountain adjacent to his owner's Scottish property) proved himself to be a bright, intelligent pupil. Confident and inquisitive, he returned to the country of his birth and Tom Dreaper's Kilsallaghan stables 18 months later.

It cannot be said that his physique inspired more expectation than apprehension. Consequently the competition among the long-serving stable personnel to 'do' Arkle was limited to a point of non-existence and his needs were cared for by a newcomer, Johnny Lumley, who thereby inherited a golden chalice.

Mark Hely-Hutchinson partnered our hero in his first two races (third in a Mullingar bumper; fourth at Leopardstown) after which Lord Donoughmore's son offered a neat line in self deprecation, 'boasting' a single claim to fame; namely to have been the only one of five to have ridden the great horse without winning on him.

For the record, the other scores were:

Liam McLoughlin – 3 rides; 1 win
Tommy 'T.P.' Burns – 1 ride; 1 win
Paddy Woods – 1 ride; 1 win
Pat Taaffe – a remarkable 28 rides; 24 wins

I would like to be able to write that the first time I saw Arkle (25 October 1962) I 'knew' that here was something special.

Unfortunately that would be right up there with some of the biggest rubbish I ever penned or dictated during 37 years with the *Daily Express*.

I'd paid a fleeting day visit to the Co Kilkenny course Gowran Park (whose ebullient director,

Left: Pat Taaffe and Arkle at Newbury for the Hennessy Gold Cup.

Jack Duggan, observed to me drily on attending the opening of Ascot's steeplechasing circuit, 'This is so good it could become the Gowran of England'!) to scout for Irish-trained Grand National prospects.

OK, Arkle won the supporting President's Handicap Hurdle very readily. But, even including a 4lb penalty for previous success at Dundalk, he was getting no less than 23lbs from that good mare and fellow five-year-old Height O'Fashion.

Pat Taaffe, who was there as a spectator as he could not do the required 10st 5lbs, used to come to the O'Sullevan Chelsea flat at times to be driven to meetings such as Cheltenham. Thus, said some, confirming his lack of nerve.

He had a particularly soft voice and, as with Lester Piggott, I often found it difficult to catch every word. But there was no mistaking the aside at Gowran, 'Wait while you see this fellow jump a fence'. The wait was not a long one.

Although Arkle had given Pat an uncharacteristic crushing fall when warming up over hurdles prior to his first serious 'school' over fences, the pilot was deeply impressed by his partner's handling of the big ones, and felt that he'd learnt a lesson that would not be forgotten.

Accompanying the stable's winning Mackeson favourite, Fortria, to Cheltenham on 17 November 1962 for his first 'chasing experience, Arkle (11-8) seemed almost embarrassed by his effortless 20 lengths superiority over the nearest of his 11 opponents in the 2½-mile Honeybourne Chase.

If all the horses who 'Could win a Gold Cup one day', stood head to tail, the line would stretch from Limerick to Lambourn – and back.

Still, even with another potential legend on the horizon in the contrastingly heavyweight shape of England's adopted Irish-born son, Mill House, bookmakers' odds against Arkle ever striking gold were already unappealingly defensive.

Come the 1963 Cheltenham Festival and the rain-soaked terrain (responsible for the abandonment of the Monday's nearby Worcester card) was barely raceable.

It did not prevent Arkle from sluicing up in the three miles Broadway Novices' – beating the Jimmy Fitzgerald-ridden subsequent Scottish National winner, Brasher, by 24 lengths.

Neither did it dim the brilliance of 'The Big Horse', Mill House, who was hailed by his ever growing fan club as the Golden Miller of the future after triumph in the Gold Cup by 12 lengths from the mud-hating Fortria.

The 'big two' would have their first encounter eight months later.

In the interim Mill House had one more run (back at Newbury) on 20 April 1963 when, under 12st 5lbs in very heavy ground, he hacked up by 8 lengths – giving the runner-up 33lbs.

Arkle reappeared twice that season, turning the prestigious Power Gold Cup (Fairyhouse) and Punchestown's John Jameson into virtual processions.

Prior to the Hennessy on 30 November 1963, Tom Dreaper sent Arkle down to Gowran for the 2½ miles Carey's Cottage Handicap Chase (24 October) as a post-summer holiday livener.

There were those who believed that the concession of up to 34lbs to some race-fit, quite useful rivals would be beyond him. They were wrong by 10 lengths – minimum.

In the 'Brandy Stakes' the English handicapper assessed Mill House (12.0) 5lbs above Arkle (11.9). Personally I found it difficult to envisage any horse being capable of lowering the Westminster colours on these terms. Pat Taaffe had ridden twice previously in the Hennessy; both times on beaten Irish-trained favourites (Zonda, second in 1960, and Olympia, fourth in 1961). Hence the 'lead' to my copy on 30 November (*see right*).

DAILY EXPRESS

IT'S ARKLE TO LAND £5,000 FOR THE IRISH

By Peter O'Sullevan

It may be third time lucky for Pat Taaffe, and a first Hennessy Gold Cup triumph for the Irish when Arkle (2.10) and Mill House clash in this afternoon's eagerly anticipated seventh running of the £5,000-plus 'chase.

The remarkable Fulke Walwyn record in the race which was inaugurated at Cheltenham in 1957 is three firsts and a third with the only three horses he has run – Mandarin (winner 1957 and 1961), Taxidermist (winner 1958; third 1961), and Team Spirit.

The Lambourn pride Mill House may well embellish the Saxon House record.

But it is the fact that Arkle goes to post with the benefit of a previous public run this season that influences me to favour him.

That and the Gowran Park evidence that he goes in the soft – and might even be a match for his ex-Irish rival at levels anyway ...

DAILY EXPRESS

Losing jockey takes flying holiday

By Peter O'Sullevan

Willie Robinson will be taking a holiday at Pat Taaffe's expense after this afternoon's Gold Cup. At least, that is Pat's firm opinion.

For over dinner in Cheltenham last night, the respective partners of the great protagonists, Mill House and Arkle, agreed that the rider of the winner (a bare 10 per cent of first prize-money comes to £800) would pay for 'an airline ticket to romantic places' for the loser.

'That Willie will be taking the trip all right,' affirmed Pat, indicating his four-years-younger rival and firm friend.

But the quiet man, who'll be aboard the 'big horse', could find no ground for his adversary's assumption.

By way of reply he sent for a timetable to learn the precise cost of a flight which he would inevitably be required to underwrite ...

The bare result of an encounter diminished as a spectacle by fog read:

1. Mill House 6.12-0 15-8 fav
G. W. Robinson

2. Happy Spring 7.10-0
100-9 8 lengths J. Lehane

3. Arkle 6.11-9 5-2 ¾ length
P. Taaffe

Irrespective of excuses advanced on behalf of the second favourite, Mill House had staged a fine performance.

From this commentator's viewpoint Arkle was unquestionably closing on the long-time leader approaching the third last fence where he lost his footing on landing and forfeited all impetus.

The extent to which this affected the outcome was a matter of conjecture. Which was abundant.

Mill House went on to win the King George VI Chase, followed by Sandown's Gainsborough Chase, without breaking sweat.

Arkle returned to Ireland to collect three more prizes – two at Leopardstown and Gowran's Thyestes Chase – under circumstances which confirmed his breathtaking talent.

On Thursday, 5 March, 1964 Mill House's versatile partner, Willie Robinson, and Arkle's staunch ally, Pat Taaffe, joined me for dinner at the modest but grandly-titled Carlton Hotel, Cheltenham, where we were staying for the Festival.

Neither of the lifelong friends could seriously envisage the possibility of defeat in what was to be the 39th running of the Gold Cup on Saturday. Not that either expressed himself in braggartly manner; for there is no more effective conduit to humility than lifetime association with racing.

From a personal viewpoint an eternal problem was created by the requirement to file 'copy' for the *Daily Express* immediately after the last race, having been isolated in a commentary box, working for the BBC, during most of the afternoon.

My aim was to have a 'story' ready for the next day 18 hours, or more, in advance.

I suggested over dinner that Pat and Willie came to a (notional) understanding that the loser on Saturday paid for a luxury holiday for the winner.

Given the generous and sporting nature of my friends, compliance was assured, as I reported on race morning (*see above left*).

Tipping-wise my heart and instinct favoured Arkle; the head and logic said, 'The Big Horse'.

Each race needs to be evaluated on its merits. Refraining from 'investment' I went with logic.

In his excellent chronicle *Arkle: The Story of a Champion*, Ivor Herbert reproduced several of my commentaries. By the time the contest for the '64 renewal developed in earnest, both Pas Seul, Gold Cup hero in 1960 and second the following year, and King's Nephew – the winner of 10 'chases, including the latest Great Yorkshire under 11st 10lbs – had faded far out of contention.

While I was saying, 'Coming down to the third last and it is still Mill House by 2 lengths from Arkle', I was *thinking*, 'You've done it all wrong here, son.'

Pat already had Irish heartbeats poised for acceleration.

Come the second last they were upsides. Rounding the home turn Willie picked up his whip. 'The Big Horse' kept going bravely, but his relatively lightweight adversary was already contemplating the extra two pints of Guinness which would lace his evening feed. 'It's gonna be Arkle if he jumps it,' I heard myself call as the Duchess' pride and joy bounded to and over the final fence and streaked up the hill; 'This is the champion,' I offered expendably, 'this is the best we've seen for a long time.'

As the triumphant duo returned to a tumultuous ovation, the judge posted the winning margin – 5 lengths. Never again, irrespective of weight concession, would the Lambourn giant get within single figures of Ireland's amazing hero.

For the record, they met three times following the 1964 Gold Cup:

1964 Hennessy (Newbury): Arkle gave Mill House 3lbs, beat him 28 lengths

1965 Cheltenham Gold Cup: Arkle met Mill House at levels, beat him 20 lengths

1965 Gallaher (Sandown): Arkle gave Mill House 16lbs, beat him 24 lengths

Nevertheless, it must be recorded that under a fine, sensitive ride by David Nicholson, Mill House overcame the demoralising impact of those defeats, as well as the physical problems which tested to the utmost the renowned skill of his handler, Fulke Walwyn, by earning an emotional ovation after victory in the 1967 Whitbread following a great exhibition round at Sandown.

Meanwhile the Irish stewards had already taken an unprecedented step in a bid to cater for Arkle's awesome talent.

They instructed the handicapper to compile two sets of weights whenever Arkle was entered. One to take effect if he ran, the other if he absented. He still won the Irish National, three weeks after his first Gold Cup, giving 30lbs and a 1¼-length beating to that tough, useful mare Height O'Fashion.

Yes, the same Height O'Fashion who had been required to concede him 23lbs over hurdles 18 months earlier. A turn around of more than 4 stone! And Arkle had been 2-1 ON to do it.

In fact the great horse started odds-on when winning no fewer than 20 of his 27 races.

A statistic which reminds me of the 1966 Hennessy – a year after he'd won the Newbury showpiece by 15 lengths at 6-1 on, when giving that grand little horse, Freddie, twice 'National runner-up under substantial weight, 32lbs.

Pat and Arkle acclaimed after the 1964 Gold Cup.

The latter race had been followed by a hat-trick which included a canter round Cheltenham for a third (30 lengths) Gold Cup victory.

Come Newbury '66, the bookmakers' intelligence service, which is widely regarded to have no superior, suggested that the world's top 'chaser had over-indulged himself during his annual summer leave with the Duchess; that he was fat to a point of obesity and surely could not be 'ready' by 26 November. Further, the ebullient Captain Ryan Price was in a mood for hat consuming if any eligible quadruped could give the stable's race-fit representative, What a Myth, 33lbs and a beating.

In the interest of both my readers, and with an unworthy thought for myself, I telephoned Tom Dreaper for enlightenment. I got Paddy Woods.

Even allowing for the natural bias of the man who rode and monitored the well-being of Arkle every day, Paddy's report was infectiously enthusiastic. He was not only totally convinced of the horse's fitness but firmly persuaded that, 'He is better now than he ever has been.'

I believe that punters who impose restrictions on themselves – never betting odds-on, for example – act against their own interest.

The only limitation should be never bet beyond capacity to pay.

Recent winner What a Myth apart, there were four more race-fit runners opposing my 'good

Arkle after winning the Cheltenham Gold Cup in 1964.

thing', including the 13-race-winning grey, Stalbridge Colonist, who had never run this distance (3¼ miles) but on whom Stan Mellor was plotting the favourite's downfall.

Nobody rides 1,000 jumping winners without being a talented practitioner and Stan, who could arrange for a horse to shift the balance of his weight, while at full stretch, like no other before or since, was always a worrying opponent.

He knew that Pat would want to give Arkle as easy a race as possible in view of his lengthy absence. So over the last three fences he sat in the favourite's slipstream waiting, just out of eyeline, for Pat to look around approaching the last. As soon as he'd done so Stan flew; hurtled with devastating impetus into the last; gained half a length in the air and virtually sealed the race in that instant.

Almost shamefaced after his triumph, Stan explained, 'I wanted to give Pat the impression that there was no danger ... it was one time I think I got it right in a race ... we did, in a sense, cheat Arkle.' Adding, 'I say that by way of underlining *his* greatness – not mine!'

Stalbridge Colonist, who was in receipt of 35lbs that day, went on to pay his own tribute by finishing second (beaten ¾-length) in the 1967 Gold Cup and third in the Cheltenham 'classic' (beaten a neck and 1 length) the following year. What a Myth, who had been third at Newbury, himself won the Gold Cup in '69.

Personally, while haemorrhaging financially, I gave the Hennessy finale full throttle as the 25-1 outsider held on by half a length. The next week a disenchanted television viewer wrote of his disgust at my commentary, from which it was patently obvious I had backed the winner, and requesting that I eschew such blatant bias in the future.

Arkle himself returned home for a couple of weekends to his draught Guinness and fresh farm

Above:
Arkle on his summer holidays ridden by Nora Pearson, mother-in-law of Fred Winter.

Main Picture:
Out on his own, as ever.

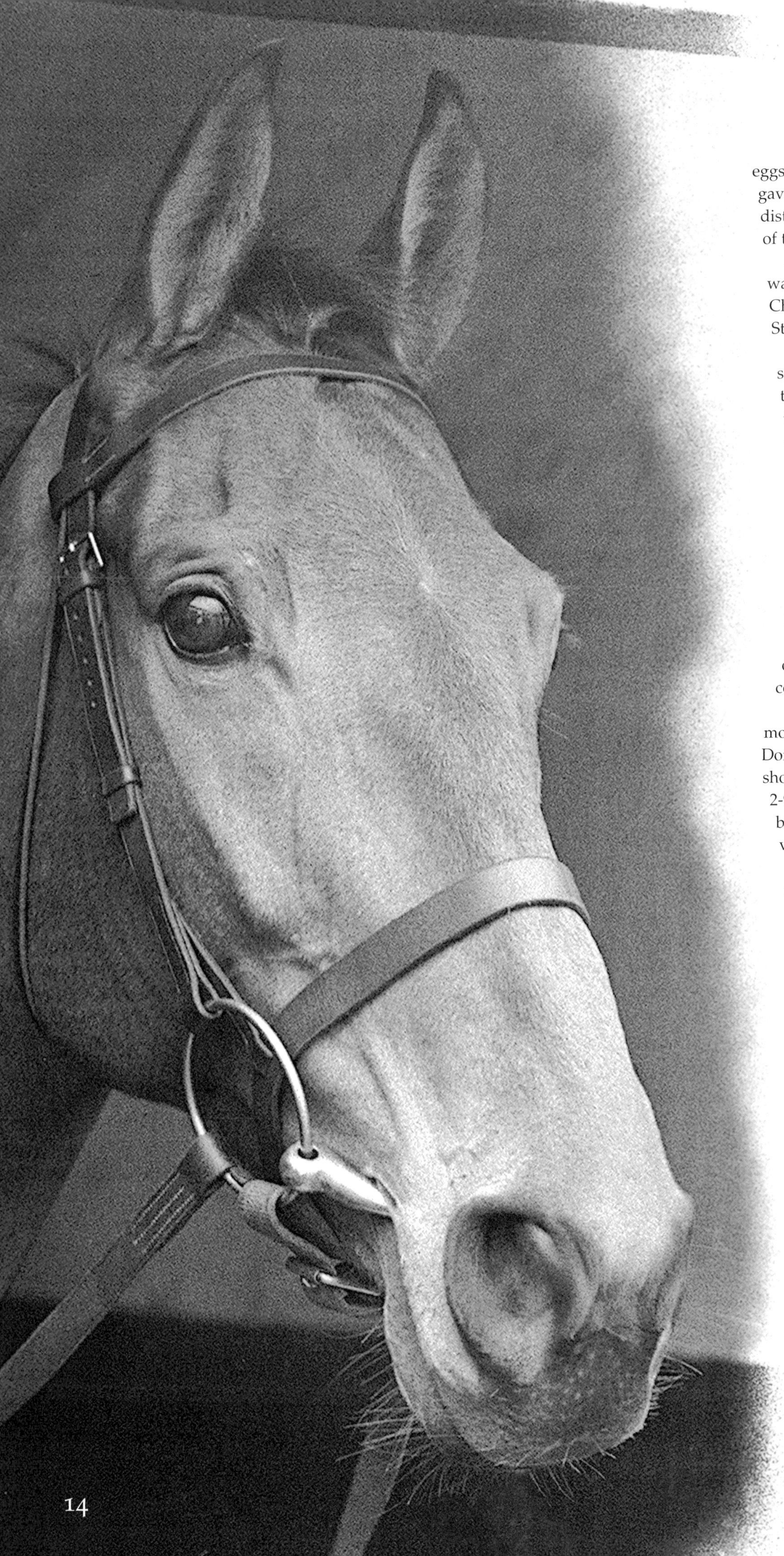

eggs before tripping over to Ascot where he gave four opponents up to 32lbs and a distant view of his backside in the big race of the week, the S.G.B. Handicap Chase.

A similarly nonchalant tour of Kempton was anticipated in the King George VI Chase – the traditional Boxing (or St Stephen's) Day feature.

To the chagrin of thousands for whom sight of Arkle was to be a post-Christmas treat, severe frost caused deferment of the big race until the following chilly day.

At this time our hero was being painted, sculpted, and serenaded in music and verse. His fan mail reflected worldwide admiration, affection – and concern.

Concern over the Herculean tasks being imposed upon him by the handicappers.

Ironically it was not while essaying one of his more immense weight concessions that 'it' happened.

After a race run in an atmosphere of mounting tension – won by 1 length by Dormant, receiving 21lbs – *Chaseform*'s shorthand comment alongside the beaten 2-9 favourite read: 'Led to 9th: led 11th tl blnd 14th: led 16th: led two out: r.o.wl: v.lame aftr r'.

Over fences which are renowned for commanding sustained respect, Arkle had belted the guard-rail of an open ditch. He'd broken a pedal bone.

The progress of Kempton's celebrity invalid was chronicled daily throughout the media; his box was smothered in get-well cards; the neighbouring box was taken over to accommodate the overspill and the presents; Tom Dreaper's charming wife, Betty, who, until the accident, had handled all Arkle correspondence, was now obliged to take on a full-time secretary to cope with the increased volume.

On finally leaving Kempton he enjoyed lovely convalescence with the Duchess before returning to his Greenogue stable.

Once fit, and clearly relishing the prospect of returning to action, Arkle was off to Fairyhouse – inspiring a

Above:
Arkle sups one of this twice-daily bottles of Guinness, proffered to him by Henry Hyde, Managing Director of Kempton Park.

Bottom Left:
Arkle and Mill House in the 1965 Cheltenham Gold Cup, by Lionel Edwards.

pilgrimage which only a visit from the Pope would emulate.

It was the popular Easter meeting in April 1968, the comeback event a 2½ miles hurdle.

The ground was undoubtedly hard and both Tom Dreaper and the horse's renowned vet, Tom Cosgrove, were anxious about it. And the Duchess doubly so.

My great friend Michael O'Hehir was fulfilling the dual role of radio commentator and course announcer, as he so often did, and was in full flow about his subject when he was handed a piece of paper which read, 'Horse does not run'.

Changing gear smoothly he expressed sympathy with all racegoers who would be deeply disappointed, while assuring them that they would be certain to accept that the best interests of 'the horse who has brought such honour to our country' must be paramount.

Would he ever race again?

The Duchess who, with Tom and Betty Dreaper and Pat Taaffe, proved themselves the exemplary guardians of a unique equine star's career, removed all doubt in October 1968. Arkle has retired, she said.

Eighteen months later, when Arkle was into his fourteenth year and by now painfully discomfited by arthritis, she had to make the ultimate decision which so many humans face in a lifetime.

The great horse received his life-extinguishing injection from a hand he knew and trusted, in a familiar environment – as should happen to all horses.

During his retirement he had paraded in front of an enraptured audience at the Horse of the Year Show.

Beforehand the Duchess was asked what music she would like to accompany him.

She smiled, wistfully: 'There'll Never Be Another You'.

SIR GORDON RICHARDS

My most vivid and abiding memory of the great Sir Gordon Richards was a fleeting cameo within a broad, vibrant canvas.

The scene: Epsom Downs on 6 June 1953. Before the sparkling young Queen and her Prince and a crowd estimated at 750,000 the shortest Knight, who brought the greatest credit to his profession in the history of British horseracing, had finally won the sport's greatest prize, the Derby.

It was his twenty-eighth attempt – and as it turned out – his last.

The defining moment in a career involving an unprecedented and surely unrepeatable 26 championships.

Above Right:
Queen Elizabeth II and the Duke of Edinburgh have a word with Sir Gordon Richards before the Coronation year Derby.

Below:
At last! Sir Gordon wins the 1953 Derby on Pinza, his twenty-eighth and final partner in the race.

Before the 174th renewal of the Derby Stakes (value to the winner £19,118.10 shillings) there was concern regarding Sir Gordon's massive partner Pinza's ability to handle the unique demands of the course.

In the event the big bay son of Chanteur II always held a handy position in the 27-runner field, positively hurtled down the hill, and was

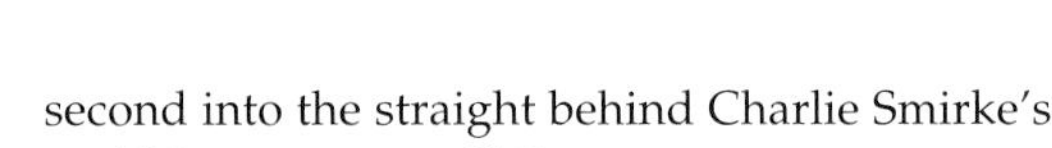

second into the straight behind Charlie Smirke's trail-blazing mount Shikampur.

Then, floating over the sun-baked ground, as though buoyed by a tide of emotion, he swept to the front at the two furlongs marker; and, accompanied by the skywards flight of the finest products of Messrs Lock & Co, Hatters (est. 1759), he beat the Queen's Aureole into second place by an emphatic, if ungallant, four lengths.

Third was Egyptian Prince Saïd Toussoun's Rae Johnstone-ridden 33-1 chance Pink Horse, whose ticket I had bought with a couple of friends at The Derby Club auction-sweep Dinner.

When I was not involved in a broadcast, like this day, I hurried from the stand on to the course, before the rope barriers around the unsaddling enclosure were secured, to interview the returning warriors.

Prior to the introduction of the film patrol camera in 1960 (four years after Ireland; two years after France) there were some desperately rough Derbys. The experiences related by interviewees were more appropriate to Balaclava than Epsom.

Now, uniquely, as the contestants pulled up in the old paddock, the jockeys formed a circle around the hero of the hour to express their admiration and delight.

It was a spontaneous and necessarily short-lived ceremony because there was an imminent race (the Lonsdale Produce Stakes; won by Scobie Breasley on Pugilist, with Sir Gordon third) to weigh out for. There followed my cameo as, flanked by two tall, amiable police horses, the triumphant duo prepared to exit the course and enter the winner's circle. Jockeys seldom carry a handkerchief and Gordon, sheepishly, used the back of his hand to wipe away a tear, left and right.

It had been a long while (32 years) since the determined young miner's son from Oakengates in Shropshire rode his first winner (Gay Lord) at Leicester. First of a lifetime British total of 4,870.

If the immensely popular and nationally revered champion's vision was temporarily blurred, he had many thousands for company.

I first met Gordon through my good friend Johnnie Dines, outstanding featherweight of his era, who won just about every significant handicap in the *Racing Calendar* – most of them on several occasions: the Chester Cup, Cambridgeshire, Ebor, Lincoln, Newbury Autumn and Summer Cups, Liverpool Summer and Spring Cups, Manchester Cup, Northumberland Plate and the Cesarewitch. And many more.

I guess it was the major confrontation between Johnnie and 'Moppy' (so called because of his thick mop of black hair which, in later years, the West End hairdresser Charles Topper used to travel to Berkshire to trim) that sealed the bond between them.

There had been two significant gambles in the 1927 renewal of the Newmarket marathon the Cesarewitch – both of them trained at Ogbourne.

Gordon was aboard the second favourite Saint Reynard, trained by his original boss Martin Hartigan, and Johnnie on Eagle's Pride, the third favourite, handled by Edwin Martin for Colonel Fred Halse who in later years trained with Walter Nightingall at Epsom.

At a critical stage of the event Gordon found himself inadvertently holding a surplus of reins as well as accommodating an alien knee behind his own. Circumstances which, Johnnie claimed, accounted for the unfortunate misdirection of his whip.

The verdict was that Eagle's Pride (7st) had beaten Saint Reynard (7st 5lbs) by a head. When enquiring into the aforementioned unrehearsed development, the stewards learned that anything which might appear to have occurred was, if not illusory, purely accidental.

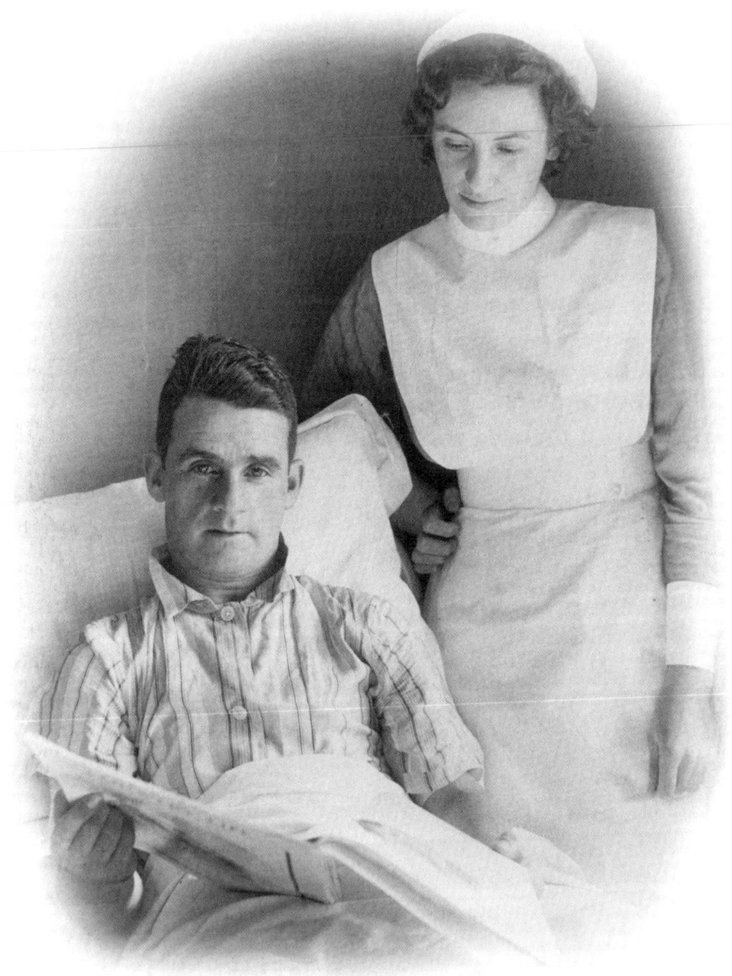

Above:
Gordon in hospital in October 1935 after a fall at Newbury.

The matter appeared to be concluded until one of the stewards, Lord Hamilton, unexpectedly turned up at the start of the next race.

Although demurely conciliatory before the panel, the two protagonists were now giving expression to their true feelings with unbridled vigour.

At a consequent further enquiry they resumed mutual protection mode and it was decided that such interference as had taken place was largely accidental. 'Largely' but not entirely, and the *Racing Calendar* reported that, exceptionally during his long and distinguished career, Gordon was 'severely cautioned'.

That year, 1927, was the season of Gordon's comeback following more than 12 months' absence through career-threatening sickness.

In 1925, six years after a lonely train journey to Swindon (change at Birmingham) which followed

Below:
The travel toiletries which always accompanied the fastidious knight.

Gordon and Tudor Minstrel after their dazzling 8-length 2,000 Guineas triumph in 1947.

a 2½-mile walk to the station, and ended in a 15-year-old's first ride in a motor car, Gordon was Britain's champion jockey.

Prospects for the future were dazzling bright. Operation for appendix removal was surely a minor impediment. However, it preceded commitment to riding engagements in the ice-laden winds of Lincoln's Carholme. Pleurisy followed. The Limerick-born Martin Hartigan, ever sensitive to the welfare of his young protégé, ordered an X-ray which revealed a patch on a lung.

Diagnosed a sufferer from tuberculosis, which was regarded with grave misgiving at the time, the young jockey was packed off to a sanatorium at Mundesley, Norfolk, in May 1926, having ridden only five winners that season; and facing doubt whether he would ride another.

Granted sufficient strength of character, an individual may well turn adversity to advantage.

Lester Piggott even succeeded in emerging from the grim experience of prison a more compassionate and thoughtful person than before sentence.

Gordon, one of eight surviving children born to Nathan and Elizabeth Richards, was raised, like his brothers and sisters, to respect strict Methodist beliefs and principles. He was 13 when he left school to be employed in a warehouse.

Neither before leaving home at 15, nor in racing stables since, had there been great scope for expanding his horizon.

Now, while receiving medical treatment over a period of eight months at Mundesley, he met a variety of fellow patients from diverse backgrounds. Among them a senior invalid, Bill Rowell, who ultimately introduced him to wider interests including fishing, boating, golf and ('most especially', as Gordon put it) to Port.

So that if you set a decanter in front of the champion jockey, he'd be odds-on to name the vintage.

Bill, from Chipping Norton in the Cotswolds, became a lifelong friend of Gordon and his wife Margery, who were married before the start of the 1928 season.

The nationally idolised champion jockey's sustained success was simply phenomenal, reflecting an insatiable hunger for winners.

Even when beaten for the title by one in 1930 he rode 127 winners, and in all achieved a double century on no fewer than 12 occasions.

Gordon's conqueror Freddy Fox, 16 years his senior, was also a Shropshire lad. Likewise, incidentally, another immensely successful former apprentice champion and rider of 2,591 winners, Edward Hide, who rode 42 winners in 1968-70 for trainer Sir Gordon Richards, with whom he formed a mutually happy and successful association.

It was a traumatic finale to the 1930 season when the protagonists went into the last day at Manchester with Freddy one up. Gordon rode the winner of the first to draw level. Then it looked as though he'd settled it by winning the November Handicap on Lord Glanely's Glorious Devon. However, the Fox partner made it a draw in round four and Gordon, who had no further rides, crept into the stand for a cup of tea. He could not bear to watch but he could not avoid hearing, and the clamour which greeted the closing stages of the Worsley Nursery Handicap told him everything he didn't want to know.

Left:
Three champion jockeys: Harry Wragg, Gordon Richards and Freddy Fox at Alexandra Park, 1928.

Below:
Gordon and an unenthusiastic moke raise funds (and a little ribaldry) for charity at Arsenal football ground, 1928.

Freddy Fox, the 1930 champion, would have been replaced by Gordon on his 1931 Derby winner Cameronian if the first Darling-Richards retainer proposal had been accepted by Gordon. Everybody needs a bit of luck.

Like Gordon, Freddy was a hero to me because he was the first jockey to take an interest in and personally support the crucial work of **The International League for the Protection of Horses**.

As with most animal welfare organisations the League, founded in 1927, owes its existence to a compassionate lady, Ada Cole.

Among its worldwide activities the International Training Team has lately initiated a project in the Gambia where the equine population has escalated dramatically from virtually zero in 1950 to nearly 70,000 by the turn of the century.

Knowledge of saddlery, farriery, veterinary care and nutrition in this region is, at best, 'rudimentary'.

The eternally active **Brooke Hospital for Animals**, another wonderful enterprise inspired by a caring lady, alleviates the suffering of horses and donkeys working for poor people in developing countries. The Brooke's eagerly welcomed mobile clinics, manned by dedicated local vets, provide care and training in the heartland of local communities in Egypt, India, Jordan and Pakistan.

The Thoroughbred Rehabilitation Centre, the original charity dedicated to the welfare of Thoroughbred ex-racehorses, was pioneered and established by Carrie Humble who directs the invaluable operation with constant fervour and has, so rightly, been recognised in the Honours List for her work. Even if the farm animals' best friend worldwide, **CIWF (Compassion in World Farming)**, is dynamically administered by a lady, Joyce D'Silva, male *amour-propre* is marginally redeemed by the undertaking's founder having been a compassionate farmer, Peter Roberts.

CIWF has long been at the forefront of a campaign to end the sickening trans-EU traffic in horses for slaughter under appalling conditions; as well as seeking to end the massive international trade in live farm animals, and to outlaw factory farming practices which discredit the human race.

Magically ridden white-faced Humorist and Steve Donoghue win the 1921 Derby from Craig An Eran.

These four enterprises, as well as long established and brilliantly governed **Blue Cross**, whose equine centres and ambulances provide indispensable service, and **Racing Welfare**, who are there for the backroom boys and girls among the 60,000 who work in the often dangerous milieu of Thoroughbred racing and breeding, are supported equally by the Peter O'Sullevan Charitable Trust.

Income is derived from the proceeds of an annual Award auction-lunch, benevolently supported by generous sponsors, big-hearted bidders and donations, and gifted orators. Also from the sale of the Trust's Christmas Card.

So that in 2004 each of the six beneficiaries received a cheque for £30,000 as a result of the card sales and the November 2003 Savoy luncheon.

Should you be interested, please (!), the Trust administrator is Nigel Payne, **Peter O'Sullevan Charitable Trust**, 26 The Green, West Drayton, Middlesex UB7 7PQ. Email: nigel@earthsummit.demon.co.uk. Registered UK Charity Number: 1078889.

Following which short commercial, it's back to you, dear Gordon, and 1930, the year of your first two Classic winners: the Oaks on Rose of England and St Leger on Singapore. Remarkably, the dam and sire respectively of his 1937 Leger winner Chulmleigh, on whom the ride only became available on the eve of the Classic through the unexpected withdrawal of his intended partner, Cash Book, no booking having been made for Lord Glanely's colt.

Soon afterwards Gordon organised a fund-raising dinner for his childhood idol and initial tutor, Steve Donoghue, who rode regularly for Martin Hartigan at the time the 15-year-old apprentice joined the stable. Typically, Steve went out of his way to help young Gordon at every opportunity. Now, sadly, one of racing's eternal heroes, the rider of six Derby winners and, like Gordon himself, 14 English Classics; a man possessed of a magic touch with horses, whom he adored, and who clearly reciprocated his affection; a man who abhorred the whip; a man of whom trainer Charles Morton, responsible for Steve's gallant 1921 Derby winning partner, Humorist, said: 'He was worth 7lbs to any horse in a race like the Derby at Epsom where he had no superior in the world', was comprehensively skint.

Steve, who regarded a contract as a basis for negotiation, was due to ride Glorioso (66-1) for Lord Derby under the terms of his 1921 retainer. But his heart had long been set on partnering Humorist (6-1) whom many had labelled a 'dog' because of his variable form. Steve loved him and was convinced that the son of Polymelus always gave everything of which he was capable at the time.

The combination of Steve's charm and Lord Derby's respect for Humorist's owner, Jack Joel, secured him the ride. And what a ride.

Steve's esteemed contemporary George Duller, the most stylish hurdles rider of his era, referred to Donoghue's 'magical "God-given hands"', with which he instilled confidence into the most nervous subject.

The ride that the 10-times champion (nine outright; one shared with Charlie Elliott) gave Humorist was widely considered his most sensitive and best. During the final, desperate lunge to the line few could have resisted a single crack. But Steve positively 'knew' that Humorist was giving his all – and more. 'I would rather have cut off my right arm,' he declared melodramatically, 'than even show him the whip.'

The neck winner of the 1921 Derby looked worryingly groggy afterwards and, after weighing-in, Steve went straight to his box to comfort him.

The product of the Joels' Childwick Bury Stud (acquired by the Marquesa de Moratalla towards the end of the twentieth century) had perked up by next morning.

Three weeks later Alfred Munnings went to Childwick (pronounced Chillick) to make preliminary sketches for a painting of the Epsom hero. It was a lovely day and the subject looked marvellous. After lunch Sir Alfred – as he became – asked if he could have the 'charming horse' out for another half hour.

As the head man approached the Derby winner's box he quickened his step anxiously. There was a trickle of blood from beneath the door. Humorist was dead.

"There was a trickle of blood from beneath the door. Humorist was dead."

Gordon achieves his 4,000th success when Abernant wins Sandown's Lubbock Sprint, 4 May 1950.

Above:
Lord Lascelles with Steve Donoghue on Oaks Day.

Below Right:
Gordon entertains fellow jockeys at a post-season dinner, 1928.

'I loved him like a child,' grieved Steve. 'To think that he won the greatest race with only one lung.'

Gordon sustained his supportive efforts on Steve's behalf so that his one-time mentor was able to equip a stable at Blewbury which was active by the outbreak of World War II. It was not the ideal period for such enterprise.

By now Gordon's unprecedented career had attained such highlights as riding 12 consecutive winners (the last at Nottingham on 3 October 1933, followed by all six at Chepstow and a further five at the same meeting the next day); and breaking Fred Archer's British record by riding 259 winners in a British season: a record he was to surpass himself in 1947, with 269 firsts.

Meanwhile, his winning margin of 187 over the title runner-up, Billy Nevett, in 1933 was another record.

Pre-1940 he rode 2,586 winners and, despite wartime restrictions, was to ride a further 2,284.

Come the war he made three attempts to join up with the RAF but was disqualified, Graded III, because of his medical history. Red Cross fund-raising activities included 'exhibitions' with his great friend, the billiards professional Tom Reece.

A reflection of the champion jockey's status was an official request for him to broadcast racecourse appeals on behalf of enrolment for National Service.

The first of these was during racing at Brighton. As you would expect of one of the best after-dinner speakers I have ever heard, he did this superbly well. He worried that he was not able to make a more significant contribution to the war effort.

Mind you, he was an inveterate worrier; hence his duodenal problem which prompted regular milk consumption.

His jockey pal Archie Burns, who invariably travelled with Gordon and worked hard on the form book for him, made sure that the Thermos was always present in the Rolls.

Mention of worry ... I once asked the champion if he thought I would *ever* get over pre-commentary nerves. 'The day you do, Peter, is the time to worry,' he suggested. 'It'll probably mean you have lost your "edge".'

1942 was his best racing year when he won four of the five Classics on Sun Chariot ('now there was a *great* filly,' he'd say) and Big Game in the colours of the King.

He'd have won the previous year's Derby, run at Newmarket, on Owen Tudor but for an accident at Salisbury the previous month.

The Duchess of Norfolk had asked him to look after a lad who was having his first ride. Gordon went over to the apprentice at the start where the young man's partner lashed out and broke the champion's leg, and put him out for the season.

It was another wretched day at Sandown on 10 July 1954, the year following his knighthood, that the filly, Abergeldie reared over with him, broke his pelvis and ended a unique chapter in racing history.

For that was the last of 21,843 domestic mounts for which Sir Gordon would weigh out before taking out a trainer's licence in 1955.

So what was the secret of this exemplary, charming man who was a statistical phenomenon?

The imperishable Charlie Elliott (three Derbys among 14 Classics), who won the Ascot Gold Cup, Gold Vase and Eclipse – all on the four-year-old Golden Myth – as a 17-year-old apprentice in 1922; the 2,000 Guineas (Ellangowan) at 18 when he shared the title (on 89) with Steve Donoghue and won the championship outright (106) at 19 when still apprenticed, had this to say: 'I believe that great jockeys are born, not made, that the ability to communicate with a horse so that he'll run for you, give you his maximum, is some kind of natural gift. But,' he added, 'you've got to work to develop it and you've got to have a lot of self confidence to make the most of it on the big occasion.' He reckoned that 'men like Donoghue, Gordon, Lester are a law unto themselves ... there's something strange and marvellous that happens between the horse and certain men who get on his back, and you can't explain it.'

Doug Smith, who perennially took second spot in the title race before Gordon's retirement, when he became champion on five occasions, considered: 'His [Gordon's] ability to keep a horse running dead straight in a desperate finish with the reins loose on his neck was sheer genius, resulting from his facility for communicating his own determination to win. No-one could copy Gordon's style without courting disaster.'

Goodwood was a particularly favoured arena for both Gordon and Lester. Time and again one would marvel at the motor circuit speed with which each was balanced and running – particularly noticeable over the flying five furlongs of the King George Stakes.

Gordon achieved the remarkable feat of winning the prestigious sprint six times in succession, from 1947 to 1952, as well as scoring in 1933 (Myrobella, one of his favourites) and 1938 (Neuvy). While Lester collected the first prize no fewer than 9 times.

When Lester was a young man I remember Gordon describing him to me as having 'a touch of genius – a touch of the devil'.

So what did Lester think of Gordon as a jockey, I asked him over lunch one day in 2004? He reflected for a few moments before responding: 'You had to be a jockey to realise just how good he was. You'd be down there at the start and, all of a sudden, he'd gone ... he'd gone.' He shook his head in wonder at the memory. 'Amazing,' he said. 'He was *amazing*.'

Training on downland turf from Beckhampton, Ogbourne and Whitsbury in turn, Sir Gordon instantly reaffirmed his gift for handling horses.

Sir Gordon (with PO'S) at his last Jockeys' Dinner, 1984.

Because his multitude of followers were accustomed to a cascade of winners from their 4ft 11½ins idol, rather than a conservative stream, there was a misconception that he had not succeeded in the new discipline.

In fact his 634 winners in less than 16 full seasons was aggregated with notable consistency. His development of the popular 11-race winner Reform, Britain's top miler of 1967, proving an outstanding example of his skill.

As he had ridden winners of the Champion Stakes – Big Game (1942), Nasrullah (1943) – so he trained one in little Reform (1967).

In 1970 with lease expiry imminent; relations with his landlord, William Hill, less than harmonious; and no alternative downland site available, he decided, reluctantly, to discontinue – becoming racing manager to the Sobell family and Lady Beaverbrook instead.

Sir Gordon died, aged 82, on 10 November 1986. Truth to tell, he never really recovered from the death of his beloved wife of 54 years, Margery, in 1982.

Scobie Breasley gave the Memorial Service address at St Margaret's, Westminster, where the lessons were read by Arnold (Lord) Weinstock and myself. Regrettably the 600 assembly heard little because a power cut, affecting the church, immobilised the organ, microphones, speakers, lighting and heating.

Scobie ended his address with the words: 'As we leave this famous church, we think of her [Margery] as well as Sir Gordon Richards, a man whose name throughout the world of sport, and beyond, will always be associated with loyalty, humility and integrity. A shining example to us all.'

RAE JOHNSTONE

William Raphael Johnstone was the first of horse racing's great international jockeys. He rode the winners of 30 classic races in Europe – 16 more than the great Sir Gordon himself – and more than 2,000 winners in nine countries.

Born on 13 April 1905 in New South Wales, Rae completed a unique hat-trick in 1948 when riding the winners of the world's top three Derbys – in England, France and Ireland – and a notable six classics in those countries during the 1950 season.

In the 37 years between riding his first winner at Rosehill, Australia, and the last at Chantilly, France, he gambled his way into poverty, and rode his way out. He broke a lot of rules, several records and a few hearts.

I first met Rae in Paris in March 1946, when I was over to interview the horse-rich industrialist and Emperor of the French Turf, Marcel Boussac.

Rae was urbane, great company, with a gently ironic sense of humour, and a serious gourmet. We became instant friends.

In July 1957, soon after he had confided his intention to retire (aged 52), Pierre Wertheimer, who had retained him to ride in France 25 years earlier, gave a farewell dinner in his honour at the Pré Catelan in the Bois de Boulogne. It was an emotional occasion attended by a host of owners and trainers from England, France, Ireland and India for whom he had ridden winners, as well as by jockeys from all over. I was charged with making a presentation on behalf of his weighing-room colleagues in England.

At the end of a delicious, candle-lit dinner in the *Bois*, accompanied by Pouilly Fuissé, Chateau Beychevelle 1953, Pol Roger 1949 and a rather exceptional Calvados, some of us, including the guest of honour, drove into Paris to a *boite* – as if we hadn't earned hangover enough already. The small assembly included Alec Head, Roland de Chambure (whose sudden death, aged 54, in September 1988 was such a loss to French bloodstock breeding and to all his friends), Frank Vogel – a mutual American friend and dedicated racing aficionado who lived in Paris – and myself.

"He gambled his way into poverty, and rode his way out. He broke a lot of rules, several records and a few hearts."

Inevitably the question of Rae's 'book' came under discussion. Ever since I had announced Rae's abrupt retirement in what the *Daily Express* referred to as 'yet another Peter O'Sullevan scoop', a literary agent had pursued Rae with relentless determination. The persistent and agreeable Stanley Barnett even had a 'plant' at the dinner to work on his target.

It seemed that everybody who hadn't got to write it was convinced that it should be written.

Frank Vogel, who had fulfilled the role of owner, trainer, manager and punter, and was an integral part of the Gallic racing set-up, was the ideal candidate. A 65-year-old retired advertising executive with theatrical and restaurant interests, and an ardent collector of remarkably young female company, he lived within a kilometre or so of the subject, whom he knew – and understood – as well as anyone in the world. He had just insisted that the colourful story would be a sure-fire film, 'with my friend George Raft in the part', when I told him: 'Frank, you are the absolute perfect ghost writer for the job.'

'Frank,' interjected Rae, 'can't keep his hands off a girl long enough to write a cheque.'

The rider of 23 Anglo-French classics and champion in Sydney, France and India, who had been in more trouble than occurred in Foinavon's 1967 Grand National, was adamant: 'Either Peter agrees to write it – without pulling a single punch – or it will not be done.'

He tilted his glass in my direction and offered: 'Maybe we could make enough to buy a horse together and ensure that I have at least one to train.' We did.

The upshot was that I started writing at 6.00am – until it was time to leave for the track – for three months. Often stopping off, *en route* to Midlands meetings, at the British Museum Newspaper Library in Colindale to check dates. And occasionally, in desperation, I made expensive telephone calls to Tokyo (where my subject had gone, at the invitation of the Japanese Racing Association, to coach the local riding talent) to establish facts.

It was written in the first person, as an autobiography, and when I expressed the first two chapters east, Rae reacted with such limited enthusiasm that, excepting the publisher's vehement encouragement to stay on course, I'd have ducked out immediately.

When he returned to Paris and flew over for dinner one evening, I set a bottle of Dom Pérignon in front of him, put on a tape of his favourite Nat King Cole, and insisted he read to the end before my wife, Pat, put the soufflé in the oven.

My reward was the unashamed tear or two at the end – and he'd only drunk one glass. Rae inscribed his book to 'My staunchest supporter, father confessor, author and best friend'.

Although my name was not associated in any way with the production of *The Rae Johnstone Story*, I'd sought permission to write it so as to avoid being in breach of contract with the *Express*. This had been granted on the understanding that the *Express* had first refusal in the event of serialisation. The option was exercised on 17 March 1958.

The reviews were heartening; the first impression sold out swiftly; the second likewise. Thirty years after publication at 18 shillings (90p), the foremost London equine bookseller at the time, JA Allen, advertised a copy in his second-hand list for £15. Better than being 'remaindered'.

Two film companies took options – unexercised. We bought a half-sister to the Paddy Prendergast-trained flying two-year-old Windy City, five lengths Gimcrack winner and Free Handicap topper. Named Just Windy, she also went like the wind. But only a puff, unfortunately.

When we ran her over 4½ furlongs at Compiègne she got four furlongs; when we ran her half a mile in Saint-Cloud's 800 metres Prix Yong Lo on 24 July 1961 she lasted three-and-a-half furlongs.

Despite her shortcomings, underlined by continued failure when we sent her to the provinces for a spell, Just Windy's family connection secured for her comfortable retirement to the eminent stud of Mme Jean Stern.

Talking of family connections ... although Rae's parents, estranged before he reached double figures, were both Australian-born, there was variety among his grandparents.

On his mother's side the father was Irish; mother German. On father's the mother was Portuguese; father Welsh. How the foregoing accounted for Rae's slightly oriental appearance (resulting in a much-disliked post-war sobriquet, 'Togo', after the Japanese Admiral) is a mystery.

Rae was 13 (1918) and a pupil at the Roman Catholic Marist Brothers' School at Darlinghurst when his father, a miner, paid one of his filial visits to Sydney to see his son. Such rare rendez-vous usually promised surf-bathing at nearby Coogee Beach, boat-spotting in the great harbour or – best of all – a ball game.

This time dad, the only gambler in the family, announced: 'We're going to Canterbury to a "meet".' His young son did not understand the significance of this information, but he did

"Named Just Windy, she went like the wind. But only a puff, unfortunately."

Rae Johnstone and PO'S on a damp day, Newmarket.

Opposite Page:
Rae Johnstone by Holt.

intercept a sharp, clearly disapproving glance from his mother.

Before this life-defining day Rae had never seen a racehorse or been aware of the sport of horse racing.

Within a few hours, intoxicated by what he termed 'the fantastic atmosphere, the beauty of the silky-skinned horses, the nonchalance of the colourful jockeys, the applause, the bustle, etc. ...' he had one ambition in life – to be a jockey.

Mum, Maisie, was not best pleased. But, made acutely aware that resistance was a non-starter, she did her utmost to further young William Raphael's hopes. Finally a willing trainer was located and Jack Phoenix, a rugged, wizened, ex-bronco and hurdles rider, tolerantly agreed to accept him *after* he'd passed his school-leaving exam.

That was mum's only proviso. No hurdle was cleared quicker.

Just after his fourteenth birthday Rae forsook the relative comforts of the Marist Brothers academy in favour of the Spartan rigours of stable life and (in theory) five years austere apprenticeship.

The terms: board and lodging plus 5 shillings (25p) a week for the first two years; seven-and-six (37½p) for the third year and 10 shillings (50p) for the remaining two.

The conditions of the apprenticeship agreement were that, wages apart, one received five per cent of the winning stakes from the Australian Jockey Club plus presents from any grateful owners. But the trainer was entitled to a percentage of both these items. So they would be paid into a joint account.

'Golly,' as he was nicknamed in the yard (because 'golly' and 'gosh' were the only exclamations he picked up in his Roman Catholic school), found the going tough. He and his fellow novitiates, having been shaken awake in their sparsely furnished dormitory at 4.30am, would be tending their horses by 5 o'clock.

Even bed was little comfort because of the bruises collected through repeated crash landings by day. Personal pride and the encouragement of Jack Phoenix kept him going.

As his featherweight frame gradually became adjusted to sustaining partnership with his mount, Jack made young 'Golly' concentrate on time, time, time, in workouts. So that working on the tan, cinders, or grass, he got to know to within a split second how long his horse had taken to cover each furlong.

Just 12 months after the start of his apprenticeship, 65-year-old Phoenix let it be known that he was about to launch a riding prodigy in 15 years old Johnstone.

He took three 'good things' to a little country meeting at Wyong, around 80 miles from Sydney, knowing that success would instantly guarantee outside rides for the boy in whom he had detected serious potential. He thought.

The trio all looked the part. They all started at odds-on. And they all lost.

One of them, Bonny Nozeen, was a mare whom young Rae 'did'. She won next time out and her jockey, Norman Bragg, gave Rae £1. It was a present that made a big impression on him and which paid a dividend in later years to every stable lad on whose horse he won.

There was a fairly useful horse in the Phoenix stable called Grey Arrow, who was expected to run at Rosehill (the course on which the great New Zealand-bred Phar Lap won his first race) on 26 June 1920.

Australian Turf writers are not given to equivocation as critics of jockeyship.

When the boss made it known that Johnstone was to ride Grey Arrow the local Turf writers assumed he had mislaid his reason. And they said so.

"When the boss made it known that Johnstone was to ride Grey Arrow the local Turf writers assumed he had mislaid his reason. And they said so."

The denigrated rider's mother had never bet on a horse. However, she was so incensed to read that with her son on board a potential even-money chance was 7-1 that she had £70-£10 each-way, and became the third gambling member of the family.

His weight reduced to 7st 3lbs by the 7lb apprentice claim, Grey Arrow won nicely. And Rae was away. Within 18 months of an unpromising beginning at Wyong he had ridden over 100 winners. So that the potential advantage of being associated with 'Tiger' Johnstone (as the newspapers now referred to him) did not escape the notice of the 'wide' element who were shortly to become his companions.

Rae was now gambling full-time – and upsetting the authorities big-time.

Jockeys are not allowed to bet in Australia any more than they are in Europe. Only in the US was a rider permitted to back a horse – his own mount.

Rae's definition of a crooked jockey was quite simple. A 'bent' jock, in his book, was one who rode contrary to instructions – ignoring a directive to win if he could, in order to get money from a bookmaker for pulling one up.

That was not his line. (Well, only once, in the outback, and that didn't work.) And because he could see little harm, save to his own pocket, in punting his own money, he was more than a little

casual in concealing his activity. Hence one stipendiary steward's avowed mission to 'get Johnstone'.

His new 'friends' were doing little for his reputation. Whip transferred to left hand (say) on receiving instructions in the paddock signified 'well fancied'. Cantering to post on the far rail meant 'put me £300 on'. If there were insufficient grounds to bet and whip remained in right hand, the 'friends' would alert a bookmaker on their own account and 'collect'. Connections would then learn on the bush telegraph that the horse had been 'stopped'.

First black mark on the Johnstone crime sheet (11 December 1921) was for 'withholding information' when he refused to incriminate a senior jockey who had 'roughed him up' (whipped him across the face and bloodied his nose) during a race. Fourteen days' suspension.

There followed a series of penalties for 'careless riding' (two months); 'interference' (two months), and, more seriously, expulsion from every course within 100 miles of Sydney. This was a sequel to the stewards' annual bank account inspection to ensure that trainers were looking after their apprentices.

The account should have been extremely healthy. Rae was approaching 19. His financial shortage was acute and the account was empty.

He had not resorted to forgery but persuaded the bank manager, a friend, to accept one signature instead of two.

When the Metropolitan ban was finally lifted he returned to Sydney with a sparkling four-timer on day one (he was also minus an appendix and plus a lovely, brunette, 21-year-old wife) and demand for his services appeared limitless.

The future looked bright as the sun's reflection on the waters of Sydney harbour. Until he was booked for Highweight Handicap favourite Myrangle King ('A leaden-headed bastard,' according to a weighing-room colleague) at Gosford on 19 October 1926.

Six furlongs on a sharp track; Rae jumped off smartly, took in behind a couple and was just wishing he'd invested personally when the horse suddenly dived for the rails. He had to snatch up to avoid impact. Even then he ran on to be third, two lengths off the winner.

Rae returned, rails paint down his boot, saddle, and the favourite's flank, to an inevitable enquiry. The owner expressed disappointment but full understanding that the jockey's action was necessary. The next day's newspaper report read:

... Drastic action was taken over the running of Myrangle King ... result W Johnstone was disqualified for two years ... the jockey has expressed intention of appealing to the AJC Committee ...

"Bert Jolley telephoned him in a state of great excitement more than a month after the fateful Gosford event – with what, he termed, 'proof positive that you are blameless.' "

However, the Jockey Club had 'had' Johnstone and the appeal was slung out.

While protesting comprehensive innocence with passionate intensity, William Raphael Johnstone accepted that his career was finished. Curtains.

His genuine friends who believed implicitly in his innocence would not lie down. One of them, Bert Jolley, telephoned him in a state of great excitement more than a month after the fateful Gosford event – with what, he termed, 'proof positive that you are blameless.'

Myrangle King, ridden by an inexperienced jockey, had bucked into the rails during a race, brought down two horses and created mayhem. The newspapers were full of it.

Jolley got an interview with the Minister of State on their behalf and personally presented Rae's case.

The minister immediately called up the secretary of the Australian Jockey Club, CW Cropper, suggesting he be granted another hearing.

The Jockey Club is a law unto itself and he didn't get that hearing. But at the next Jockey Club meeting, on 6 January 1927, WR Johnstone was reinstated.

Of course he was profoundly grateful for the faith and support of friends, especially Bert Jolley. But he returned in a mood of sullen fury, deeply resenting the detail that only a million-to-one chance 'replay' had rescued him from oblivion.

There are few more potent incentives to crime commitment, he reflected, than being condemned for something you haven't done.

As mentioned earlier, he only acted 'crook' once and I retell this story diffidently, since it is natural to assume that one crime will be followed by a repeat. It wasn't. But Rae was insistent that he didn't want any whitewashing when it came to the book.

Anyway, riding-wise, he returned in top form and, thanks to loyal and confident support from trainers like Pat Nailon, who had a powerful string, he was soon top in the Sydney area once more. But his marriage had foundered and he was a long way from discovering the key to uninterrupted gambling success.

In fact his financial situation was patently unhealthy, which accounted for instant agreement when, in November 1927, a friend proposed chartering a three-seater and heading 300 miles north to exploit his talents at the two-day country meet at Armidale.

The first-day programme left them a credit deficiency with one bookmaker which, positively, could not be met.

Something just *had* to be done on the following afternoon. Something and somebody.

They sat up most of Wednesday night going through the form of each Thursday runner. Everything pointed to Our Rep (third under 9st 9lbs top-weight that day) being a 'good thing' when he turned out again on the morrow. And Rae was to ride him. There was a guaranteed front-runner in the six furlongs Flying Handicap worth £20 to the winner, £5 second. Not, as you'll infer, a contest of the highest calibre.

Rae had already been convicted for 'stopping' a horse that he did not stop and it had been widely, and incorrectly, assumed that there had been other instances. He would show them that he could stop one all right. The jocks on the only other two 'possibles' agreed to be 'on' the front-runner. Meanwhile his pal told the bookmaker, whose account looked like being such a source of embarrassment, that he could 'go down the book' with Our Rep, who would NOT win.

Feeling a right heel, Rae cantered to the start anxious to get the escapade behind him.

They lined up and were 'off'. The front-runner struck well and quickly established a good lead with which none of those who counted had any intention of tampering. At half-way the leader looked round to see how the opposition was faring and promptly kicked on as if the winning post was a few yards away. So with a quarter of a mile to travel he is beginning to die in his tracks – out to the wide.

The rest of them realised that the only way they could avoid taking an active part in the contest was to dismount and start a card game.

This being an impractical solution there was only one thing to do about it, Rae figured, and that was to get on with it. So he slipped past his money inside the last furlong and then got caught in the last stride.

The irony of the situation was that, had he won, then, despite guilt, he'd have been in the clear. The evidence of victory would have been sufficient to refute any suggestion of not doing his best. But he didn't win. And there was an investigation, at which he was far from being in the clear.

The stewards reached the proper conclusion that he had been solely responsible for organising the whole disorganised affair. For a reason he could not explain, the 'heel' derived masochistic pleasure from the verdict – guilty.

The *Referee* of 23 November 1927 recorded the findings simply:

Dear Peter
Learning to ski at 50
here I am having my 2nd lesson.
Acapulco is a wonderfull place.
Was at the opening of Santa Anita
yesterday, will most likely hang
around here till the end of Jan
love to Pat Rae

Postcard from Rae in Acapulco, showing him learning to water-ski at 50!

AGAIN IN TROUBLE

At Armidale last Thursday the successful jockey WR Johnstone was dis-qualified for two years. His mount, Our Rep, was beaten a head by Benzol in the Flying Handicap and the stewards having been dissatisfied with Johnstone's riding took the action stated. The joint-owners and trainer were exonerated. Up to last week Johnstone was the leading jockey in the Metropolitan area.

The miscreant resolved to keep as fit as possible; did plenty of swimming; acquired a hack; re-created in his mind every race he'd ridden, contemplating what he might have done to achieve better results; carefully studied films of all the principal races, and caught up a little on reading.

"The rest of them realised that the only way they could avoid taking an active part in the contest was to dismount and start a card game."

Pierre Wertheimer and Rae post Lavandin's Derby, 1956. 'Lulu' Chataignoux (associated with '47 Ascot Gold Cup winner Souverain) in background.

By the start of 1930 he was back in the winner's circle with regularity, repaying the confidence of supportive trainers.

Then, out of the blue, came an offer from Aussie trainer Alec Higgins to ride for him in India.

It seemed an irresistible opportunity to broaden experience. He owed a lot of tax and would not be able to leave without clearance from the Inland Revenue. This involved selling every disposable possession. Further, although he and Ruby were separated, he needed her signature ('If you want to be crazy and throw away a guaranteed future, it's up to you,' she sighed) because a husband could not skip the country without his lawful wedded's authority.

Pat Nailon was more vehement. 'You're insane,' he announced despairingly. 'Flemington's big-money meeting is coming up and you'll have a favourite's chance in the Caulfield and Melbourne Cups.' But he was booked on the P&O's *Narkunda* – with stewards to wait on him for a change.

Alec Higgins was a star of a trainer. 'He had an instinctive appreciation of the requirements of every horse in his string,' said Rae. 'He knew precisely how to vary their feed, which he surveyed meticulously; how much work to give them; how to cater for any physical weakness and – importantly – how to place them in their right class so that when the money was down they were seldom far away.'

Rae enjoyed an unbelievably successful run with the stable in India where a personal highlight included an invitation to ride second jockey to Steve Donoghue in England for Sir Victor Sassoon. The lowlight was being refused a riding permit.

So he went to Ireland, receiving great hospitality among the racing community and realising an ambition when attending the Eucharistic Congress in Dublin. Thence to England where his lifelong idol, Steve Donoghue, instantly befriended him. They both shared love of horses, aversion to the whip, and the gambling contagion.

In June 1932 Steve was going to Paris to ride The Satrap for Lord Derby in the Grand Prix. Why didn't Rae come along? His luggage had been registered ahead to Venice where he'd board the ship for India. Still, why not?

On such slender threads is the course of life determined.

At Longchamp on Sunday 26 June he met debonair Pierre Wertheimer who invited him to his box and, a few glasses of champagne later, made a startling proposal.

Proprietor, with his brother Paul, of one of the most significant stables in France – then in the hands of Albert Swann at Chantilly – Pierre enquired of Rae: 'Why don't you stay over and ride my brother's and my horses?'

"They both shared love of horses, aversion to the whip, and the gambling contagion."

Rae with fellow work riders and trainer Charles-Henri Semblat, Chantilly 1950.

Marcel Boussac leads in Rae and Talma II after the 1951 St Leger at Doncaster.

He explained that his luggage was by now boarded in Venice on his India-bound ship.

'If I get your bags unshipped, will you stay?' he pursued.

Rae had already fallen in love with Paris; to ride in Europe was his goal. He needed no time for reflection. The response was an unqualified affirmative, and in his first full season wearing the long-running blue and white Wertheimer colours (1933) Rae had become champion jockey of France. And again in '35 and '38.

He'd accepted a retainer in England for Lord ('Old Guts and Gaiters') Glanely, on whose Colombo he'd won the 1934 2,000 Guineas and finished third, as 11-8 favourite, in the Derby. Following the latter event he'd been the target for unrestrained newspaper criticism which is routinely reserved for riders born outside mainland Britain.

Exceptions among horserace writers were Quinney Gilbey ('It was lack of stamina that beat Colombo. The interference did him more good than harm – had Johnstone not been forced to check he'd have run himself out sooner than he did') and fourteen-times amateur champion and breeding authority John Hislop ('Colombo was beaten simply through his inability to stay 1½ miles'). Ironically, Rae had been offered £10,000 by an English bookmaker to 'stop' Colombo at Epsom. From the rider's viewpoint, there was not enough money in the world for the approach to qualify as temptation. Significantly, the Royal Ascot race selected for Colombo's redemption was over a mile – and he failed in that too.

Rae was informed by Lord Glanely that there was no question of breaking his contract but he (Glanely) would employ Gordon Richards when available. Rae had appreciated the directness, accepted a clear invitation to call it a day, forfeited a £3,000 contract after half a season, and returned to France. Not before he'd been lured to the Piccadilly Hotel on some pretext to discover Gordon Richards, Steve Donoghue, 'Brownie' Carslake, Johnnie Dines, 'Brusher' Herbert, Jackie Sirett, Freddy Fox, Bobby Jones, Harry Jelliss, etc. ... assembled in a private dining room to give him a great surprise party.

Asked by a reporter at the airport if he had any final word on Colombo, he'd replied: 'Yes, just this. If he'd been ridden in the Derby by a jockey, he'd have won 10 minutes.'

He'd won the 1935 French and English 1,000 Guineas on, respectively, The Nile and Mesa, but been beaten on the latter in the Oaks. The Wertheimer filly had a poor run in a rough race and Rae's self-criticism was enthusiastically endorsed in the press.

In the same year Rae and Steve had flown south together to ride in the Grand Prix de Marseille. They'd agreed that – one to be in the first three – the loser would foot the bill for the finest *bouillabaisse* in the area that night.

The account became Steve's when Cozzida, Rae's first ride for Marcel Boussac, became his 100th winner of the season. The *oursins* which preceded the *bouillabaisse* did not count as food, we told each other. The *bouillabaisse* certainly was not fattening, we agreed, and the chilled Vin Rosé of Provence could hardly be rated as hard liquor. So a little *Marc de Provence* was fully justified.

Steve cancelled his rides in England the next day and they agreed to meet up in New York, when their respective seasons ended, to discover whether the *bouillabaisse* of Marseille could be equalled. It couldn't.

Rae travelled widely in the ensuing years, responded to personal appearance invitations – as from the Jockey Club of the Argentine where he rode successfully on the new turf track, San Isidro, outside Buenos Aires. But travel opportunities were shortly to be restricted. War and a turning point in the life of WR Johnstone were imminent.

The French ultimatum to Germany had expired at 5pm on 3 September 1939, Deauville had emptied like the stands after the last race and the lovely girl who had occupied Rae's heart for a while now had driven from Paris to join him. They had the restaurant, Chalet Normand, to themselves. Rae's Australian passport had expired while he was in India and he'd obtained a British replacement.

He said it was because he thought a uniform would impress his fiancée that he presented himself before an unappealing recruiting official, who reacted: 'We have no vacancies for toy soldiers, try England.'

Rae and professional dancer Mary Soube, a devout Catholic, were married on 12 March 1940 and the bridegroom renounced gambling. Just as well; before an earlier season, when financially 'on the floor', he had requested his Wertheimer retaining fee in advance. After the substantial sum had been produced he popped into the Casino on the way back to his Auteuil flat and arrived at the appartment penniless.

On 5 May 1940 racing had stopped in Paris. The Belgian Army had capitulated at the end of the month; the Germans had reached the Somme and Aisne-Oise Canal crossings on 5 June, prompting the Italians to declare war, bravely, five days later. Tension ran high as the grandstand at Saint-Cloud.

Rae and Mary packed the Delahaye Coupé and took the road to Spain. They were not alone. The frontier was closed and the last ship for England had left St Jean-de-Luz.

Alien Johnstone was well served for a while by his only identity paper – a French jockeys' licence – but not indefinitely. Having driven west to the Côte d'Azur they'd stayed at the Hotel Ruhl in Nice until the funds ran out and the car was sold.

The Italians were moving in from the south-east frontier. Rae was among 50 civilians, including Americans, Belgians, British, Greeks, Hungarians and Poles, who were rounded up by the Italian Army Guard one day and stripped of

Rae and his wife Mary relaxing in their flat overlooking Auteuil.

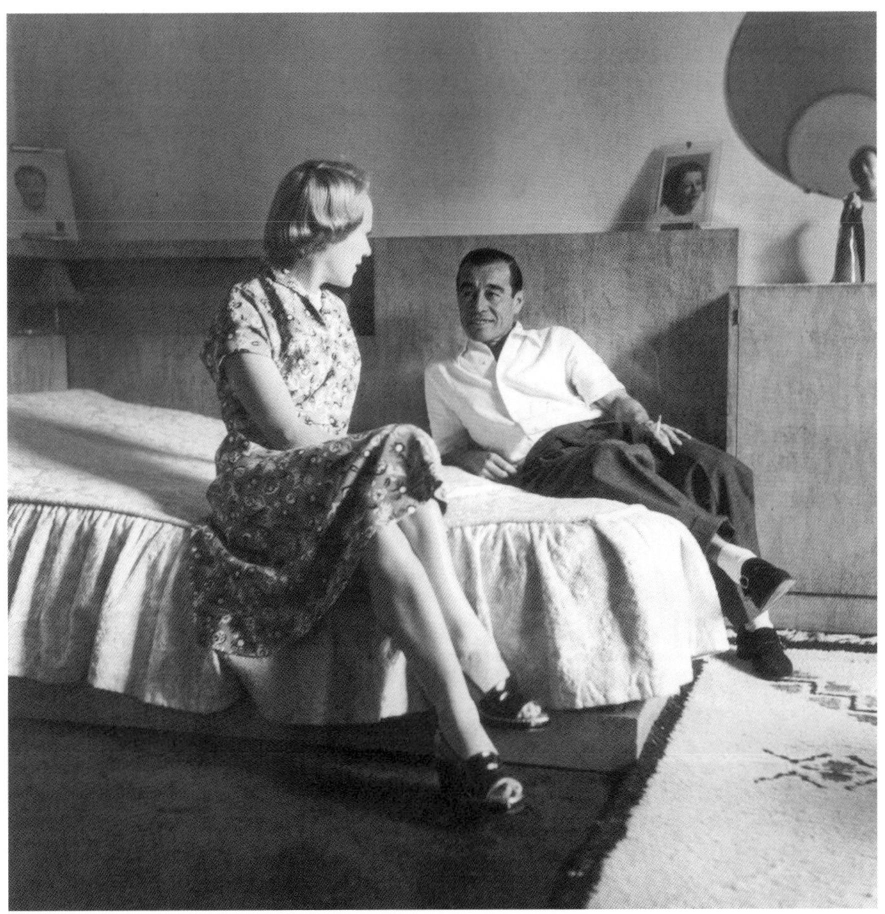

EXIT THE CROCODILE

Jockey Willy Rae Johnstone, an international sporting figure, retires—wearing the same colors he bore in Paris 25 years ago

by WILLIAM McHALE

In the soggy heat of the weighin room of Paris' Longchamp race track a couple of weeks ago, a little seam-faced jockey named Rae Johnstone turned to a British friend, said, "This is my last ride, Peter." Making a final adjustment to the blue and white colors of Owner Pierre Wertheimer, he strode briskly to the paddock, mounted a slate-gray filly named Midget and rode her to a hard-fought second place. Just 25 years before, almost to the day, Johnstone had ridden his first race in France. The owner was Pierre Wertheimer and the horse finished second.

Between these two near wins, Willy Rae Johnstone piled up a quarter-century record of victories which fixed him as one of the greatest international jockeys of modern times. Before arriving in France in 1932, he had already won 600 races as champion jockey of Australia and India, and he added some 1,400 more before his retirement. Among these are 30 "classics," including three English Derbies. In a single year, 1948, he won the English, French and Irish Derbies, plus the Grand Prix de Paris. He has raced in 11 countries—France, England, Ireland, Australia, India, Egypt, Italy, Argentina, Belgium, Germany and the U.S.—and has won victories in all but the last two.

"My greatest thrill," says 52-year-old Johnstone, looking back over a life-time ... "was winning my first ... in 1948." ...

My Love was trained by Richard Carver, now 73, a member of one of those British racing families which has lived in France for generations (his grandfather trained in France during the reign of Napoleon III. As a 2-year-old, My Love had never won a race and Carver was dissatisfied with his jockey, so he asked Rae to have a try. Johnstone's answ... him: "Guvnor, I'll do ... tion: that you'll let m... Derby." The Derby ... in the offing, but Jo... on My Love that h... friend and patron... pleaded: "Mons...

JOHNSTONE ON SICA BOY, AFTER WINNING THE PRIX DE L'ARC DE TRIOMPHE, EUROPE'S RICHEST RACE, AT LONGCHAMP, PARIS, IN 1954

EXIT THE CROCODILE

continued

that horse, I'll ride him and win the Derby for you." The Aga was able to purchase only 50% of the horse, but his faith in Johnstone was justified: the following year, My Love gave the Aga's chocolate and green colors their fourth Derby victory.

Johnstone's keen sense of horseflesh has been honed over a tough career almost unmatched for longevity, variety and brilliance. Warren G. Harding was in the White House as President of the U.S. when Johnstone started racing as a 16-year-old apprentice in Australia, and he became national champion before he was out of his teens. After a decade of success in his home country, Rae went to India, then blooming in the genial autumnal years of the British raj. "That was real living," sighs Johnstone reminiscently. ... colorful uniform... had tw...

horseplayer's paradise. He became a familiar figure to Parisians in the winning enclosure behind the magnificent cream-colored stand of Longchamp, in the red brick rural loveliness of Le Tremblay. He wore the racing colors of France's most famous owners—Boussac, Aga Khan, Volterra.

REFORMED WHEN MARRIED

Young, cocky, successful Johnstone backed his own mounts heavily with his own money, tossed many a purse to the croupiers in Deauville and other gilded gambling halls. All this stopped abruptly when Rae married his present French wife, Marie, in 1940, and he hasn't gambled since. During the Nazi occupation, Rae was tossed into a French concentration camp ... emy alien. He esca... was in th...

Le Crocodile because he came from behind to eat up the opposition. On his losing days they also called him "robber," "crook" and "bum," because he refused to lash a horse with his whip if he thought the animal had no chance to win. In a typical Johnstone-fashion run for the money, he humped his back like an angry cat, worked his arms and knees in a tremendous burst of energy to urge the horse on. But he seldom did more than flick the horse with his whip. "I just waved the whip in front of him now and then, to let him know it was there," he says. "There's no sense in beating a horse to death. If he hasn't got a win in ... whip it out of ...

Rae notes one big gap in his 36 years on the track: "I never rode a great horse. I've ridden lots of good ones, but never a great one like Native Dancer or Citation or Ribot." He nearly had a chance for a go on Native Dancer in 1954 when Alfred Gwynne Vanderbilt asked Rae to ride him in the Prix de l'Arc de Triomphe, but the big gray broke down before he could cross the Atlantic (Johnstone won the race anyway, on Sica Boy).

A frequent visitor to the U.S., usually on his way to a winter vacation in Mexico, Johnstone has raced here only three times, with no luck. He knows Eddie Arcaro very well and admires him as a track technician but has mild doubts about the efficacy of the acedeuce style Eddie affects. "Of course, it makes more sense to ride that way in America, where all the tracks are exactly the same and you go around them all to the left," he says. "In Europe there are no two tracks exactly alike—you can go around them to the left or to the right, and in one, Maisons Laffitte, you can go around clockwise and counterclockwise on the same afternoon."

Aside from the quality of the horses and the skill of the men who ride them, Rae doesn't have much use for racing in the U.S. "It's too monotonous," he says. "There's no atmosphere. As far as I can make out, people go to races in America to eat sandwiches and hot dogs and to bet on a number."

Much better, in his opinion, is the ambiance of the Paris tracks he will never ride again—the rolling, richly green, up-and-down courses; the flower-bordered, tree-shaded paddocks filled with the buzz of knowledgeable conversation and the slim shapes of chic women. Most of all he will miss Chantilly, the forest-enclosed training area 25 miles from Paris, where jockeys come each morning to try out their mounts by dawn's light. "Every time I did it for 25 years," says he, "it was a thrill to drive to Chantilly, to see the morning sun break through the trees arched overhead, like light coming through cathedral windows."

The summer days which used to begin with a predawn ride to Chantilly have no pattern for Rae now, and it's strange not to be saddling up at Longchamp when the afternoon shadows begin to lengthen. Beyond a trip to Australia to visit his mother, Johnstone has no plans for the future, only a few regrets about the past. "I've made some mistakes and run some bad races," he says. "I wish I had run nothing but good races." END

JULY 22, 1957

a Time Inc. weekly publication

25 CENTS
$7.50 A YEAR

SPORTS ILLUSTRATED

THE YANKEES

5 big questions answered for the first time

HANK BAUER

Above:
Rae returns after winning his first Derby on My Love in 1948.

Opposite Page:
Article on Rae in **Sports Illustrated**, 22 July 1957.

all identity. Herded into open trucks, and handled with all the sensitivity exercised in the twenty-first century by the Mafia-controlled horse slaughtering industry, they were driven to barracks in Sospel, high in the Maritime Alps. This was 'home' and 'hell' until the 1943 Italian surrender, when the Guard fled.

While temporarily and blissfully reunited with Mary, worse was to follow. Holed up in a back-street Monte Carlo appartment block, he was picked up by the Gestapo and sent to a vast (800 inhabitants) Prisoner of War camp in the Vosges mountains at Giromagny, 600 kilometres north of Monte. His daring escape nine months later, while being transported to potential oblivion in Germany, reflected the courage and resourcefulness of both Madame Johnstone and the resolutely brave Maquis.

By the time they regained their desecrated appartment in the Avenue Maréchal Lyautey, overlooking Auteuil, where racing continued without interruption during the war and occupation, Rae had only the rags and porous shoes in which, with beard and foot-long hair, he stood in an alarmingly overweight 10-stone frame.

Rae visited the Turkish baths and got tidied up – on tick. He wrote to Charlie Elliott, who immediately sent over pyjamas, shirts and warm sweaters. And they set out on the road back.

Come the 1945 season and Rae achieved the ultimate passport to popularity in the weighing room by attaining a personal record – 47 consecutive losers between 24 April and 1 June! For it is a lot easier to sympathise with a colleague's failure that to condone his success.

The French racing public were convinced by now that '*Le Crocodil*', as they called him, had lost his teeth. Maisons-Laffitte trainer Joseph Lieux was far too shrewd to share this opinion. He had Rae riding work for him regularly and on 3 July

Galcador and Rae Johnstone led in by Marcel Boussac after the 1950 Derby.

he launched his favourite two-year-old and favourite jockey on his favourite course. The power-packed youngster, Sayani, and his resurgent partner, Rae Johnstone, cruised to victory at his trainer's local track.

Rae reckoned that this son of Lord Derby's stallion Fair Copy was one of the best horses he ever rode – especially after the 1946 Cambridgeshire in which (well backed ante-post at 28-1, he still started 25-1) he established a weight-carrying record for a three-year-old (9st 4lbs) despite being so badly hampered at the start that he pitched on to his nose. By the time he was balanced, 'the other 28 looked like Shetland Ponies in the distance,' said Rae.

Meanwhile, in the '45 season he enjoyed a stroke of luck. Marcel Lollierou, who usually rode the filly Nikellora, a narrow 'Diane' winner but last of 13 in the Grand Prix, was 'claimed' by his number-one stable on the eve of the Prix de l'Arc de Triomphe – the first to be run again at Longchamp since 1942. René Pelat asked: would Rae ride? He certainly would, especially since the filly was an outsider and he'd be able to wait with her.

The team of Marcel Boussac, who had headed the owners and breeders winners' statistics since 1939, owned three of the 11 runners. Coupled in the Pari-mutuel betting at 10-1 ON, they were headed by multi-successful Ardan, unbeaten in six runs that season and winner of the 1944 Arc, run at Le Tremblay.

Rae planned to sit in behind and observe the action. One of Madame Couturie's pair, Galène, forced the pace but 'Jacko' Doyasbere on Ardan was close up behind. Entering the home straight the pair had a short, sharp tussle before Galène cracked. Then three-year-old Basileus, second in the French Derby, had a go and 'Jacko' beat him off. It was now the very useful Chanteur's turn; the effect being that of a series of boxers jumping into the ring fresh to have a slug at the champion before they were floored by him. And floored Chanteur was, like the others.

Rae waited to 'pounce' with Nikellora and try and 'do' him with one sharp run so that she did not get involved in any drawn-out battle. Sometimes events run for you, he reflected. 'Jacko' spotted the last challenge looming and immediately called on Ardan for one extra effort. But he'd been fighting hard, and for long enough. There was no more fire left and the mare got up to win by ¾ length, with a reinvigorated Chanteur only a short-neck behind Ardan in third.

Rae was 'away' now. The weight was fine, thanks to Mary's Gallic talent in the kitchen. Freed from gambling fever he was, he felt, riding better and evaluating form more dispassionately.

Nine years later Rae rode an Arc de Triomphe winner, Sica Boy, trained by René Pelat's son, Pierre. The winner's owner, Mme Jean Cochery, also did a good training job in teaching her parrot to announce: 'Sica Boy's won it,' when addressed before or after the event.

In the interim he'd won a succession of classics, both sides of the Channel, including avenging Derby defeat on Colombo by attaining one of the most satisfying triumphs of his career on My Love in the 1948 Epsom renewal. 'Satisfying' because he'd fallen in love with the colt on their first encounter and assured one of his idols, HH Aga Khan III, that he should buy him because Rae would win him the Derby. M Leon Volterra would only part with 50 per cent but he won at Epsom and Longchamp (the Grand Prix) in the Aga's colours.

After steering me and both my *Express* readers impeccably in the 1950 classics, Rae foundered on 27 May because he was very, very doubtful about Galcador getting the Derby trip. I'd backed Galcador largely to recover losses over his two more qualified stable companions, Pardal and Geraphar, who had each encountered training problems.

I wanted to oppose Prince Simon, the very warm favourite, and L'Amiral apart, could not go along with the claims of any other. Rae said: 'Peter, you're just riding with your money. You wouldn't tip him if you hadn't backed him.' I was not so sure, but Roger Poincelet gave me a lot of encouragement for L'Amiral – powerfully reinforced by stable companion Amour Drake winning the Coronation Cup. Weakly, I changed allegiance to L'Amiral and forfeited a clean sweep in the classics.

Rae was bitterly critical of his winning ride on Galcador. 'I came too soon, Peter, ages too soon,' he insisted. He was furious because on the flight back to France, as the team sat around the conference table in Boussac's giant private plane, he'd reiterated his conviction that the horses were working too hard at home. Late sub Galcador, who had not undergone a 'preparation', was proof.

On the contrary, said the Boss; 'with a preparation he would have won by two lengths.'

Although Rae went on to win the St Leger on Scratch in the orange, grey cap in 1950 – his fourth British classic of the season – and the next year in the same colours on Talma, that was the beginning of the end of an always uneasy association.

Five years before Talma's success Rae and Mary had returned 'home' by flying-boat (eight days between take-off from Poole harbour, Dorset, to putting down in Rose Bay, Sydney!) to fulfil a promise to his mother, who was now a racehorse owner and no mean gambler.

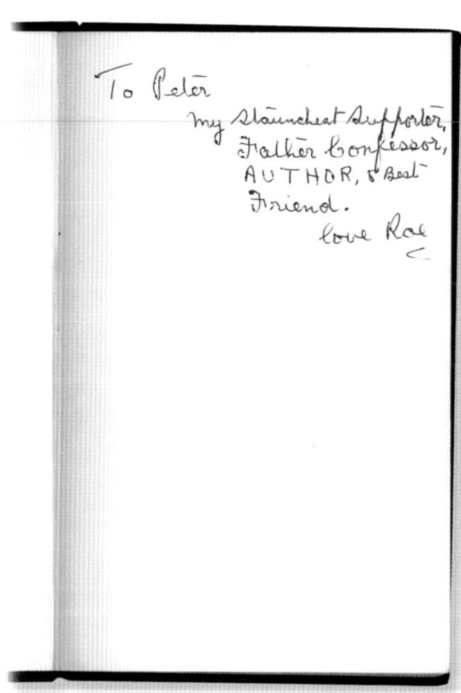

Inscription in a very special copy of **The Rae Johnstone Story.**

Rae's old mentor Jack Phoenix, a sprightly 86-year-old, had retired. He went racing with his one-time apprentice and enquired: 'Do you still tell trainers how to train their horses; do you still waste all the time you used to on your clothes?'

Rae didn't like to tell him that his Parisian tailor José actually made him two sets of suits – one for the racing season; one for the close period when he was 10lbs heavier; that his shirts were made by Sulka in the Rue de Rivoli; shoes and riding clothes in London.

'I guess so,' he answered.

Although Marcel Boussac won the French Derby a remarkable 12 times, Galcador was his only success at Epsom. Now, in 1956, Rae had his last chance for a third triumph at the scene of his unwarrantably lambasted defeat on Colombo 22 years earlier.

Unhelpfully, he was enduring a prolonged losing streak in May '56 while I was trying to persuade his former patron, Pierre Wertheimer, to put him up on currently riderless Lavandin (*see Alec Head chapter*) next month.

The portents were clearly favourable if he was to go to The Curragh and win the 1,000 Guineas on the Wertheimer filly Pederoba on 10 May. He did, and won his sixth Irish classic in the process. So I took a chance in my Friday 11 May column in the *Express* and wrote:

1. LAVANDIN
2. MONTAVAL
3. ROISTAR
COPE'S
DAVID COPE

Left:
Lavandin and Rae's photo-finish Derby triumph from a deceptive angle.

Below:
Post Lavandin Derby. The personnel at Charco's Bistro deliver a floral extravaganza to Cranmer Court.

Opposite Page:
Lavandin, ridden by Rae Johnstone, wins the 1956 Derby, with Montaval second and Roistar third.

Sequel to Rae Johnstone winning the Irish 1,000 Guineas on Pederoba for Messrs Wertheimer and Head is that he will ride Lavandin in the Derby. And win.

That 6 June triumph was surely one of the emotional high points of Rae's multi-faceted career. A charming postscript was that when we returned to my London flat from Epsom, the entrance looked like a section from the Chelsea Flower Show. Six months earlier Rae and Mary had dined with us at the local bistro (Charco's) and I'd toasted the forthcoming Derby victory of Johnstone and Lavandin. The waiters were all on at 33-1!

Rae and I finally had our winner together when he trained Grey Lag, ridden by Aussie Roy Higgins, to win at Chantilly on 11 September 1963. Tragically, a year later, William Raphael Johnstone collapsed and died from a heart attack while walking up the grandstand steps at Le Tremblay.

Less than a month before, he'd had a comprehensive insurance-related physical check-up. 'I'm odds-on to go the distance,' he'd reported to me delightedly.

Knowing Rae, he'd have reacted: 'So much for odds-on chances.'

Forty years on, in May 2004, our hero was inducted to Australian Racing's Hall of Fame.

From all the staff
John (EAVESDROPPER)
Mick.
Alfonse
Teddy.
Cyril.
&
Nora (Washer upper)
We all had a bash 33 to 1.
(The Boss Didn't.)!!!

PADDY PRENDERGAST

Legendary contemporaries Paddy Prendergast, born Co Kildare 1909, and Vincent O'Brien, born Co Cork 1917, were responsible for putting Irish racing on the international map.

In an intensely competitive sport this indisputable attainment owned nothing to combined effort; everything to independent, singular talent.

Son of a horsewise dealer, who would commit to remarkably accurate memory every characteristic of a horse he had assessed, Paddy not only inherited his father's gift but added his own unique brand of sorcery. The result was a trainer of utterly exceptional talent and achievement.

The sparsely chronicled early days of Patrick J Prendergast – widely known as 'Darkie' – offered little clue to the glory that lay ahead. Unlike his brother 'Red Mick', who won the 1936 Irish National while riding with a broken collarbone on Joe Osborne-trained Alice Maythorn, 'Darkie' was better known for injuries than winners during his career in the saddle.

In 1930 he tried his luck in Australia where his first son, Kevin, was born on 5 July 1932, returning to the UK the following year. He then worked at Epsom's Grove Stables for the shrewd trainer Harry Hedges, whose yard landed a Cesarewitch gamble with Fet, ridden by Midge Richardson, in 1936.

When World War II sadly became a long odds-on prospect, Darkie decided to join up and presented himself to an RAF panel. Not only did the injuries sustained while a jump jockey –

Right:
Young Darkie at Harry Hedges' Epsom stable.

Left:
PJP as an apprentice, top row second right.

Below:
The hurricane-paced Windy City

which included a broken neck and arm fractured in eight places – disqualify him from any aspect of Air Force service, his accent proved an even more emphatic handicap. Maiming 'mainland' civilians was a popular IRA activity at that time.

So the offer of a subsidised crossing to accompany a mare purchased by an Irish stud became an irresistible invitation.

On arrival home in Kildare he contacted an old friend, Mick Connolly, who had just begun training, and rented a few boxes from him.

Our hero was 32 when he successfully applied for his first trainer's licence from the Irish Turf authorities in 1941. In the same year, on 30 September at Goffs Sales, Ballsbridge, a yearling who was to become his utterly dependable meal ticket for a decade was knocked down at 30 guineas to Messrs Kerr & Co. On behalf of his first owner, Sam Henry, Paddy bought the son of Sea Serpent out of Dinah's Daughter for £200.

From then on whatever the season, whatever the going, whenever required, Pelorus was there, ready and willing to assume responsibility for redressing the shortcomings of others and to sustain the slender Prendergast team.

It was as if this versatile performer wished to show his appreciation of his first and only trainer who would cycle through Newbridge with fodder on the handlebars. 'The grub is borrowed and the bike isn't mine,' the rider would admit with the cheerful confidence of a man whose belief in the horses in his care is unbounded. As it well might be.

Having won the Troytown Chase at Navan on 26 November 1949 under the outstanding Martin Molony, the evergreen ten-year-old Pelorus returned to the level and collected the Naas November Handicap.

As well as his gift for nurturing talent, one of 'Darkie's' great assets was the ability to spot potential – irrespective of pedigree. Consistently he reversed the usual trend by purchasing swans at the price of geese.

By the time the war ended he was positively 'flying' and ready to fire a salvo or two across the Irish Sea. A forerunner was a 350 guineas Denturius filly, Port Blanc, who, ridden by the stylish England-based Irishman Michael Beary, won Goodwood's Harvest Stakes by 4 long-looking lengths, carrying her pretty head in her chest, on Friday 30 August 1946.

The ebullient 'Darkie' had long enjoyed friendship with the More O'Ferrall family whose Anglo-Irish Bloodstock Agency, with its extensive transatlantic contacts, helped to expand the ever-developing number and distinction of the stable's patrons.

By 1951, during a preview of the season on behalf of the *Daily Express*, I was reporting from 'the biggest stable in England or Ireland [Walter Nightingall's 73-horse Epsom yard was the largest in England] – the 85 horse-power team of Paddy Prendergast.'

Further, I was drawing attention to a 700 guineas, unfashionably-bred yearling named Windy City who, in full flight, would make 'a gale-force wind appear sluggish by comparison.' Or as 'Darkie' put it to the colt's one-time cowboy, leather-countenanced, highly

Right:
Within two years of Windy City, Paddy wins the Gimcrack again with blistering-paced The Pie King.

Below Right:
Wakefield-born popular US champion Johnny Longden aboard Blue Sail, the horse who split the Anglo-Irish Turf authorities.

entertaining, horse-hustling owner, Ray Bell: 'There isn't a two-year-old foaled who could blow wind up this fellow's tail.'

Ray was more accustomed to dishing such a pitch than being on the receiving end and he accepted the assessment with world-weary grace. And appropriate disbelief.

The difference was that Ray Bell's trainer's contention was proved by four well-coordinated hooves to be right on target.

After sensationally explosive success by an easing down 5 lengths in Chester's Oulton Stakes, there were those who doubted whether, given his amazing speed, six furlongs would be within his capacity. Ridden by Gordon Richards he won the six furlongs Gimcrack by the same margin. And headed the Free Handicap.

Regrettably the 700 guineas yearling, who was sold to the US for $165,000, was injured while running second in the Santa Anita Derby and consequently retired to stud.

Within two years Ray Bell was back in the winner's circle at Goodwood, Ascot and York via the blistering speed of The Pie King, a 1953 juvenile speed merchant. The 1,850 guineas yearling's victories in the Richmond, Coventry and Gimcrack were achieved by an aggregate of 10 lengths.

This was the era of the sensational Blue Sail affair, which has been touched on elsewhere but less than fully detailed.

A late-developing two-year-old with a stamina-charged pedigree, by Tehran out of a Blue Peter mare, Blue Sail did not race until August of his juvenile year, 1953. He finished eighth in a Navan maiden over six furlongs and seventh over the same trip in The Curragh's more competitive Railway Plate a month later.

It was fairly obvious that Blue Sail would be suited to a longer trip, making Ascot's searching one mile (at the time the distance of the Cornwallis Stakes) an ideal target.

'Darkie' made no secret of the fact that he liked to bet, an admission which made him 'suspect' among many dwellers in the upper reaches of middle England in the twentieth century. For, believe it or not, so concerned were the Board of Governors of the British Broadcasting Corporation to protect the citizenry from this perceived vice that there was a comprehensive embargo in respect of any mention of betting. This was only relaxed (for Starting Prices) in 1958 after ITV initiated the service. It was another two-and-a-half years before mention of pre-race markets was forced on the Corporation by ITV relaying this information at both the race meeting they were transmitting and the BBC's!

Anyway Paddy (his hair less dark by now) not only liked to bet, he preferred to take as much precaution as possible against loss. He would have found out at home that Blue Sail warranted support over eight furlongs.

The colt (backed from 3-1 to 5-2 favourite) ran an excellent race but not quite good enough to beat Denys de Rougemont's Jack Leader-trained filly Plainsong (supported from 8-1 to 6-1), who benefited from the sex allowance and Tommy Gosling's overweight on the favourite to win by a neck.

The Ascot Stewards initiated an enquiry into Blue Sail's form and, not being satisfied by the explanation offered, passed the case on to the Stewards of the Jockey Club. The latter then published in the *Racing Calendar* a notice to the effect that: 'The running of Blue Sail in the Cornwallis Stakes on 10 October was inconsistent with his previous running in Ireland, that horses trained by PJ Prendergast would not be allowed to run under their Rules, and that no entries would be accepted from him.'

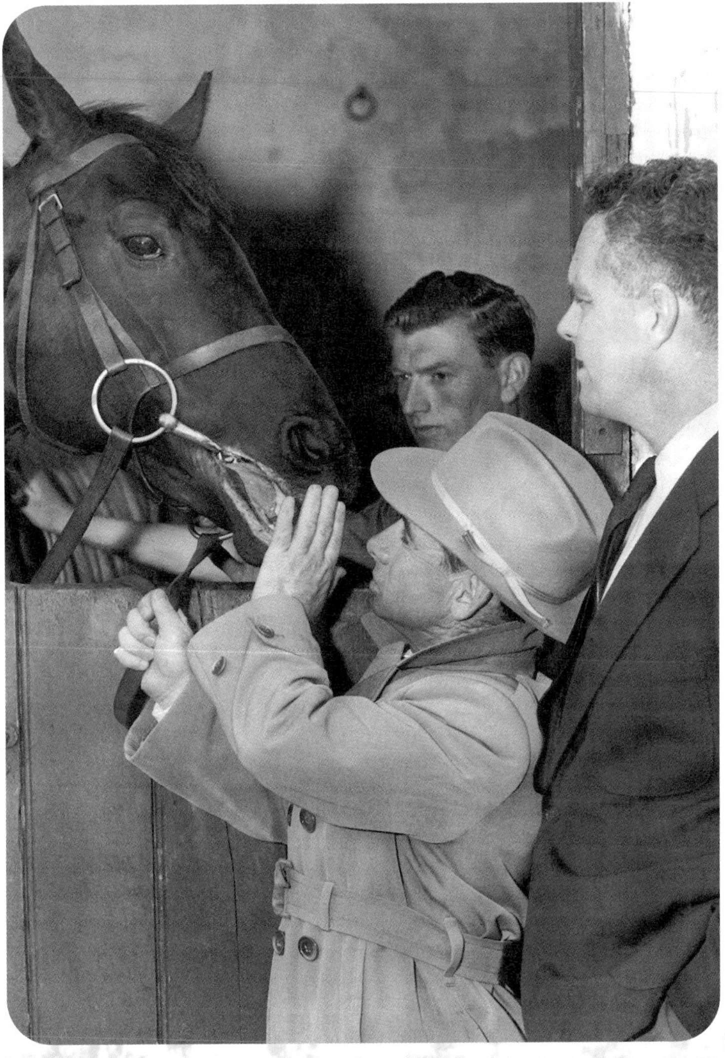

Left:
Regarded by owner Max Bell, Johnny Longden has a word with Blue Sail – or vice versa?

Below:
Ron Hutchinson, 32, on Martial (noseband, right), his first ride for the Prendergast stable, foils Aussie compatriot George Moore on 'good thing' Taboun, 1960 2,000 Guineas.

Incensed by a slur upon their competence (the inference being that Blue Sail had been 'hooked up' in both his Irish runs) and the insult to Ireland's leading trainer, the Turf Club of Ireland combined with the Irish National Hunt Committee – since Paddy was licensed by each of them – to conduct an exhaustive joint enquiry into the Jockey Club ruling.

They interviewed every senior official relevant to the case including the British (Geoffrey Freer) and Irish (Major Dick Turner) top handicappers; Stewards' Secretaries; witnesses who saw Blue Sail run in all three races; jockeys Paddy Powell Jr, Rae Johnstone and Tommy Gosling. Also, of course, PJ Prendergast.

There followed an unprecedented rebuff to the English authorities which read:

The evidence before the Irish Stewards showed that their three senior officials were satisfied with the running of Blue Sail in Ireland. The Form Books of both countries were examined and the Stewards took note of the fact that at Ascot the race was over a distance of one mile, and that the race in Ireland, at The Curragh, in which Blue Sail ran, was over six furlongs and 63 yards. The Irish Stewards were of the opinion that, on the evidence given before them, there was no unexplained discrepancy.

When the ban was lifted inside a year, Blue Sail headed a York-bound armada which included the winners of the first two races at the Ebor meeting; Panalley (Tommy Gosling) Prince of Wales's Stakes; My Beau (Tommy Carter) Nunthorpe; as well as Gipsy Rover (Rae Johnstone) Rous Selling Stakes and Blue Sail himself, 10 lengths winner of the Voltigeur under Bill Rickaby. Well backed, too.

York, Chester and Goodwood became for Paddy the 'holidays with pay' meetings which he would target annually. Target and plunder. So that by 1963, following another decade of remarkable achievement, Patrick J Prendergast became the first trainer based in Ireland to win the British title with winners

of 19 races worth £125,294. He did it again in 1964 with 17 races worth £128,102. And then completed an amazing hat-trick in 1965.

British classics winners alone in this period, following 2,000 Guineas victory in 1960 with Martial (32-year-old Ron Hutchinson's first ride for the stable) included Pourparler ('64 1,000 Guineas); the breathtaking Noblesse ('63 Oaks) and Cecil Boyd-Rochfort reject Ragusa ('63 St Leger).

As well as the classics there were two successes in the Eclipse and two King George VI and Queen Elizabeth Stakes at this time. And, of course, a posse of flying two-year-olds.

Paddy not only had the gift of spotting potential stars – he bought Ragusa for 3,800 guineas for Jim Mullion at Ballsbridge after Cecil Boyd-Rochfort had turned him down as an undersized yearling – and nurturing their talent, he inspired lifelong loyalty among members of the perennially successful team.

Christy Roche joined his boss as a 15-year-old and achieved four apprentice championships with the stable. He later became champion jockey five times before turning to training himself.

What made his old governor special, I quizzed Christy during the 2004 Cheltenham Festival?

'He was well before his time, an innovator,' said Christy. 'He concentrated on a horse's mind as much as his fitness. He liked them to be relaxed and confident, especially the fillies. He was brilliant at keeping them stress-free. The fillies would have a pony companion and he'd have them out (for two hours) on a lead rein from the pony's rider. The filly not mounted. That way they'd be exercised without knowing they'd done any work. He could judge their ability even before he had them in the yard. Didn't he buy the 1978 Irish '1,000' winner for 3,000 guineas at Goffs (Kill) as a yearling? And what about Ballymore?' asks Christy rhetorically, by now well into his stride.

Yes, Ballymore represented some achievement.

Too backward to run at two, he was prevented by lameness from running in an Irish 2,000 Guineas prep race in 1972. Lester was offered the ride but he preferred Flair Path, trained by Paddy's tall second son (born 19 March 1935) 'Long' Paddy. So Christy rode the newcomer whose first serious gallop was delayed until 10 days before the classic.

The English '2,000' winner High Top was odds-on and Flair Path 5-1. Ballymore (33-1) won comfortably from 13 rivals. Earlier in the afternoon elder son Kevin had won the '1,000' with 20-1 chance Pidget (Wally Swinburn). Not a bad family double.

From my journalistic viewpoint, one of the problems of annual stables touring was to contrive a fresh approach.

In 1965, while on holiday in Switzerland, I rang Paddy to make a date and hear his latest news. His potential classics youngsters had swept the board as two-year-olds, winning six of their eight races, and I anticipated my volatile friend giving full rein to his renowned unbridled enthusiasm. Remarkably, the three-year-old he was bubbling about was a colt who had not yet run.

After calling in at Rossmore Lodge on 15 March I wrote in the following day's paper the piece reproduced on page 46.

When phoning 'copy' I'd asked the art department to put a chef's hat on a good photograph of PJ Prendergast. The object was to flatter him from a new angle.

Above:
1963 Oaks: Noblesse and Garnie Bougoure first – and the rest ...?

Left:
Ballymore at the finish of the 1972 Irish 2,000 Guineas at The Curragh.

Opposite Page:
Top:
Pourparler (Garnie Bougoure) wins 1964 '1,000' for long-time Paddy supporter Lady Granard.

Middle:
Christy Roche, five times Irish champion jockey before turning versatile trainer.

Bottom:
A staunch and happy association: owner-breeders Jim and Meg Mullion and the man himself.

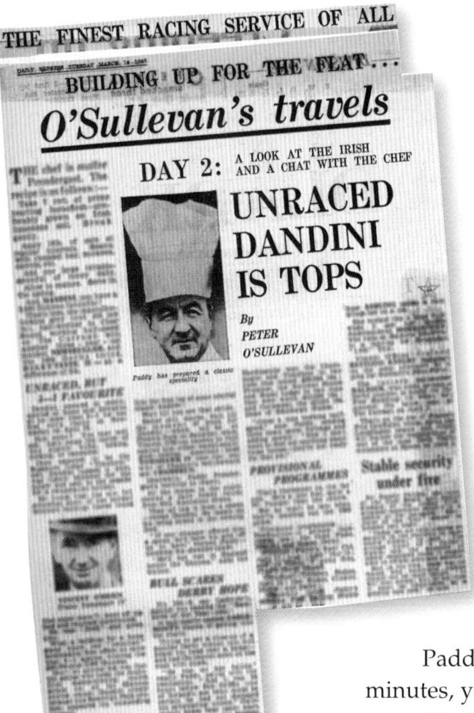

THE FINEST RACING SERVICE OF ALL

BUILDING UP FOR THE FLAT...

O'Sullevan's travels

DAY 2: A LOOK AT THE IRISH AND A CHAT WITH THE CHEF

UNRACED DANDINI IS TOPS

By PETER O'SULLEVAN

When I rang Paddy a week later he was hopping mad.

'You've made me look an idiot,' he fumed, 'a right blithering ee-jit.' I couldn't think what the hell he was raving about and said so. It was the hat.

Anyway, to cut it short, we ended up putting the phone down in unison, and starting a long period of non-communication. Until Saturday 26 June.

On that day I had just received the 'all-clear' from London after commentating the Irish Sweeps Derby victory of Paddy-trained Meadow Court at The Curragh and was hurrying down to ground level to congratulate Bing Crosby ('After listening to Paddy talk about your horse for two minutes, you just had to feel sorry for the opposition,' he once told me) and ran straight into Paddy.

Totally forgetting our rupture, I grabbed his hand and was about to shake it when he seized my left arm in a firm grip and threatened: 'If you don't come to the party tonight, I'll never speak to you again!'

I said I thought we weren't speaking now.

'That,' he said, 'was a green-eyed, jealous, so-called colleague of yours, putting in the poison and saying you'd made me a laughing

Above:
The offending photo, 16 March 1965.

Below:
Correspondence from Rossmore Lodge.

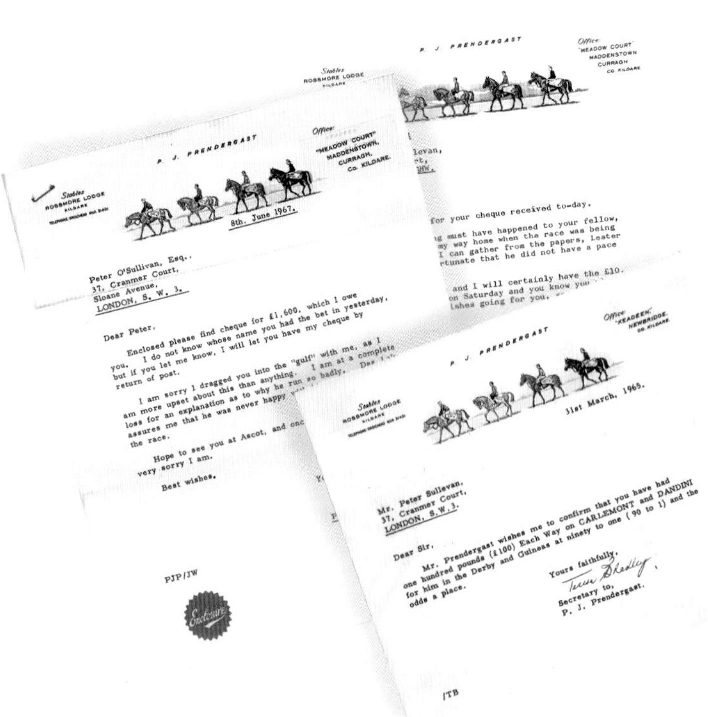

P. J. PRENDERGAST

Stables ROSSMORE LODGE KILDARE

Office: "MEADOW COURT" MADDENSTOWN, CURRAGH, Co. KILDARE.

8th. June 1967.

Peter O'Sullivan, Esq.,
37, Cranmer Court,
Sloane Avenue,
LONDON, S. W. 3.

Dear Peter,

Enclosed please find cheque for £1,600, which I owe you. I do not know whose name you had the bet in yesterday, but if you let me know, I will let you have my cheque by return of post.

I am sorry I dragged you into the "gulf" with me, as I am more upset about this than anything. I am at a complete loss for an explanation as to why he run so badly. ... assures me that he was never happy ... the race.

Hope to see you at Ascot, and onc... very sorry I am.

Best wishes,

PJP/JW

...for your cheque received to-day.

...g must have happened to your fellow, ...my way home when the race was being ... I can gather from the papers, Lester ...rtunate that he did not have a pace ...

...and I will certainly have the £10. ...on Saturday and you know you ... ...ishes going for you, ...

P. J. PRENDERGAST

Stables ROSSMORE LODGE KILDARE

Office "KEADEEN" NEWBRIDGE. CO. KILDARE.

31st March, 1965.

Mr. Peter Sullevan,
37, Cranmer Court,
LONDON, S.W.3.

Dear Sir,

Mr. Prendergast wishes me to confirm that you have had one hundred pounds (£100) Each Way on CARLEMONT and DANDINI for him in the Derby and Guineas at ninety to one (90 to 1) and the odds a place.

Yours faithfully,
Teresa Bradley
Secretary to,
P. J. Prendergast.

/TB

DAILY EXPRESS

UNRACED DANDINI IS TOPS

By PETER O'SULLEVAN

The chef is *maitre* Prendergast. The recipe is as follows:

Take 7cwt of prime yearling horseflesh – preferably grown on Irish limestone soil. Break gently.

Apply 16lb of oats at regular intervals. Season with chopped hay, molasses, carrots, etc. Add one large (s)table-spoonful of honey daily.

Allow to mature. Serve in the spring.

And, DANDINI, you have a 2,000 Guineas favourite!

That's him, the masculine-looking grey (cost £6 per lb), half-brother to Clear Sound, working half-speed on The Curragh with another three-year-old maiden, Newsrullah, and the 1964 Derby third, Dilettante II – at a difference of 5lbs.

UNRACED, BUT 5–1 FAVOURITE

Dandini, unraced in public, untried at home and favourite at no more than 5-1 for the first colts' classic at Newmarket on April 28 ...

Don't let anyone kid you that the genius who holds the Anglo-Irish stakes-winning record struck out all his Guineas entries except Dandini simply because this Sovereign Path product appeared his outstanding prospect.

I'll bet he withdrew the proven stable stars so as to remove the temptation to train the Derby hopes too early. Dandini is bred for mile running.

So I came to The Curragh expecting to write down the grey talking horse. Instead I found myself reaching for the phone and making him the first leg of some playful classic doubles! ...

1967, ridden by Des Lake, never raised any hope of ending an 80 years' sequence of failure for maidens. Paddy and I were 'on' the ultimate 8-1 third favourite to Royal Palace at long odds.

Typically, when promptly forwarding his cheque for £1,600, he wrote:

I am sorry I dragged you into the 'gulf' with me, as I am more upset about this than anything. I am at a complete loss for an explanation as to why he ran so badly. Hope to see you at Ascot, and once again I cannot say how very sorry I am.

There was no evidence that Paddy's Epsom expectations were ever modified by disappointment. When he rang during May 1971 to ask me to put him 'a towsand' on Lombardo for

stock. I shouldn't have listened to the git. He'll not be entering my yard again.'

Paddy added for good measure: 'You'll get your money back over Dandini in the last.' At 5-4, and with Lester putting up 5lbs overweight, I decided to sit that one out. And missed a winner. But I didn't miss the party at which, when it came to singing Irish songs, Paddy was rated no more than 2lbs behind Bing.

The Derby was the only classic to elude him on either side of the Irish Sea and Dominion Day in

the Derby, I had to remind him that he'd already requested £1,000 on Credit Man ('and have a word with Saint-Martin about riding him') a week earlier. There was a moment's hesitation. 'I can't separate them,' says he, 'they'll be first and second.' They were last and fourth respectively.

It was a sad day for a multitude within racing, and beyond, when on 20 June 1980 I had to stand before the Royal Ascot Press Balcony television camera and pay tribute to Paddy Prendergast, who had just died following bravely fought illness.

Within half an hour I was calling home the winner of the Winsdor Castle Stakes, Cooliney Prince, trained by our hero's youngest son, 'Long' Paddy.

Your man would have approved of that.

Above Left: Meadow Court (Lester Piggott) wins the 1965 Irish Sweeps Derby, evoking a memorable sing-song involving part-owner Bing Crosby and trainer Paddy Prendergast.

Above: Elder son Kevin, as well as 'Long' Paddy, maintains the great Darkie tradition.

Left: Radical racing journalist Richard Baerlein and PO'S at a celebration of the great trainer's achievement.

SCOBIE BREASLEY

Thursday, 23 March, 1950 was a bitterly cold, wet day at Aintree where Lord Bicester's fine nine-year-old Finnure, ridden by future champion jockey Dick Francis, had just defied the testing ground on the Grand National course to win the Champion Chase.

Conditions for the next race, at 3.45pm, run over one mile for 21 three- and four-year-olds, would be even worse.

'*She's* looking worried,' observed a stipendiary steward, pointing to an attractive, smartly dressed, clearly anxious lady who was pacing the weighing-room precinct. 'That's Breasley's wife,' he added.

Remembering that Rae Johnstone had asked me to look out for his fellow Aussie, who'd been brought over to England by millionaire miller Jimmy Rank; and that famed Melbourne commentator Bill Collins ('his wife's a cousin of mine') had requested likewise, I went over and asked if there was anything I could do.

May Breasley's concern was that 'my poor Scobe' would have no idea where lay the least unfavourable ground. So I entered the weighing room and asked a good friend, Charlie Elliott, who wasn't riding in the race, to have a word with him.

My 'copy' in the next day's *Daily Express* was captioned:

DAILY EXPRESS

SCOBIE LISTENED, THEN WON

Quiet, unassuming, Melbourne champion Scobie Breasley accepted wise counsel before making his first English ride a winning one on Promotion. Renowned for his habit of sticking to the rails at home, Breasley listened intently to Charlie Elliott's advice to avoid the soft ground on the inside and challenge in the centre.

Mrs Breasley and her young daughter, Loretta, hope to see Mr Rank's new jockey do it again in this afternoon's Spring Cup.

"Pat Quinlan taught him the almost supernatural ability to judge furlong after furlong to a split second."

Unfortunately the ground had deteriorated further and Scobie's Spring Cup partner, Jock Scot, could not handle it. But his second UK ride for his new boss, Decorum, had already bolted up, following a typical late Scobie flourish, in the opener, at 100-9 too.

The 36-year-old cavalier from Wagga Wagga (more or less between Melbourne and Sydney), who became an instant friend, was fulfilling a long-cherished ambition when accepting a retainer in England.

Not that it was by any means his intention to uproot permanently. Before the completion of two seasons, during which he rode 73 winners in 1950 and 60 in '51, he was getting homesick. And although the second season included classic success in the 2,000 Guineas on one-time 370 guineas yearling Ki Ming, he decided to return 'home'.

Much to the regret of a legion of admiring followers and friends.

Born on 7 May, 1914, the second son of a sheep drover and trainer of trotters outside the New South Wales town of Wagga Wagga, Arthur Edward Breasley spent his early life among the ponies and horses who fired both his imagination and determination to follow the career of his elder brother, 'Bonny', a very useful all-round rider, and become a jockey.

Apprenticed to the Melbourne trainer Pat Quinlan, who taught him the almost supernatural ability to judge furlong after furlong to a split second, he rode his first winner, Noogee, in 1928 on his nineteenth ride. Two years later he achieved his first major success when winning the Sydney Metropolitan Cup on Cragford as a 16-year-old apprentice.

That victory promoted an immediate enquiry. As a result the placings remained unaltered but the impetuous young rider received a two months ban – emphasising the similarity between the early career of the future Melbourne champion and his British counterpart, Lester Piggott.

For each of them controversy was a constant galloping companion.

Unexpectedly, it wasn't long before the mutual competitiveness of these supreme parallel talents would be renewed on the 'battle field'.

Sadly, Jimmy Rank had died while Scobie and May were *en route* for home and Druid's Lodge was acquired by the successful businessman and rumbustuous racing enthusiast, Jack Olding. Wisely retaining Noel Cannon, he charged his trainer with the immediate task of luring Arthur Breasley back to England.

The Melbourne champ was already into his renowned stride on familiar territory – winning a fifth prestigious Caulfield Cup in 1952. However, the incentive to go west again was positively irresistible. Back in England in 1953, he was in instant demand – Herbert Blagrave taking a second retainer after Noel Cannon and Joe Lawson coming in at number three.

Scobie's fourteenth ride of the season, Fellermelad (25-1) opened his and Druid's Lodge's score on 10 April, closely followed by the Newbury Spring Cup winner, Prince d'Or, for Derrick Candy, the next day. But the highlight of the month was a first triumph in the Royal colours after Noel Murless invited him to ride Gay Time for the Queen in Newmarket's March Stakes on 30 April. Signal for one of our cheerful dinner parties which Rae Johnstone flew over to attend.

Around this time Scobie and I took to having a short telephone chat on most mornings – a 'call-over' of the day's card – which was, hopefully, a mutual benefit.

It was surely helpful to me when he reckoned that his lovely-looking 1954 1,000 Guineas partner, Festoon, could reverse placings with her Kempton conqueror Key (favourite for the first fillies' classic at Newmarket). Hence a winning *Daily Express* selection which I was able to reciprocate a while later when Etienne Pollet rang towards the end of April 1966 saying: '*J'ai besoin d'un jockey pour dimanche.*'

He explained that the filly he needed a jockey for was a very 'light-mouthed' daughter of Right Royal, named Right Away.

She would have a good chance in that Sunday's Pouliches (French 1,000 Guineas).

As soon as he said 'light-mouthed', I reacted, 'What about Breasley?'

'Good heavens,' he exclaimed. 'He's older than you and I combined, isn't he?'

'Wait 'til you see him ride,' I countered. 'He handles a horse as Yehudi Menuhin does a violin, and Patek Philippe doesn't keep better time.'

'I suppose you're right about him suiting this filly,' he reflected – a little grudgingly, I thought.

'Can you get him?' he asked. I thought I could. And did. And after Scobie, who was a few days short of his 52nd birthday, had won his first French classic on his first ride for the stable – beating the great French jockey, Yves Saint-Martin, by an unhurried length – Etienne proclaimed: 'What a fabulous jockey that is!'

Whenever the 'fabulous jockey' achieved another landmark in his outstanding career my thoughts tended to rewind to the traumatic afternoon (Monday, 3 May, 1954) when not only his career but his life as an active individual appeared terminally compromised.

Scobie Breasley, wearing the Queen's colours in Coronation year, is led in after winning the March Stakes at Newmarket on Gay Time.

Below:
Scobie with Lester Piggott.

It was only three days after winning the 1,000 Guineas that Scobie was riding in the opener at Alexandra Park where the deceptive camber of the North London circuit often gave grounds for concern.

Like this particular day when, following a long dry spell, overnight rain, welcomed on the infield allotments, made the racing surface perilously slippery.

Just half a mile out the ominously named filly Sayonara lost her footing while leading her closely pursuing eight rivals, crashed to the turf, and pitched Scobie's unhelmeted head into the metal upright which supported the rails.

The filly was quickly on her feet (and racing within a month) but Scobie was disturbingly motionless. The duty doctor was soon on site but, according to my report, it was 20 minutes before the ambulance arrived.

A fractured skull, optic paralysis and near-total loss of balance did not augur well for an athletic future. Nor was the London Clinic patient greatly encouraged by the medical prognosis that, apart from ending his career in the saddle, he would be unlikely ever to walk again unaided.

But the deceptively mild and gentle Arthur Edward Breasley was raised in a tough school.

Fortified by May's daily visits bearing the finest East End-smoked salmon, and other essential nutrients not readily available in the notorious Devonshire Place residence, Scobie commenced recovery.

The intervals between searing headaches became longer; the determined expeditions across his hospital room less akin to the initial efforts of a novice 'chaser.

Re-homed to Roehampton, he was still prone to capsize over invisible obstacles in the house when beginning a daily rehabilitation routine at Wentworth Golf Club. For miles and miles, he walked and walked, exercising that wiry frame to the limit.

By the first week in July he was returning, bronzed, from Cannes; flying his car from Le Touquet to Lympne, and commuting to Druid's Lodge to ride work. Back in action for the Goodwood Summer meeting, he won the Trundle Handicap on 10-1 chance Victory Roll (putting up 3lb overweight at 8st 3lbs) and the Chesterfield Cup astride Prefect (100-8), both trained by Noel Cannon and carrying the 'Yellow, black hooped sleeves, black cap' of Jack Olding.

Goodwood ended on a Friday at that time. On Saturday he moved on to Epsom for a double. There followed a clutch of winners at Brighton,

"A fractured skull, optic paralysis and near-total loss of balance did not augur well for an athletic future."

Scobie on home turf in Australia, riding Zonda. The photo is in the Australian Racing Museum and Hall of Fame, of which Scobie is Patron.

Salisbury, Newbury, Bath, etc. ... before a foursome at the Doncaster St Leger meeting. And, for a man unlikely to be able to walk unaided, he was really up and running.

1954-55 was a significant period in the lives of three of the most renowned riding talents of the century. While Scobie restructured his career after that life-threatening accident, forgoing the most coveted retainer of the time; poor Gordon's (Sir Gordon Richards) incomparable sequence at the head of his profession was terminated by multiple injury; and the babe of the trio, 18-year-old Lester Piggott, won his first Derby – and the Triumph Hurdle for good measure.

Acknowledging the honour of being offered the number one job for Noel Murless (later Sir Noel), Scobie did not wish to relocate to Newmarket or to undertake regular trips thence to ride work.

So, to their mutual great benefit, Lester accepted Noel's offer.

Scobie and Gordon had already established close rapport during the former's first visit in 1950. Likewise had May Breasley and Margery Richards. So it was a special delight for Scobie to be offered, and to accept, a first retainer which endured for more than a decade until Sir Gordon retired.

Because each of this remarkable trio enjoyed a far more prominent profile in the saddle, there is an unjustified tendency to regard them as unsuccessful trainers.

The truth is the opposite. For in their respective second careers – including classic, group and premier international prizes – they aggregated more than 1,000 victories worldwide. And relished the opportunity for sustained association with the horse.

Reverting to the mid-1950s, it was then that I got Scobie his first ride for Vincent O'Brien (likewise for Lester come to that) leading to a horse-and-jockey association which reached a dramatic climax on Tuesday, 11 November, 1958 in the USA.

Scobie had experienced a couple of sightings of Ballymoss the previous year when, ridden by the versatile and talented 'TP' Burns, he had run second to Crepello in the Derby; and when winning the St Leger.

On the first occasion Scobie was aboard the Sir Gordon-trained Pipe of Peace – on whom he thought he should have won – and on the second he was runner-up to Ballymoss while riding Sir Gordon-trained Court Harwell at Doncaster.

Ballymoss and Breasley were first united in the Coronation Cup where they scored comfortably; thence to six lengths victory in the Eclipse, followed by three lengths success over the Queen's Almeria in the King George VI and Queen Elizabeth Stakes.

For their fourth association the sparkling double act was faced with near-flooded terrain at Longchamp for the 5 October Prix de l'Arc de Triomphe. Despite the outcome of the previous year's Leger, run on a decidedly soggy Town Moor, it was firmly believed that the 'soft' was anathema to the son of Mossborough.

Poor Vincent was not only advised that withdrawal from the £46,439 prize was not an option, I had to tell him that his bets couldn't be cancelled either.

Rae Johnstone, uncharacteristically horseless for this year's renewal of France's most significant race, paddled into the weighing-room to give Scobie the benefit of his unrivalled local knowledge. The gist of his laconically imparted counsel was – stick to the narrow strip of ground, paint-close, against the rails, and NEVER move off it.

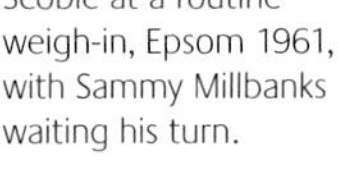

Scobie at a routine weigh-in, Epsom 1961, with Sammy Millbanks waiting his turn.

Scobie had to push, push, with hands and heels, to both reach and hold his place on the inner in the early stages. Then, for a painful spell, he looked like being crowded out altogether.

He stuck to the rails and, suddenly, as the field fanned out running into the home turn with under three furlongs to go, he was isolated in his muddy glory against the rain-washed fence.

Then, beautifully balanced by his pilot, Ballymoss surged forward, like a powerboat on a benign sea, and the race was all over.

Among the 50,000 crowd there were enough Irish present to transform the unsaddling enclosure into a Cheltenham Festival-style gala.

I figured if Scobie ever came out of the shower he would have to agree that wasn't a bad occasion on which to ride his first winner at Longchamp.

And so to Maryland for the sixth running of the £35,000 (1½ miles on turf) Washington International at Laurel, featuring 10 runners representing seven nations.

The banner headline across the front page of the following day's *Daily Express* read: 'BIG RACE SENSATION'. The sub-heading: 'Peter O'Sullevan, only British daily newspaper racing expert on the spot, tells of the most dramatic finish ever'.

Well, it may not have been the most dramatic finish EVER, but it sure did provoke pandemonium. The 40,000 racegoers, already warmed by the Maryland sun, but now thoroughly overheated, were still booing the result half an hour after the start. And what a start.

In deference to the European visitors and others unfamiliar with US starting stalls, the unpromisingly named official at the despatch end,

Eddie Blind, was instructed to effect a 'walk-up' flag start.

The intention was commendable; the upshot chaos.

Drawn on the inside Viktor Kovalev on Zaryad, who was intended to be pacemaker for the main representative of Soviet horse factory No. 33, Garnyr, repeatedly broke the ragged line in anticipating the 'off'. Likewise Venezuela's Escribano. Meanwhile Germany's Orsini, evidently frustrated by this pantomime, embarked on a vain attempt to dislodge an imperturbable Lester Piggott – making such a nuisance of himself that he was expelled to the outside.

When Mr Blind finally lowered his starter's flag an over-zealous official still had a firm grip on Zaryad who, in consequence, was hopelessly left.

Running to the first of the hair-pin bends on the tight seven-furlong circuit (where, 'two jocks ahead of me were having a fight,' reported Lester later) Ballymoss was badly baulked. Into the home stretch on the first circuit and ex-English Tudor Era led, followed by Irish representative Tharp and veteran US jock Eddie Arcaro; then Australia's Sailor's Guide and 19-year-old Cincinnati prodigy Howard Grant. The inside 'rail' was a hedge and Orsini, having slammed into it, bounced off the birch into Ballymoss. The favourite now really 'had it to do'. He made swift progress as Scobie snatched the rail on the home turn, but he'd spent all his energy getting there.

Tudor Era passed the post first from Sailor's Guide with Ballymoss third. An instant protest was lodged by the 'Sailor's' rider for having been 'fouled repeatedly' by Bill Harmatz on the 'winner'.

After debating the complaint (which was vehemently supported by Eddie Arcaro) for 25 minutes, the officials lobbed a metaphorical firework amidst the volatile horseplayers by relegating a popular and well-supported local horse in favour of the antipodean visitor whose connections were shocked and embarrassed by their jockey's action.

The announcement of the revised placing was a signal for both amplified clamour and a hectic scramble for discarded mutual tickets. Meanwhile I was phoning 'copy' and fielding an urgent BBC TV request for a recorded interview to camera with Scobie who said, before we went on air, 'It was bloody rough out there.'

Ballymoss's proprietor, John McShain, showed himself to be what the Aussies term, 'a good winner', by quitting the scene without a word to his jockey who clearly had an unfortunate run.

The British champion (title winner for the first time in 1957) was never invited to wear the American owner's colours again.

Just for the record ... three weeks after the event, I was able to report:

DAILY EXPRESS

The eighth running of the Laurel International (11 November, 1959) will be held 'over a new turf course', announced the executive yesterday. The circumference of the track will be increased by a furlong. The front and back stretches will be widened to 80ft. The turns will be 100ft wide and well banked. For the International only a new finish line will be introduced to lengthen the run-in considerably. The hedge, which formerly represented the inside running rail, will be replaced by an aluminium rail. The inside turf will be preserved specifically for the International ...

A feature of the next few years – during which Scobie won three further champion jockey titles – was the head-to-head conflict with his 21 years junior rival, Lester Piggott, who was born on the day Scobie and May were married.

There were occasions when the rivalry between the two supreme exponents of their profession became earnestly intense; competitiveness heightened by the transparent fearlessness of each. But only a hoofprint below the surface, there existed a durable level of mutual admiration. So that when Scobie realised a lifelong ambition at the age of 50 and won the Derby on Santa Claus (Wednesday, 3 June, 1964) I quoted Lester, 'We were all pleased he'd done it. He deserved it, and I tell you I am really glad for him.'

Paddy Prendergast, trainer of the third, fourth and sixth, characteristically shrugged off his own disappointment and exclaimed,

Scobie at Haydock, 1968.

Above and below: The Derby start, 3 June 1964 – and finish, with Santa Claus and Scobie drawing away to win from Indiana (Jimmy Lindley) and Dilettante (Peader Matthews).

'That was one of the finest races I've ever seen ridden at Epsom – if he hadn't nursed him like that he'd never have won.'

Epsom senior steward, the Duke of Norfolk, was the first in line to offer his sincere congratulations. The Queen sent for him to express her delight. And what of 'connections'?

Darby Rogers, father of successful trainer Mick, who had won in 1958 with Hard Ridden, had walked down from the stands seething with indignation. A respected figure, who combined experience with reticence, he was convinced that the winning rider had done everything to get beaten; that quite simply he was 'not off'. Scobie was never invited to ride Santa Claus again or any other horse in the stable.

Unaware of the reason until I told him some years later, Scobie recalled, 'I remember how well I was going at the foot of the hill and saying to myself, "Hang on now, don't lose your head, take your time". I thought I rode him alright. He did it nicely. Now you come to mention it, I thought the old captain seemed a bit funny afterwards.'

I guess that is just about the most staggering reaction to a classic ride in my experience.

Another bizarre sequel concerned a court action by Scobie against the *Sporting Life* and its correspondent, Tom Nickalls, and the subsequently demised *Daily Herald* and Don Cox. As both publications were owned by Odhams Press the actions were heard in London's High Court simultaneously.

Personally, I was affronted on Scobie's behalf when reading the *Life* on 18 October, 1961 after his partner Operatic Society (backed from 5-4 to 4-5) had been beaten by champion hurdler Another Flash (9-4 to 3-1) in Hurst Park's seven-runner Byfleet Stakes, and (Lt Colonel) Tom Nickalls – who had a gift for mishandling words – wrote, 'Curiously enough Breasley never seems to shine on odds-on chances.' The comment implied that he was either 'bent' or incompetent – or both. Statistics ruled out incompetence.

Scobie returns after Santa Claus's Derby victory, 1964.

After receiving a letter from Scobie's solicitors, Tom Nickalls wrote a note in the *Life* to the effect that he owed an apology to Mr Breasley who was a fine jockey and had won on 36 odds-on favourites during that season and lost on only 19.

Privately, I felt it would be best to accept a less than full apology given the uncertain course of 'justice'. But I wasn't the injured party and Scobie was seriously angry. The outcome? His 74-year-old Lordship found for the plaintiff against the *Herald*; the defendant (with costs) in respect of the *Sporting Life*. Net cost to Scobie – over £5,000.

I am reminded of racing sage Dick Whitford's assertion, 'I'm certain better justice comes out of the Jockey Club than from the courts of the country.'

In November 1964 we flew to Australia together in a Qantas Boeing 707. By way of celebrating that year's Derby triumph, the Victoria Racing Club had invited him as an honoured guest to take part in the renowned racing festival which features the Melbourne Cup – the richest race prize in the southern hemisphere and the greatest traffic-stopper in the sporting world – and the Victoria Derby, the oldest established race in Australia.

My assignment was to report on Scobie's 'home-coming' for both the *Express* and the local *Herald*; then to cover the Washington International and the clash between Kelso ('He'll have to run for President if he wins this; there will be no other target left') and US champion Walter Blum's partner, Gun Bow.

Wagga Wagga's most famous son, treated with the reverence of a cherished national idol, had just switched from champagne to Bordeaux with his duck and declined a second Peach Melba on the last lap of a long flight when, on the back of the menu, he calculated that, since his first win at Werribee in 1928, he'd lost three and a half tons. Like this: he'd been riding for 36 years and taken off a minimum of 1lb a day – up to 3lbs on a hot day – so at an average of 150 days' race-riding a year, and allowing for 1½lbs a day, that is 8,100lbs.

It was a great bonus to be able to go to scale at 8st in colours without having to undergo any significant weight-reducing measures. 'It makes that Lester all the more a bloody marvel,' he reflected.

The matter of Scobie's participation in the Derby and 'Cup' – the only major race on the Australasian circuit to have eluded him so far – was becoming an embarrassing issue. While his hosts hoped very much that he would be in action, they had no control over the owners and trainers involved. Racing was more parochial in that era and the fact that there was no stampede to unship regular and tried partners in favour of a 50-year-old grandpa was due, in part, to the thought that he might be ring rusty round the tight home track.

However, on our second morning, there was a very promising looking invitation on behalf of a Derby hope, by the '57 Eclipse winner Arctic Explorer, who had won his maiden nicely. I had rented a self-drive, as usual wherever I went, and we drove out to Caulfield for Scobie to ride 'work'.

"'That was one of the finest races I've ever seen ridden at Epsom - if he hadn't nursed him like that he'd never have won'."

Charlottown and Scobie beat Pretendre (Paul Cook) in a photo-finish for the '66 Derby.

The trainer, Charlie Sanderson, was one of the old school and appreciated the benefit of alliance with Arthur Edward Breasley. While Scobie set off in the early morning light on the sand track, Sanderson said, 'This'll interest you, I've asked the "old fellow" to come even time [15 seconds to a furlong] over six furlongs. He won't have done this for a long time. We'll see how much he's forgotten.' At each marker the trainer pressed his watch. 'Spot on' is an inadequate description. He just was not a hundredth of a second out. To me, a miracle.

It wasn't a morning for superfluous discussion. We had each made a serious assault on the production of one of the country's finer vineyards on the previous evening. For a time we proceeded in silence broken, finally, by Scobie declaring, 'I won't be riding THAT horse.' Surprised for the second time that morning, I asked if he had an alternative prospect. He had not but would rather be in the stands than on HIM.

Prominent in the betting, he was named Bering Strait. I enquired what was wrong with him. 'I don't know,' replied my fellow traveller, 'but he's a bastard.'

Searching enquiry among my colleagues in the Flemington Press room yielded no stain on Bering Strait's character. Nor were there grounds for questioning his ancestry. Among race-writers and radio reporters there remained those who reckoned 'the old fellow's' reject as fair value. But Scobie, who had literally ridden before he could walk, somehow sensed an alien vibration.

Starting stalls were not yet introduced in England. Here, as they flashed open for the start of the richest Victoria Derby, there was a collective intake of breath as Bering Strait dived across the only horse on his inside, pitched, and hurled his rider, Ian Saunders, into the running rail.

Scobie knew I'd be late back to the car park because I had 'copy' to write as usual. When we finally met up he was drinking with friends in the evening sun, having been to commiserate with the injured jock. He filled me a glass of cool champagne, raised his own and smiled, 'Good health, Pete, I told you that horse was a bastard!'

He courteously came to the airport to see me off to the US the next day, reflecting that it would be hard to match Derby-winning year, 1964, in the future. Yet, remarkably, 18 months later, under a caption, 'SALUTE TO GRANDPA THE GREAT', I was writing:

"He filled me a glass of cool champagne, raised his own and smiled, 'Good health, Pete, I told you that horse was a bastard!'"

DAILY EXPRESS

For as long as the Derby remains the greatest of all horseraces, the 187th in the series will be remembered by all who saw it – on Downs or screens – as a testament to the supreme all-round artistry of the grandfather from Wagga Wagga, Scobie Breasley.

Nor does any tribute to the 52-year-old Australian detract from the brilliantly confirmed potential of his 32 years younger rival Paul Cook. "I was thrilled with the way he rode Pretendre," was the generous reaction of veteran trainer Jack Jarvis.

But it was the range of talent of the maestro, whose athletic example should invigorate the over-50s, that landed Charlottown in the winner's circle yesterday.

The early portents for Lady Zia Wernher's son of Meld (first Oaks winner to produce a Derby winner since 1921) were ominous in the tense preliminary.

First the tell-tale sign of apprehension as he sweated up in the paddock. Then the long period of anxiety as his off-fore had to be replated. Yet immediately he was united with his imperturbable partner in the rainswept paddock he was relaxed and cool.

The transmission of confidence was probably as much the determining factor as the remarkably tender ground-saving ride he received from flag fall to winning post.

Charlottown was Scobie Breasley's first winning ride in the Wernher colours – a ride that would have been Ron Hutchinson's excepting the owner's belief that the colt reacted less than perfectly to his style. Nor in his natural disappointment were there any hard feelings from 'Hutchie'. As it was he initiated a golden day in the life of first-year public trainer Gordon Smyth on the two-year-old Flying By, and completed it on fully reformed Barrymore in the last.

"For as long as the Derby remains the greatest of all horseraces, the 187th in the series will be remembered by all who saw it as a testament to the supreme all-round artistry of the grandfather from Wagga Wagga, Scobie Breasley."

Charlottown and 'Grandpa the Great' led in after the 1966 Derby.

Right:
A happy duo – Scobie and Cyril Mitchell after Be Friendly wins at Kempton.

Opposite Page:
At the launch of **Calling the Horses**: left to right, Jimmy Lindley, Scobie Breasley, Geoff Lewis, Joe Mercer, Brough Scott, PO'S, Edward Hide, Lester Piggott and Peter Scudamore.

I should add that Scobie only accepted the Charlottown ride after an absolute assurance that, irrespective of his decision, Ron Hutchinson would be replaced.

Charlottown was no easy ride, as he emphasised when ridden by Scobie (for the last time) and beaten a length, without excuse, in the Irish Derby. Four days later, as jockey and owner, we were sharing Kempton's winner's circle with Be Friendly after Scobie's first ride in my colours.

Just over three weeks later, as Lady Zia Wernher and my wife, Pat, shared the televised delight of England's World Cup triumph while staying at Bailiffscourt, one of our favoured south coast hotels, Scobie and Be Friendly staged a smooth repeat at Epsom. They looked set for a sequence when poor Scobie crashed out again.

He was back in time to resume the successful vein in Kempton's opening big race of the 1967 season, the 2,000 Guineas Trial; for Royal Ascot's

CALLING THE HORSES
PETER O'SULLEVAN
CALLING THE HORSES
PETER O'SULLEVAN

King's Stand Stakes and the Vernons. But, come 1968, he'd begun to wind down a little.

When he cabled from Barbados on 1 February '68, 'Cannot decide between Minho and Sir Herbert Lincoln stop please advise stop love to both from us Scobie', I responded in clear favour of Sir Herbert, and wrote in the *Express* (3 February), under a caption:

DAILY EXPRESS

SCOBIE PICKS HIS LINCOLN PARTNER

Scobie Breasley will ride Sir Herbert in the Lincoln. The most significant Spring Double riding engagement to have been made so far means that the 53-year-old maestro will be teaming up with Peter Easterby for a second time in the Doncaster handicap.

The previous occasion was 1965, when the jockey-trainer partnership scored with Old Tom.

Further significant details are that before leaving for his Barbados holiday home Scobie had expressed a doubt whether he would return for the opening meeting of 1968 'unless there was a chance of a really good ride in the Lincoln', in which he was also offered the mount on current ante-post favourite Minho ...

No sooner was the ink dry on my ante-post voucher than Sir Herbert ruled himself out through injury, and his intended pilot decided to prolong his holiday in Barbados. Minho finished tenth.

By now, since I wanted to run Be Friendly as a five-year-old when Scobie would have retired, Cyril Mitchell, the horse's trainer, became obsessively anxious to put up younger super-sub, Geoff Lewis, on a permanent basis. But come what may, it was firmly agreed that the Vernons Sprint Cup was sacrosanct. It was a target frequently toasted throughout 1968 between Scobie and myself.

Be Friendly would be the final ride of his career. Although the four-year-old was odds-on to succeed in the six-horse renewal on 9 November at Haydock, where the coloured racecard frontispiece featured the partnership winning in 1967, Lester Piggott had volunteered his last race mount, Harbour Flower, trained by his father-in-law Sam Armstrong, to Scobie – in case Be Friendly failed. 'I want him to go out on a winner,' said Lester simply.

The wind of fortune which was expected by the weathermen to disperse Haydock's very local shroud of fog could never raise a canter. 'RACING ABANDONED', read the *Manchester Evening News*.

At least there was no fog in Barbados on 3 March 1993 when, at 78, Scobie Breasley trained the winner of the prestigious Cockspur Cup yet again; and announced his retirement to Australia where he celebrated his ninetieth birthday on 7 May 2004.

Good on you Scobe!

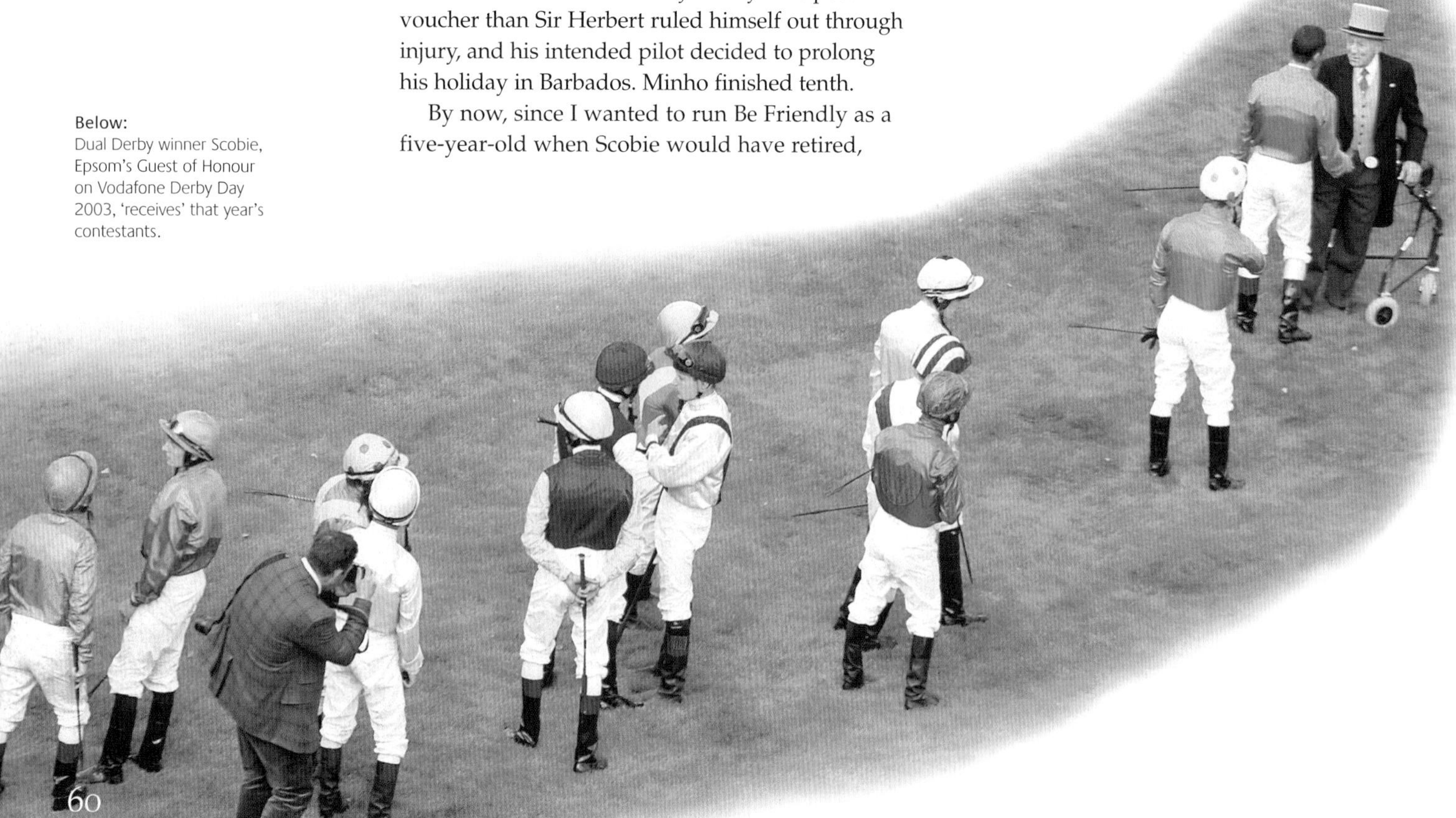

Below:
Dual Derby winner Scobie, Epsom's Guest of Honour on Vodafone Derby Day 2003, 'receives' that year's contestants.

BE FRIENDLY

A lingering kiss from the delectable sixties pop idol, Sandie Shaw, as she presented me with a gold trophy, did nothing to dispel the feeling that Haydock's 2.30 on Saturday, 5 November 1966, had simply been an extravagant dream.

A dream containing such improbable ingredients as a fine and exuberantly athletic chestnut two-year-old named Be Friendly, carrying my undistinguished black and yellow colours, ridden by an apprentice who could not claim his allowance, striding clear of the season's acknowledged top senior sprinters inside the final furlong – according to my BBC television commentary – to win the richest all-aged race ever staged in Britain by a comfortable two lengths, receiving a vociferously generous ovation in the process.

The dream further included such unlikely embellishment as Be Friendly at odds of 15-2 (10-1 to early customers) landing the O'Sullevan nap and becoming the middle leg of a 57-1 *Daily Express* treble completed by another swift-rising young star, Persian War, at Sandown, where the gallant Freddie won the Gallaher Gold Cup.

The subsequent, gratefully received, avalanche of telegrams (it was the era of hand-delivered messages) and mail (literally by the sackful) inevitably evoked reflection on my involvement as a small-time owner – thus far.

When Pretty Fair, ridden by French jockey friend René Emery, trained by Charlie Bell, won the Castle Selling Hurdle (£186 first prize) at Windsor, on 11 March 1954, he was the first of 16 horses in 15 years to achieve a place in my colours.

Admittedly they were for the most part 'rescue' horses – the shameful export for slaughter traffic was a feature of tawdry countrywide markets – or gifts: or purchases at up to three figures which always began with the numeral 'one'.

Far from heralding a change of fortune in his proprietor's career as an owner, Pretty Fair, who had been bought in after the 'seller' for 110

Below:
Just Friendly after the Mynne Selling Stakes, Epsom 1958.

guineas, indicated unmistakably, during several subsequent appearances, that he had no further interest in impersonating a racehorse. In fact, a lady owner of substantial proportion had offered me £100 for him as a hunter.

However, fearing that his slightish frame might be unsuited to the task, I gave him to a lissom young friend instead. He carried her for many years with the Cottesmore with mutually happy zest, and sure-footed gratitude.

In 1957, while the O'Sullevan 'livery' was being borne by a filly (Big Sister) of singularly uncompetitive disposition, we dined one evening at the house of an American actress friend of my wife, Pat. Our hostess's stockbroker husband, Stephen Raphael, had been a prominent devotee of the Turf before the Second World War when he trained with George Lambton and Billy Laye. He had not owned a horse, or any part of one, for over a decade.

The port had already completed more circuits than the runners in a long-distance chase at Plumpton when Stephen posed a question which would lead us, within a decade, to joint ownership of one of the sprint stars of his era.

Yes, I'd be delighted to welcome him in his proposed role of 'back-seat' partner: a situation, he suggested, which would enable me to enter the yearling market with 50 per cent more ammunition than previously. Still only a few metres above the bargain basement, I figured, but offering potential for improvement nevertheless.

Our first runner, 600 guineas purchase Just Friendly, competing on the first day of the 1958 Flat season, scrambled home by the length of a well-smoked cigarette in Lincoln's Stonebow Selling Plate.

She followed up with a less heart-stopping success in another 'seller' at Hurst Park. After which Cyril Mitchell and I said: 'Snap'.

We had both spotted an ideal race in a fortnight at Ally Pally, or, to give the highly individual frying-pan-shaped circuit its little-used proper title – Alexandra Park.

The Enfield Plate, five furlongs, ideally catered for maiden two-year-olds – 'selling' races excepted. So we would enjoy an experience advantage over many of our 18 rivals as well as the conviction that the stable's chestnut daughter of Ballyogan was improving almost hourly.

The start took place among the patchwork of diligently tended allotments, out of sight of the grandstand and, apparently, of the starter.

Backed from 6-4 to 10-11, Just Friendly was drawn in the most favoured berth, 19.

Unfortunately her regular partner, Ken Gethin, a renowned 'job' jockey, good friend and no mean judge, was taking a turn and facing in the wrong direction when the dispatcher pressed the starting lever. It was related afterwards that Ken's language caused the official's guide dog to faint.

Amazingly the 3.30 favourite still ran home sixth.

The sensible ploy would have been to wait awhile and see how she was treated come the 'nursery' season. But there was a Derby eve 'seller' at Epsom in which, excepting further intervention by fate, Just Friendly would be very, very hard to beat.

Oscar Wilde once observed that he could resist anything but temptation. I recklessly considered a gamble in the Mynne Selling Stakes – winner to be sold for £100 – to be irresistible. Even if we had to go up to 1,000 guineas to buy her back, granted success.

Before their ill-conceived emasculation in 1963, 'selling' races were a source of drama and entertainment.

There was a surfeit of both elements associated with Epsom's 2pm on Tuesday, 3 June 1958.

Staff Ingham-trained, Scobie Breasley-ridden, comfortable Windsor maiden winner, Lady Cobbler, was the initial 6-4 favourite in the eight-horse field, followed by 9-4 Just Friendly and 4-1 well-fancied Rhythm Queen.

After some lively exchanges the front two changed places and JF became the 6-4 market leader.

Binoculars trained on the crest of the precipitous five furlongs chute, I saw our filly swerve as the tapes rose.

Ken Gethin, already putting up an unexpected 1lb overweight, lost both pedals. Meantime, Lady Cobbler was flying down the hill into a commanding lead. The 3-1 offered about Just Friendly could have been trebled without takers. Yet, remarkably, having picked off her rivals one by one, there she was, inside the last 150 yards, skating up. 'Led cl home', reported *Raceform*, with the accurate detachment of the uninvolved.

While the principal sauntered nonchalantly into the winner's circle, which would shortly become a sale ring, I found elation giving way to apprehension.

As if there had not been anxiety enough for one day, this was when my worries would really begin.

The easy-going winner of the Mynne Selling Stakes had barely completed a round of the tight

"Binoculars trained on the crest of the precipitous five furlongs chute, I saw our filly swerve as the tapes rose."

"I raised my hat to our adversary and gave Just Friendly a final, grateful, farewell pat."

Opposite Page:
Be Friendly and Tony Boyle preparing for take-off.

Below:
Cyril Mitchell, an instinctive, unorthodox and gifted trainer.

little ring when our 'budget' of 1,000 guineas (my bid) was already reached – and breached.

At that time any sum bid beyond the stipulated selling price (in this case £100) was divided equally between the owner of the second and the racecourse; the auctioneer receiving the guineas.

By the time the lady racegoer, who coveted the focus of ringside attention, had bid 1,500 guineas, the victory represented a loss – including prize-money but excepting bets – of £1,250.

I tried another fifty. Sixteen hundred nodded Mrs Margot Lorne, proprietor of a model stud in the former productively cultivated Rhodesia. At least it would be a fitting home.

I raised my hat to our adversary and gave Just Friendly a final, grateful, farewell pat.

While awaiting shipment, the daughter of Ballyogan was placed in the very capable care of 'Towser' Gosden (father of outstanding trainer, John) for whom she won a 15-runner Lewes 'nursery', under 9st top-weight, without breaking sweat. By 4 lengths too. No wonder she won three 'sellers'.

It was not long afterwards that I fell in love (on the rebound?) with a charming grey filly from the first crop of the very genuine northern-trained colt Quorum (later sire of Red Rum, no less) at Newmarket's September sales.

820 guineas she cost. A bargain. Not that her racing record inspired unqualified admiration.

Friendly Again ran in 34 races on the Flat, over hurdles and fences, between the age of two and six, reaching the frame 18 times and winning twice; once over hurdles at Lingfield; once on the level over 13 furlongs in a Sandown apprentices' 'selling' handicap. She always gave her utmost and never allowed failure to weaken resolve. She had a marvellous temperament, a sometimes undervalued characteristic, which is invariably reflected in families.

There was stamina, distaff-side, and I convinced myself that, allied to a swifter sire than the excellent miler Quorum, her dam, Lady Sliptic, just might produce the goods.

So provided he looked the part – and he did, though some purists 'crabbed' his hocks – the chestnut colt by the fast and fertile Skymaster out of Lady Sliptic just had to be bought. Even at 2,800 guineas. And he was.

County Limerick-born Be Friendly's first stable yard in England was adjacent to a public house at Burgh Heath, Surrey, in a once rural area which would shortly become a housing estate.

In the brief time before Cyril Mitchell relocated his team to Downs House, Epsom, within a furlong of the Derby start, the youngster had established himself among his two-year-old contemporaries as the indisputable leader of the pack.

He was exuberant, powerful and, as his strength developed, a right handful.

From day one Cyril, a former tough, grafting jump jockey, recognised Be Friendly's need of a strong lad who embodied the qualities of both firmness and patience.

His nomination, Tony Boyle, was inspired and in the opinion of Cyril's five times amateur champion son, Philip, who ultimately succeeded him, probably crucial.

As in most firm relationships, horse and lad had their differences. But there was a strong bond of mutual affection between them, highlighted when they travelled together to France (five times). Be Friendly liked to fly with his head resting on Tony's shoulder.

Within several weeks of the opening of the 1966 season, now located at Doncaster, Cyril, who did not enthuse freely, was convinced that the Downs

2

House youngsters were 'alright' – especially the Willie Madden-bred product of Lady Sliptic, Be Friendly.

By way of reinforcing his judgement, he sent the youngster along one March morning with an older horse, Espeekay, who was due to run shortly. Disregarding convention, to which he accorded low priority, he had the senior receiving 15lbs from the junior.

Irrespective of this unorthodox concession Be Friendly ran away from Espeekay who, nevertheless, galloped to face-saving victory over 17 rivals in the six-furlong Canterbury Handicap at Lingfield on 25 March.

If ever the portents for a successful launch were favourable, surely it was now. But, somehow, legitimate expectation has a habit of foundering in the small world of racing as the graceful central player reminds mortals of his structural fragility.

First a glancing blow from a high-spirited stable mate transformed him into a box-ridden patient – invalidating a series of well-considered entries. Then, sufficiently recovered to venture forth, he trod on an alien object and suffered a stone bruise.

There followed a bout of 'flu which swept through the yard like a plague.

I began to dread hearing Cyril on the other end of the 'phone and we agreed that, in future, provided it was justified, any call was prefaced by, 'He's OK', before we discussed jockeys, entries, etc.

Entries, in fact, included Lingfield's Appleblossom Stakes on Saturday 14 May. Unfortunately I was due to commentate for the BBC at Ayr that day and when I rang Cyril from Scotland on Friday night he was very downbeat. After confirming the blood test fine, he added:

Scobie and Be Friendly move steadily to the start.

'But I won't have a shilling on him tomorrow.'

Another two-year-old, Gay Knight, he'd run that day – backed from 10-1 to 5-1 – had finished last. Not a good sign.

Often only the exertion of a race reveals recovery from a virus to be incomplete.

Still, it seemed mad to me not to have an 'interest'. Despite the rumours that this was a very 'hot' race, featuring some youngsters who could not just catch pigeons but do so without moving out of first gear. I had a 'pony' (£25) each-way at SP with most of the rails bookmakers at Ayr and one or two of the boards operators.

Jimmy Lindley, whom I had written of a fair while back as 'one of the brightest young apprentices I've ever seen', was aboard. His instructions: 'Get as near as you can, but don't knock him about.' I never wanted one 'knocked about'.

Anyway, he was third (25-1) and when, at half way on the drive back to London, I called Cyril, he reported: 'He hasn't turned a hair, enjoyed himself, and Jimmy said he'd be better for the race.'

Unusually, pre-race rumour proved well founded. The winner, the Duke of Norfolk's Luciennes, trotted up next time out in the Caterham Stakes at Epsom, starting at 9-2 on, and even the sixth, On Your Mark, turned the Great Surrey Stakes (Epsom) into a procession before winning Royal Ascot's Windsor Castle by six lengths.

Our reappearance was delayed – this time by sore shins – until 6 July and the Wren Stakes at Kempton.

Earlier in the season I'd warned Scobie that he might have to take a first ride in my colours this year.

'Is that right?', he reacted, trying politely to suppress the note of disbelief in his voice. Since then he'd ridden 'work' on Be Friendly and expressed gratifying approval.

Among the opposition this day were a Noel Murless-trained debutant brother to the very speedy Abelia, named Cholo, a first ride for the stable by Lester Piggott since a controversial 'split' two months previously; and Bloody Mary – a highly regarded US-bred daughter of an unbeaten Molecomb winner.

There were only seven runners, so our fellow had to be in the first two to justify my each-way selection.

Scobie returned with a broad smile and full of apology. Through my unsteady binoculars Be Friendly had broken smartly and always seemed to be holding them, despite hanging slightly in the closing stages.

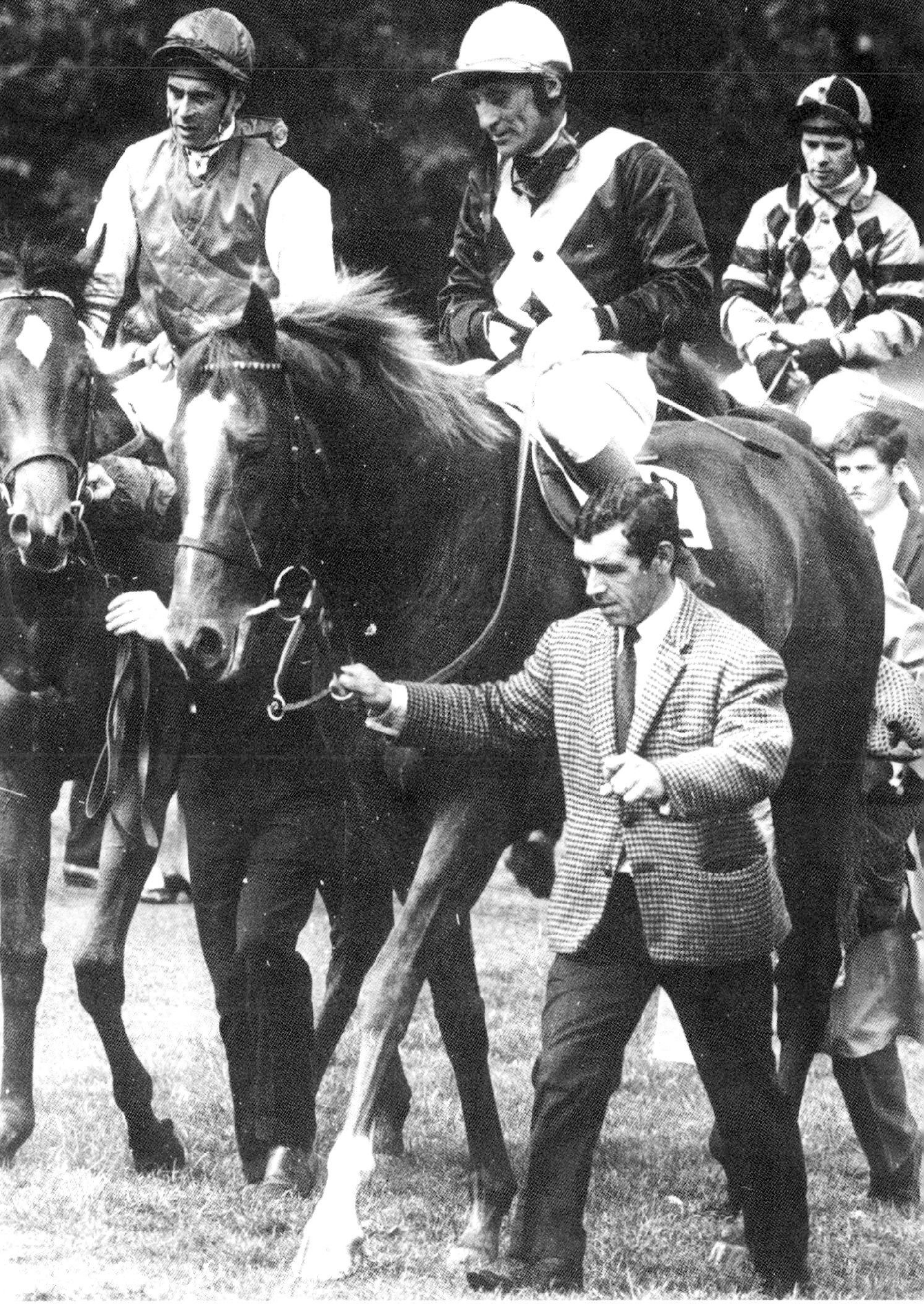

Be Friendly and Scobie after being beaten a head by Manacle (Brian 'Ernie' Taylor, left) at Kempton, 11 May 1968.

The maestro from Wagga Wagga very seldom used his stick, so I shared my equine hero's surprise when, inside the last furlong, he picked up his whip and gave him a couple. They won by two lengths.

Dismounting from his fourth successive winner of the afternoon, Scobie explained wryly, 'I must have had a rush of blood to the head being so keen to win for you.' He added: 'At least the colt took it very well. Didn't seem to resent me at all.'

On the day, 30 July, that England's footballers won the World Cup, Be Friendly confirmed that he bore Scobie no ill-will by conveying him to the winner's circle after Epsom's six furlongs Box Hill Stakes. Then, the following month, disaster.

Scobie, who had already survived a career-terminating prognosis following an appalling accident in 1954, suffered another sickening crash. This time at Newbury.

Counted out for the season, he agreed that I would be right to consider a good claiming apprentice for forthcoming 'nurseries' because, said he, 'The colt is a very easy ride.' Adding, on another occasion I was visiting him in the London Clinic: 'You may find that he is even better, possibly much better, when there is "give" in the ground.'

I'd been quite impressed by Colin Williams, a young man apprenticed to a particularly charming Newmarket trainer, Jack Leader. So I canvassed the opinion of a few jockey pals – every one of whom was positive. Even Lester opined, 'He's all right' – a very high rating on the Richter scale of Piggott praise.

Our colt was in the always intensely competitive Highclere Nursery at Newbury with 8st 6lbs. That looked to be a perfectly fair assessment, but it would look fairer still with a 5lb reduction. I rang Cyril and asked what he thought of Colin Williams. 'Never bloody heard of him!' was the reply.

The going was again on the fast side and we were drawn unfavourably low (3) in the 16-runner field, starting third favourite (13-2 from 8-1). Colin made his way gradually towards the stands side,

Be Friendly congratulated by PO'S after 1966 Vernons.

5 November 1966: Be Friendly and Colin Williams led in by Tony Boyle, with Philip Mitchell, after winning inaugural Vernons November Sprint Cup.

struck the front over a furlong out, but was caught close home and beaten ¾-length by 20-1 chance Early Turn (drawn 16) who was totally unfancied, despite a featherweight, and not even plated.

Cyril kept his admiration for jockeys well under control and, anticipating criticism, I got my retaliation in first by asking in the unsaddling enclosure: 'The boy did nothing wrong, did he?'

'Absolutely nothing,' he responded. 'He'll do me anytime.'

So Colin was booked for the recovery mission over the same course and distance (5 furlongs) in the Wantage Nursery on Saturday 22 October. 7-1 third favourite in the 22-runner field, we were unfavourably drawn (4) again, but 'holding' terrain would put Scobie Breasley's theory to the test.

Both my readers looked like collecting a furlong out. And they did.

'A different horse altogether on this ground,' pronounced the young pilot from Cascade, Glamorgan. 'Absolutely smashing!'

The runner-up, Miss Wolff, had been a 3 lengths course winner first time out and, while giving her 23lbs, Be Friendly conceded similar weight to some strongly fancied opponents.

I had long shared the enthusiasm of immensely popular and innovative course clerk John Hughes for the introduction of an event on the lines of Longchamp's Prix de l'Abbaye, in which top two-year-olds met their seniors.

This was to be the inaugural year (1966) of the Vernons-sponsored, richly endowed, November Sprint Cup to be run over the six furlongs Haydock dog-leg for competitors of all ages.

The entry had been made in a spirit of wild hope. Now that 'Himself' had got so far so well, what was there to lose by running? Especially since it usually comes up mud at Haydock at the season's close – as it did at Manchester.

The more I thought about it the more convinced I became that, provided he reacted positively to his latest effort, we must have a go.

When ringing Cyril in the morning to renew congratulations and seek a health bulletin, I learned that our hero was in exuberant spirits, indulging a contented roll in his personal sandpit.

Right:
Be Friendly's second Vernons (1967) trophy presented by Susan Hampshire.

Below:
A foggy day at Haydock Park. PO'S, Pat, Scobie and Pucci – in doggy bag – put a brave face on it, 9 November 1968.

'Hang on, hang on,' reacted Cyril when I expressed my wishes. 'We can't do that. When he got beat in the Highclere I took him out to save you a tenner.'

So that was that. Until, three days later, Be Friendly's handler rang to report that 'the secretary' (his wife Robbie) had slipped up somehow and the forfeit form had been found, unposted, under the blotter. 'So if you still want to go to Haydock, we can.'

Pragmatically it seemed absurd to put up an apprentice, who was not eligible to claim his 5lb allowance because of the value (£5,000+) of the race, when such experienced talents as Edward Hide and Ron Hutchinson were available to ride at the prescribed weight for two-year-olds. It would be tantamount to volunteering a 5lb disadvantage.

On the other hand, Colin knew the horse and had confidence in him. And how extra appealing if the two youngsters could combine to launch each other into the big time. I would understand if Cyril demurred. He didn't. 'Suits me,' he reacted without a second's hesitation.

So at 7am on the damp morning of 5 November 1966 there we three (Alex Bird, Colin Williams and myself) were, walking the soggy (happily) six-furlong course at Haydock – the

verdant site mid-way between Manchester and Liverpool.

Although it involved forfeiting ground (approximately 1½ lengths – deceptively less than it appeared), I favoured crossing over to the stands side at the turn, inside half a mile from home, and asked professional punter friend Alex, a leading exponent of the stratagem, to help me explain it to Colin.

The 22-year-old rider, opposed by four in his partner's age group, including impressive Ascot winner, Green Park, and the top senior sprinters in the country, was an instant convert.

He reckoned that the ploy earned him the dramatically emphatic victory which inspired an avalanche of domestic telegrams, emanating from the Workhouse to Clarence House; one of the first overseas cables coming from a convalescence address in Barbados:

> Thrilled by wonderful news of Be Friendly's great triumph stop love to you both from us Scobie

While leading a generous chorus from Ireland was one from 'Dad' – Skymaster.

In view of the stamina in his dam's pedigree, would Skymaster's son stay a mile? Scobie didn't think so. However, as the new season approached, following a few months break, we decided to at least up the trip to seven furlongs.

Left:
Be Friendly and Scobie win Kempton's 2,000 Guineas Trial – just! – in March 1967.

Below Left:
Scobie and Be Friendly, Tony and Philip, after victory in Royal Ascot's King's Stand Stakes, 1967.

Unfortunately for me the obvious option, Kempton's 2,000 Guineas Trial, coincided with a BBC request to commentate at Teesside (Stockton) that day – 25 March.

I was not obliged to accept but, as I continually complained about the Corporation losing TV coverage, it seemed inappropriate to opt out of the least appealing dates. I went North.

In fact Scobie wanted to ride another horse, Starboard Watch, on whom he had also been unbeaten the previous year. However, he allowed himself to be talked out of that, and according to Tom Forrest in the *Sunday Express*:

> Scobie's triumphant return on Be Friendly made yesterday's 2,000 Guineas Trial a smash-hit with the first day crowds at Kempton. Breasley hadn't ridden since his crashing fall at Newbury last August 13. For a 52-year-old whose back was still rumoured to be weak, the Australian artist produced a Herculean finish to snatch back the lead from Quy by a short head.

Thereafter we never exceeded six furlongs. As it was, when I called Scobie to congratulate him, he gave all the credit to his partner, saying: 'He knew when I needed help and he gave it to me. It was his "class" that pulled him through.'

Be Friendly accepts appreciation after his King's Stand effort.

Five weeks later, within two days of his 53rd birthday, Scobie survived a horrific three-horse Newbury pile-up from which he was lucky to escape with severe bruising and a broken collarbone. So Freddy Head took over in Longchamp's Prix de Saint-Georges on 18 May.

Despite unhelpfully quick ground, he shortened from 15-2 to 5-2 in the 11-horse field which included two fellow English travellers.

'I've never been so fast in my life,' exclaimed Freddy, adding that when he let him down he hopped from leg to leg on the fast surface. He was beaten half a length by the local champion Yours.

Scobie was back well in time for Royal Ascot's King's Stand Stakes before which the rain fell just in time; and Be Friendly avenged Longchamp – winning by a ½-length, cleverly, from Yours.

Apart from the heaven-sent weather break on 23 June, resulting in 'a great and thoroughly popular end to a great Royal Meeting', according to my colleague Len Thomas of the *Sporting Life*, it was a summer of discontent for those of us who anguished over sun-dried turf.

The July Cup at Newmarket was our next obvious target on a day when Scobie was contractually 'claimed' to ride at Brighton. We kidded ourselves with an assortment of delusory racing euphemisms (there's no 'jar' in the ground, etc.) and let him down by letting him run.

Super-sub Bill Williamson reported afterwards, 'The way I was travelling I thought he'd pick up the winner as soon as I asked him, but he just couldn't use himself on the firm ground and went from cantering to struggling in a few strides.'

It was the first time in 12 outings that Be Friendly had been unplaced. *Mea culpa*.

The sun which, normally, I would have travelled a long way to relish, finally gave itself a break towards mid-September, making the Ayr Gold Cup a possibility. Enough for me to ring John Banks and make a small investment. To win it he would need to overcome the highest weight for a three-year-old since Old Reliance won in 1938, not to mention the biggest field in the history of what was then Britain's richest sprint handicap. And he would be without Scobie, who was required by a retaining stable at Kempton.

As I drove up to cover the meeting for the *Express* and BBC TV, rain in the lowlands raised hopes of favourable ground and three days before the big one the course walked like a dream – a dream that was soon to become a nightmare as the sun reappeared with powerful rays.

Lord Sefton had generously released that renowned raconteur and talented jockey Geoff Lewis from his Kempton runner, Aura, and Scobie's deputy and very good friend was to travel north by overnight train with Cyril.

On the eve of the race, to be run on Friday 22 September, I told my colleagues in the Ayr press room that I was tipping Be Friendly each-way. But that Geoff was to ride him in the morning, and if he was not fully satisfied that the colt could come to no harm under the conditions, he'd be withdrawn – irrespective of penalty.

Before the 'work' the duo came within inches of parting company as Geoff's ebullient first-time partner erupted with explosive energy. The 31-year-old ex-pageboy and future ally of the redoubtable Mill Reef confessed, 'I thought he'd lost me for certain.'

More importantly, he was emphatic: 'There's no way he could come to any harm on this ground.'

Of course the low draw (4) was a worry in a 33-horse field – both before and during the race. Scobie had firmly advised Geoff to 'give him a chance', and not to go too soon.

In the event, after two furlongs he became worried that the stands side group were getting away from him. So he gave Be Friendly a nudge and 'in a few strides I was there,' he related afterwards, adding: 'I knew I'd done it all wrong but he didn't bother, just kept going. The best six-furlong sprinter I've ever sat on.'

Starting at 100-8 he won by 2 lengths, virtually easing up. The 22,000 crowd gave him a right

Be Friendly (Scobie Breasley) wins his second Vernons in a dramatic finale from the talented Mountain Call (Russ Maddock), 1967.

welcome and I loved the good-humoured Scottish voice in the throng around the unsaddling enclosure, whence I sprinted from the commentary point: 'What would he have done if it had rained, Pete?'

The celebrated surgeon Arthur Dickson Wright, a real racing aficionado and great fan of Skymaster's heroic son, wrote afterwards: 'I've been racing for many years without ever hearing a winner given such a tumultuous reception.'

In contrast to the Ayr Gold Cup – for which the intended stalls had to be dispensed with because of the size of the field – the nine-runner renewal of the Vernons Sprint Cup was a nightmare to call.

Scobie was back on board – against the wishes of Cyril who, with an eye to the future as he put it, wanted to stick with 22 years younger Geoff Lewis – and the serious danger appeared to be a very useful two-year-old Mountain Call, winner of five races, including at Deauville, and due to receive 18lbs from us. His excellent Australian rider, Russ Maddock, not only knew him well but, having partnered Green Park in the inaugural running, knew all about the vagaries of the course which was later turned into a far less interesting straight six furlongs.

I had the temerity to ask Scobie to walk the muddy course with me. Needless to say, it did not take him long to get the message.

Right:
Dead heat at Chantilly between Be Friendly (Geoff Lewis) and Klaizia (Freddy Head).

Below:
Longchamp defeat: Scobie explaining to Cyril and PO'S why he was slow from the stalls.

As Be Friendly preferred to be 'dropped in', Mountain Call was predictably first to the stands rails, the senior in the wake of the junior.

In a race which was swiftly reduced from nine runners to an intense duel, my commentary was riding with Scobie's dilemma.

He wasn't going well enough to come off the fence and challenge. Yet if he didn't do so he'd got no chance – unless Mountain Call finally tired and edged off the rail as he did so. Scobie stayed where he was, knowing he was doing right; knowing he'd get plenty of 'stick' if the ploy failed. Well inside the final furlong Mountain Call rolled. For several strides the two brave chestnuts ran head to head. Just before the line Be Friendly thrust his head forward on a muscular neck and it was a photo. Be Friendly by a neck. Neither deserved to lose.

Mountain Call was no slouch. Never out of a place in 11 runs as a three-year-old, his six successes included Newmarket's Palace House and Challenge Stakes, the Cork and Orrery at the Royal Meeting and Deauville's Prix Maurice de Gheest.

Racing is a hard game and come 1968 it has to be said that, apart from my Chelsea neighbour and friend, Greville Baylis, and myself, it was difficult to find anyone who did not believe that Scobie was now 'over the hill'. He'd been beaten on Be Friendly in successive races in England and France and Cyril felt (strongly) that, by indulging loyalty to a friend, I was prejudicing the livelihood of those who were committed to the career of the stable star.

The jockey question did not arise next time, 24 July, because Scobie was 'claimed' for Sandown. So Geoff Lewis was back in action for Chantilly's five furlongs Prix du Gros-Chêne in which, racing from a usually disastrous draw, he dead-heated with Suzy Volterra's useful filly Klaizia. Then, regrettably, Scobie was beaten a ½-length on him in the Nunthorpe after, in Cyril's view, 'putting the horse into the race too late.' Our fleet-footed conqueror was So Blessed whom we met on five occasions, scoring three-two in Be Friendly's favour.

I had written a 'Farewell to Scobie' piece in early August, following the four-times champion's long-debated decision to retire at the end of the season, and reaffirmed the hope that he would exit triumphantly by winning the Vernons again on Be Friendly. It was a frequently toasted target between us.

Be Friendly and Geoff Lewis hit the front prematurely in the 1967 Ayr Gold Cup, but still win cosily.

Meanwhile there was the Ayr Gold Cup and the Prix de l'Abbaye de Longchamp. He had a daunting 9st 7lbs top weight in Scotland as well as still being without his ground. Ayr is a lot further from Roehampton than Kempton, where Gordon had runners but would, I happened to know, let him off.

Cyril considered that if Geoff deputised again in Scotland he should also have the ride at Longchamp to avoid any more swapping around. It was time I made a concession, and that seemed perfectly fair.

Whilst Be Friendly and his less distinguished brother, Stay Friendly, were being boxed up for the long haul north, Scobie opted for a less arduous trip to the local circuit and Geoff booked his passage to the land of Burns.

Backed down to 5-2 favourite (100-8 bar) despite the absence of rain and the requirement to concede up to 35lbs to his 20 rivals, BF positively radiated confidence as he moved to the start like a lion.

Drawn 12, Geoff had him perfectly positioned at halfway, but he just didn't seem to be moving with normal fluency. Two furlongs out and I felt something was wrong and hoped my concern was not reflecting in commentary. Petite Path, a grey filly owned, bred and trained by Ron Mason and his wife, streaked home to become the first-ever winner of the Queen Mary and the Ayr Gold Cup.

Be Friendly, sixth, had apparently arrived at the start with a 'twisted plate' (near-fore shoe hanging off). There was no equipment to address the situation. Nothing for it but to wrench off the footwear so that he 'ran' in three shoes.

The senior starter, Alec Marsh, observed, 'It's like a professional runner trying to perform with one bare foot,' adding: 'My team in the south always includes a qualified blacksmith with necessary equipment.'

A bitterly disappointed Geoff Lewis (disappointed on behalf of his partner as much as anybody) lamented: 'He just could never find his action.'

So responsibility for recovery of self-esteem and sponsorship of the 900-mile round trip now rested upon the less substantial shoulders of his younger brother. I would not like to have been in Be Friendly's (three) shoes on the return journey after Stay Friendly (admirably handled by my long-time friend Edward Hide) had scooted home 6 lengths to the good in the Craigmore Selling Handicap.

Above:
Be Friendly (Geoff Lewis) after winning Longchamp's Prix de l'Abbaye, 1968.

Below Right:
Terence Gilbert's vivid interpretation of Be Friendly winning at Royal Ascot '67 and the Abbaye '68.

Pity about that shoe. John Joyce had laid me £2,000-£120 the double!

Ian Balding hosted Be Friendly's final pre 'Abbaye' workout when generously offering the facility of Kingsclere's fine peat moss gallop. Our hero arrived in France both fine-tuned and about to wear blinkers, to which Skymaster products seemed so well suited, for the first time since a solitary occasion as a two-year-old.

I collected Geoff from his Paris hotel in my self-drive at 7am on Sunday 6 October, so that we could walk the five-furlong Longchamp course in tranquility. We had drawn the ace position (11 of 11) in the international field in which the Aga Khan's seven-race-winning (including the French 2,000 Guineas) Grey Sovereign colt, Zeddaan, was odds-on in British bookmakers' ante-post lists as well as local forecasts. As we walked the sprint track, we agreed the marker at which Geoff was to 'let him down', but not before.

On the evidence of our soaking feet the going was no problem.

When Geoff rode into the unsaddling enclosure after the race and I greeted him hurriedly before running to the Prix de l'Arc de Triomphe commentary point, he said in mock apology: 'I'm sorry mate, I haven't let him down yet.' And that was the truth.

Even to this hopelessly biased, heart-in-mouth observer, there never appeared the faintest requirement for him to change gear.

Maybe Roger Nataf was putting it a bit strong (good on him!) when he wrote in *Paris Turf* of the 1968 winner of Europe's richest (£13,000) speed prize: 'One of the best if not the best sprinter in the world during the last 20 years.' But fewer would dispute Geoff's quote in the *The Observer*: 'When it's soft and he's right, he's unbeatable.'

The Longchamp verdict was two lengths victory over the game French two-year-old A Croquer, with Lester Piggott-ridden So Blessed third, ahead of Ireland's Desert Call. Zeddaan (who'd only just come back to sprinting) was seventh; Pentathlon, last year's winner from Germany eighth; the King's Stand winner D'Urberville ninth and Klaizia, with whom Be Friendly had dead-heated on very different ground at Chantilly, last.

Immediately after the Arc broadcast, during which I made fleeting reference to the Abbaye result, I hustled to the unsaddling enclosure to interview the associates of the brilliant winner, Vaguely Noble, and was intercepted by Phil Bull, who was in earnest conversation with Bill Hill,

2—EVENING STANDARD, SATURDAY, NOVEMBER 9, 1968

FOG BEATS BREASLEY

JACK WATERMAN: Haydock Park, Saturday

Scobie Breasley's brilliant career as a jockey fizzled out tamely here this afternoon as fog wiped out the last day of the 1968 Flat season.

The announcement of final abandonment because of thick fog came at 3.30 after paying customers—those who had bothered to stay—had waited, wondering why the stewards had persisted in a Canute-like attitude to the weather which had palpably borne no evidence of likely improvement for hours.

After a decision to put racing back half an hour, the visibility, down to about 20 yards, gradually got worse. The chases were abandoned and further inspection announced. The sun, visible like a dull sovereign above the haze, disappeared altogether. Then the stewards gave in.

The important Vernons November Sprint Handicap would have decided the top sprinter—Be Friendly, So Blessed or Mountain Call.

Mr. Peter O'Sullevan's Be Friendly has been widely expected to give 54-year-old Breasley a victory on his retirement day.

The Jackpot pool of £3428, carried forward from yesterday, will now be carried over to the next Jackpot meeting in March.

founder of the bookmaking business which bears his name.

'You know what you should do, don't you,' inquired the boss of *Timeform* without waiting for a reply. 'You should retire your horse right away and syndicate him for £3,000 a share and put William and me at the top of the list. In fact, we'll pay you for two shares now if you want.'

The capital valuation which this represented was modest by twenty-first century standards, but in 1968 it was seriously meaningful.

To recognise good advice is one thing, to accept it is another. As far as I was concerned, the joy of owning a good horse with a zest for racing was to have him race; while to syndicate was to run the risk of losing control. Whatever the future, it appeared that only fate could obstruct the realisation of his next target, a Vernons Sprint hat-trick and a simultaneous dream exit for Scobie Breasley on Saturday 9 November.

I was staying at a motel on the East Lancs Road for the last meeting of the season and, when I drove to the course at 7 o'clock on the morning of the race, there were patches of fog swirling round the grandstand. A record crowd was confidently expected and when Tony Boyle led out the odds-on favourite for Haydock's showpiece, I remarked to him apprehensively, 'I hope this fog doesn't get any thicker.'

Be Friendly's lad heeled the resilient turf, gave his horse an affectionate pat on the neck, and responded, 'It's the only thing that could beat him – nothing else will.'

Readmission tickets were issued when the gates opened at noon, so that, in the event of abandonment, payment was valid for a future occasion. Peering out from the stands the fog was dense enough to obscure even the outline of the last fence.

The first two races (due to be run over the 'chase course) were in turn postponed, then abandoned.

The weather forecasters expected significant early-afternoon improvement, inspiring the stewards to request the big-race jockeys to weigh out in readiness for action.

Looking down on the bleak scene from my commentary point, I noted bookmakers offering an unappealing '6-4 Be Friendly, all in, race or not.' Appreciating that all my sympathy should have been focussed on Scobie, I could not help casting a mercenary thought to my £1,000-£100 voucher Be Friendly for a Vernons hat-trick, struck with John Banks these many months ago.

By three o'clock it appeared odds-on that the horse whom the *Daily Mail* had referred to as 'the undisputed sprint champion of Europe' would return to Epsom without getting his feet wet. And so he did.

Within less than two miles of the course I switched off the Jag's fog lights. Bright sunshine lit the motorway.

Be Friendly (Geoff Lewis) before winning the Palace House, 1969.

I was convinced, by both his performance (at Longchamp, particularly) and ever more powerful physique, that he was better than ever; and that he could even improve further. Of course it was commercial sense to retire him to stud on a spectacularly high note as a massively compelling four-year-old.

But should we be ruled by 'commercial sense'?

Be Friendly had been 'courted' for many months as a potential stallion by (Capt) Robert Elwes on behalf of his excellent Ennistown Stud, near Kilmessan, in Co Meath. Robert renewed his proposals at the hastily convened dinner party I gave at Chez Conti in the Rue Lauriston after the Abbaye. I reported to my wonderfully indulgent partner, Stephen.

Reacting generously, as ever, he acquiesced to keeping him in training but hoped that, to protect his investment, I would agree to the sale of one of his two legs. And, if so, maybe I could find a buyer? I thought that was a fine and magnanimous compromise and, to sustain the balance of our partnership, sold one leg to Robert Sangster and one to mutual friend Jeremy Hindley – then a successful Newmarket trainer – so that we became a partnership quartet.

With hindsight I'd have settled for paternal retirement. Who could guess that the capricious English climate would select 1969 to put the purveyors of sun lamps and tanning paraphernalia out of business?

As it was, the always eagerly awaited *Timeform* Annual renewal reported in the *Racehorses of 1968* survey:

> Be Friendly's host of admirers – including Bert at the garage – will welcome the news that he is to remain in training in 1969 ... A fine, handsome colt, Be Friendly is a consistent performer, a great battler and a smashing sprinter, deservedly one of the most popular to have raced in this county for many years.

It was a notable achievement on the part of Cyril Mitchell ('he's been doing exercises in his sand pit') to have 'Himself' fit enough to tackle his first '69 target, the Sceptre Stakes at Kempton where, 'on ground much too firm for him' (*Evening News*), he 'ran his heart out in his usual game fashion to take the Sceptre Stakes by a head' (*Sunday Telegraph*).

The surface remained resolutely unfavourable for his next planned sortie, the prestigious Palace House Stakes on Wednesday 30 April at Newmarket where, wrote Michael Phillips of *The Times*:

> Although better sprinters than Be Friendly are seldom seen, he is faced with the formidable task of having to give 10lb more than the weight-for-age allowance to the three-year-old Acquit who, earlier this month, won a competitive handicap at Ascot by 5 lengths without coming 'off the bit'.

Be Friendly (Geoff Lewis) beating old rival So Blessed in Palace House '69.

"Yes, he was really great once again; but for how much longer would he be willing to extend himself on an unforgiving surface?"

Even so, the *Sporting Chronicle's* eminent authority, Peter Willett, was able to report on the following day:

Be Friendly whose courage never flags, restored some sanity to top class form by giving his usual impeccable performance, running on gamely as ever to hold off the challenge of his old rival So Blessed, with the Irish horse, Excessive, third, in front of the three-year-old Acquit.

Yes, he was really great once again; but for how much longer would he be willing to extend himself on an unforgiving surface?

As if in response the buds of May were subjected to such a drenching in the north that Chester was abandoned, waterlogged, as the Dee overflowed; likewise Teesside, Newcastle and Pontefract were flooded. At York a monsoon trench was excavated in a bid to drain the Knavesmire's deep black mud.

On 15 May 1969, the *Sporting Life* (1 shilling, or 10p) led with:

Top sprinter Be Friendly, who is in cracking form, looks a good thing to gain his third win off the reel this season in the Duke of York Stakes.

I wasn't working (writing apart), just worrying, and when I watched him led out in the morning I thought he looked a little out of sorts.

'He got the scent of a young lady in stables last night and he's been a bit naughty,' explained Tony delicately. There's always something new to worry about. That excellent young rider Sandy Barclay, a devout Be Friendly admirer, had already given me cause for concern the previous afternoon. Referring to the going, which was on the heavy side of unraceable, he offered: 'You wouldn't want to be too disappointed if you were beaten on this going. Under these conditions the greatest horse in the world could lose.'

The time for the Dante Stakes (1¼ miles), two days earlier, was a record 100 lengths slower than average, and there had been sustained rain since.

There were only four runners and he was 9-4 on, followed by previous victim, Great Bear, at 5-2.

The race was run in nightmare slow tempo with Great Bear and Ron Hutchinson splashing along in Be Friendly's slipstream until easing out over a furlong from home and sluicing by. The distances: 5 lengths, same and 8. 'He just couldn't get any sort of grip on the ground,' said a disappointed Geoff Lewis.

From there on he could get a grip alright, just as tyres get a grip on a dry motorway. But right up to, and including the Vernons finale, the surface remained uncompromisingly firm. So that after running third (still beating So Blessed) in the King's Stand at sunlit Royal Ascot, he didn't run again in England for three months.

In the week before the Vernons on 1 November our fellow received a heart-warming supply of good-luck tokens in the form of four-leaf clover, heather, mini-horseshoes, etc. ... A group from Halifax writing to say their van would be placarded 'Be Friendly Supporters Club'.

Aubrey Renwick wrote in the *Life*: 'I would dearly love to see Be Friendly end up his brilliant racing career on a successful note', adding prophetically, 'but the going seems unlikely to be soft enough for him'. It wasn't.

For just a few strides two furlongs out I gave him a chance in commentary, but he couldn't match the acceleration of my heartbeat.

Not on that ground. As the television re-run illustrated, he repeatedly changed legs as soon as extra effort was required.

Cyril Mitchell reflected, 'He was only able to have one gallop at Epsom which he really enjoyed.'

Still, referred to by Miles Napier in the *Irish Field* as 'one of the bargains of all time', he left the course with record European earnings for a sprinter of £43,880; winner of 12 races (including a dead-heat) and placed in another 10 from his 29 runs.

Richard Baerlein claimed in *The Observer*:

No horse has ever been run more openly. The public have been informed up to the last possible moment of how he was likely to perform. They have known what he's had for breakfast, lunch, tea and dinner, and over the last four years he's been a great benefactor to those who have listened or could read ...

Hearteningly his fan mail after failure, following gallant effort, in his last Vernons, matched that inspired by his initial triumph. Now, in a short while, he would be off to the Ennistown Stud where his half-sister, Friendly Again, was already a matron.

Tony Boyle accompanied him on the flight and stayed a few days in case he was homesick.

Soon settled in and quick into his stride at stud, he was a joy to behold in his new environment ('Eats, oats and loves?', to paraphrase Ms Truss). Every time I snatched a few hours to fly over and feed him a polo (it had to be the mint with a hole; when I forgot his favourite and bought a substitute he declined irritably) he looked better than ever.

Robert Elwes became a good friend and we shared delight in the stallion's high fertility and subsequent volume of winners which progressed annually until, distressingly, Robert became gravely ill.

The stud was placed on the market. Meanwhile Robert Sangster contacted me, as a partner, to report that he had received a very substantial offer for Be Friendly from South Africa. He insisted that the economic argument for sale was overwhelming – particularly since the stallion income was subject to a high income tax level for UK residents.

I was frankly horrified by the thought of losing all control over the horse's future and told him so.

Robert could have easily swung the vote. But he said: 'If you want to be sentimental about it, I'll forget it.' So HE became ANOTHER of my heroes!

Robert Elwes strongly favoured a move to Frank Hillman's Old Fairyhouse Stud at Ratoath, which was where he went and, continuing to enjoy outstanding success, remained until the end of the '78 covering season when the stud changed ownership.

So, a mature 15-year-old, he returned to the land of his racing days and the welcoming, impeccably-run The Elms Stud of Richard and Meg Bowers, in Northamptonshire.

He had developed a faint lung problem towards the end of his stay in the well-irrigated country of his birth and, although this had no impact on what are prosaically called 'stud duties', it would be nice to have him so much closer to Chelsea.

On 16 May 1979, following the previous day's three-length triumph of the grey Friendly Fun at York, the *Sporting Life* reported that 'this 255th victory for Be Friendly offspring will have been well received at his new home in England'. It was, and there would be many more to come.

TLC might have been invented for him. It was liberally supplied by his 'lass', Maureen Caddick, whom he clearly idolised and *vice versa*. But nothing could arrest the advance of the tormenting cough that increasingly racked his frame – as distressing to hear as to experience.

By 1981, now 17 years old, he had been retired from 'duties' and, at the last count by the *Official Statistical Abstract*, the super-fertile chestnut had sired winners of 325 races valued at more than £550,000 worldwide. And already 30 of his daughters had themselves produced winners. The great heart was beating regularly but the flesh was becoming heart-breakingly weak. There was no involvement of mercenary insurance to consider. Just 'Himself'.

"... 30 of his daughters had themselves produced winners"

We agonised for weeks, for days, for hours, before his sympathetic vet Bob Bainbridge regretfully pronounced the only course of action.

On the day the deed was done the horse whom Scobie Breasley described as 'the greatest sprinter I ever sat on' was led into his paddock by Maureen and his gentle executioner. While they made a fuss of him, and I stood by – a surrogate Judas – the deep, rasping cough disturbed a cock pheasant. He pricked his ears as the bird scuttled across his line of vision. And it was all over.

Now, thanks to the inspiration and initiative of Haydock Park chairman, Bill Whittle; the generous sponsorship of Stanley Leisure; and the artistic talent of ex-jockey Philip Blacker, a life-size bronze of Be Friendly is a focal point at the famed Lancashire circuit.

PO'S and sculptor Philip Blacker with the Be Friendly bronze at Haydock Park.

DR VINCENT O'BRIEN

Come 4 November 1958, on the evening of which we were sharing a flight from London to New York, Michael Vincent O'Brien, 41, racehorse trainer extraordinary, had already proved himself to be a horsemaster of legendary talent.

He had trained the winners of four Cheltenham Gold Cups (including three in succession); three successive Grand Nationals; a hat-trick of Champion Hurdles; and had virtually taken over both divisions of the Cheltenham Festival's highly competitive Gloucestershire Hurdle since 1952. This year's representatives being Admiral Stuart (division one) and Prudent King (division two), both successful under TP Burns – as brilliantly versatile as the Ballydoyle horses. Incidentally 'TP' rode five of the 'Gloucester' winners; Vincent's ever-supportive brother 'Phonsie' four, and Pat Taaffe one.

By now the score on the domestic front included the Irish Derby (twice), Irish Cesarewitch (five times), Irish Cambridgeshire and Irish Lincoln (twice each) as well as the Irish National, Leopardstown 'Chase, Thyestes, Galway Hurdle, etc. ...

The airline steward had refreshed our glasses a few times before the conversation turned to the horse who was the reason for our transatlantic crossing – the great Ballymoss, who was hot favourite to end a notable career on a high by winning the Washington DC International in his owner John McShain's home country on Veterans Day, 11 November 1958.

Vincent and I were born only 11 months apart; we both married in the same year (1951); we skied together during all-too-brief winter breaks. We'd been good friends since the glory days at Cheltenham. I'd often bet for him there and since.

During my annual stables' tour in England, France and Ireland, winner-prospecting for the *Daily Express*, I'd noted the meticulously planned expansion at Ballydoyle where the personnel's bicycle shed was soon replaced by a car port. In 1953 I'd written: 'It is not in accord with tradition for classic winners to be trained in Tipperary, but I am fast developing the opinion that with Vincent O'Brien, one of Ireland's youngest trainers, almost anything is possible.'

In 1957 I knew Vincent had a good opinion of the colt Ballymoss, (whom he'd bought on behalf of John McShain for 4,500 guineas at the '55 Doncaster Bloodstock Sales) despite a relatively unspectacular career as a two-year-old. So it was no big surprise when my friend and colleague Michael O'Hehir, a top racing journalist and interpreter of the sport via radio and television, rang in May to say he thought we should have a little 'interest' in Ballymoss for the Derby. Coincidentally, within a few minutes, I received similar counsel from another source.

The son of Mossborough out of a mare Indian Call, bought by breeder Richard Ball for 15 guineas at Lord Glanely's dispersal sale, was quoted among the 33-1, 50-1 or 100-1 others – depending on the bookmaker.

Below:
Ballydoyle

6, OLD BURLINGTON STREET
LONDON, W.1

TELEGRAMS: ADHERBAL, TELEX, LONDON
TELEPHONES: REGENT 6700 (10 LINES)

DIRECTORS: M. STEIN, H. GREEN, S. RADLEY, A. G. BURNETT, S. R. BRIGHT, T. J. MOLONY, C. STEIN, H. J. BUCKMASTER, I. STEIN, I. A. R. PEEBLES, F. R. KAYE, THE EARL OF WESTMORLAND

11 July 19

Dear Sir/Madam,
According to your instructions we have obtained for you :—

RACE	HORSE	WIN	PLACE 1, 2, 3
King George VI Queen Eliz Stks.	Ballymoss	2500 500	312 10

Yours faithfully,

P. O'Sullivan Esq.

6, OLD BURLINGTON STREET
LONDON, W.1

TELEGRAMS: ADHERBAL, TELEX, LONDON
TELEPHONES: REGENT 6700 (10 LINES)

20 May 1957

Dear Sir,
According to your instructions we have obtained for you :—

RACE	HORSE	WIN	PLACE 1, 2, 3
Derby	Ballymoss	2500 25	833 6 8 25

Peter O'Sullivan Esq. Yours faithfully,

No. M 67874

6, OLD BURLINGTON STREET
LONDON, W.1

TELEGRAMS: ADHERBAL, TELEX, LONDON
TELEPHONES: REGENT 6700 (10 LINES)

28 May 1957

Dear Sir,
According to your instructions we have obtained for you :—

RACE	HORSE	WIN	PLACE 1, 2, 3
Derby	Ballymoss	2000 40	666 13 4 40

LADBROKE & CO., LTD.

Member of Victoria Club, National Sporting League and Turf Guardian Society, Limited

Telephones: BALHAM 1288, CROYDON 6117-6118 (Private before 11 a.m.)
Telegrams: NIGHTLIGHT SOUPHONE LONDON

"HURST VIEW GRANGE," 149, PAMPISFORD ROAD, SOUTH CROYDON, SURREY

No. AZ4434
Time 9/40 AM
30 5 1957

Dear Sir,—I confirm that I have laid you the following, viz.:—

AMOUNT OBTAINED		AMT. INVESTED	NAME OF HORSE	TO WIN OR 1-2-3	NAME OF RACE
£1000	TO	£10	Ballymoss	W	Derby
£250	TO	£10	"	123	"

Mr. Peter O'Sullivan

Yours faithfully,

D. Upex Ltd

18709

MEMBERS OF VICTORIA CLUB AND NATIONAL SPORTING LEAGUE

TELEPHONE: REGENT 0761
TELEGRAMS: UPEX REGENT 0761

17, SAVILE ROW, LONDON, W.1.

P. J. O'Sullivan Esq. TIME 24th May 1957

Dear Sir/Madam, According to your instructions we have executed the following for you :—

£	s.	d.	To	£	s.	d.	Horse	Win/Place	Race
1000				10			Ballymoss	Win	The Derby
333	6	8		10			"	123	"

Yours faithfully,
p.p. D. UPEX

DAVID COPE LTD
LUDGATE CIRCUS, LONDON, E.C.4

Telephones: CENtral 4272 (Private Branch Exchange)
Telegrams: CHIPPY, TELEX, LONDON

ANTE-POST VOUCHER No. J 2028

Managing Director: ALFRED COPE

Dear Sir,—In accordance with your instructions we have obtained for you at 20 May 1957

AMOUNT OBTAINED		AMOUNT INVESTED	SELECTION	PRICE	WIN OR PLACE	EVENT
2500	To	25	Ballymoss	100/1	Win	Derby
833	To	25	"		123	

Total amount invested £50

DAVID COPE, LTD.
Alfred Cope
Managing Director

GENUINE NO LIMIT

JACK WOOLF AND CO. (Turf Accountants) Ltd.

743

Managing Director: J. M. WOOLF · Directors: H. WOOLF L. WOOLF

MEMBERS OF VICTORIA CLUB, LONDON, NATIONAL SPORTING LEAGUE and T.G.S.
DIRECTOR OF BOOKMAKERS' PROTECTION ASSOCIATION

Telegraphic Address: "SCEPTRE" BIRMINGHAM
HERALD CHAMBERS
MARTINEAU STREET
BIRMINGHAM, 2

Booked at 12-0 NOON
24-5 1957

Dear Sir, We beg to say we have obtained the following for you :—

£	s.	d.		£	s.	d.	Horse	Win or Place	Race
1,000	0	0	TO	10	0	0	BALLYMOSS	WIN	DERBY
333	6	8	TO	10	0	0		123	

Yours faithfully,
pp. Jack Woolf & Co. (TURF ACCOUNTANTS) LTD.

To PETER O'SULLIVAN
Address

A/c. No.
Checked by

Amount Invested £20/0/0

Some Ballymoss-inspired ante-post vouchers

Above:
Vincent and Jacqueline, Royal Ascot 2000.

Below right:
Ballymoss and Scobie power through the Longchamp mud to a Cheltenham Festival-style reception after winning the 1958 Prix de l'Arc de Triomphe.

Below left:
Vincent O'Brien, 1957.

Aware that the faintest whiff of support for a potentially 'live' outsider could swiftly ruffle the market, I phoned Vincent to enquire if he wanted to be 'on'. After a little deliberation, he didn't. The horse had come to himself nicely without any pressure, as his infinitely patient handler liked him to do; but he'd suffered a stone bruise which had interrupted his preparation. Vincent felt that he would 'still give a good account of himself,' adding that he wouldn't put me off backing him, though he felt there would be better opportunities later.

Among the better-looking vouchers I collected, and still hold (*see page 83*), were:

£2,500 - £25 each way David Cope
£2,500 - £25 each way Ladbroke
£2,000 - £40 each way Ladbroke
£1,000 - £10 each way Jack Woolf
£1,000 - £10 each way Dick Upex
£1,000 - £10 each way Albert Williams

There were a few more 50s and 40s. And what a race Ballymoss ran.

I'd selected Lester's partner, Crepello, but must admit my pocket was wrestling with readers' interests when in a rough race, as so many Derbys were in the pre-film patrol era, Ballymoss went two lengths up in the straight and for a few strides looked to have it won. Until Lester pressed the button and Crepello grabbed him late. At least it was still a-quarter-the-odds-a-place in those days. Enough to pay for a few dinners at Le Coq d'Or and The Caprice. And, incidentally, what a training performance by Noel (later Sir Noel) Murless with a fragile-legged horse who ran twice only at three and completed the 2,000 Guineas-Derby double.

The next race for Ballymoss was the Irish Derby in which he trotted up (at 4-9). There followed defeat on York's 'dead' ground which, as I discovered later with Be Friendly, can be death to any horse. Then the first of our betting dramas featuring the oldest British classic, the St Leger.

It was now reasonably assumed that heavy, or even soft, going was anathema to Ballymoss. So, meticulous as ever, before giving me the green light to bet £1,100 each way during the afternoon previous to the final classic, to be run on Wednesday 11 September 1957, Vincent walked every yard of the extended 1 mile 6 furlongs circuit.

When we met outside the weighing-room, as arranged, he expressed satisfaction with the terrain and, looking no happier than he ever did as a big race approached, signalled the go-ahead.

If Ballymoss hadn't been bogged down on Knavesmire, where he was beaten by one of tomorrow's rivals, Brioche, who clearly handled the ground, he'd have been a good favourite. As it was, 5-1 was the general offer, 11-2 in places.

I figured that the 100-16 rate (sixes with the fractions) would be the most I could possibly hope for. The vouchers, still among my expendable memorabilia, read:

£4,000 - £640 each way Max Parker Ltd
£2,000 - £300 each way Laurie Wallis Ltd
£1,000 - £160 each way Jack Woolf Ltd
£800 - £128 each way Dick Upex Ltd
£100 - £16 each way Stafford & Co Ltd

Having written my 'copy', napping Ballymoss, I had no sooner telephoned it from the Earl of Doncaster Arms than the heavens opened.

I didn't see Vincent until the next afternoon when I was about to leave for the radio point out in the country, on Rosehill, where Raymond Glendenning would hand over to me from the grandstand. The trainer of my nap, brow furrowed, related anxiously: 'I've just been out there; he's got no chance in this. We'll have to get out of the bets.'

I regretted that I'd no time to get to the rails and negotiate, and handed him the list of bets, explaining that he was currently a firm 5-1 chance and there should be no problem.

Vincent is basically shy and didn't want to go into the ring; and anyway the horse was uppermost in his mind. 'Let's leave it,' he

shrugged. So we did. There were no mobile phones; no betting exchanges in that era.

And yet, somehow, the whiff of ebbing confidence leaked into the ring so that, by the 'off', Ballymoss had eased to 8-1. He may not have been aware of that. But he was clearly conscious of the difference between 'dead' on the Knavesmire and 'soft side' at Doncaster.

Appropriately, the infinitely dependable TP Burns rode Vincent's first English classic winner.

However, reverting to 1¼ miles for Newmarket's Champion Stakes on 17 October was less successful. Having pulled hard early on, he faded way out of contention, finishing a distant sixth of seven behind runaway six lengths winner, Rose Royale II.

When settling (instantaneously, as ever) the stable commission, Vincent wrote: 'Thinking over Ballymoss's running at Newmarket I do not think there can be any doubt that his poor showing was due to the shock he must have got as a result of kicking the rails.'

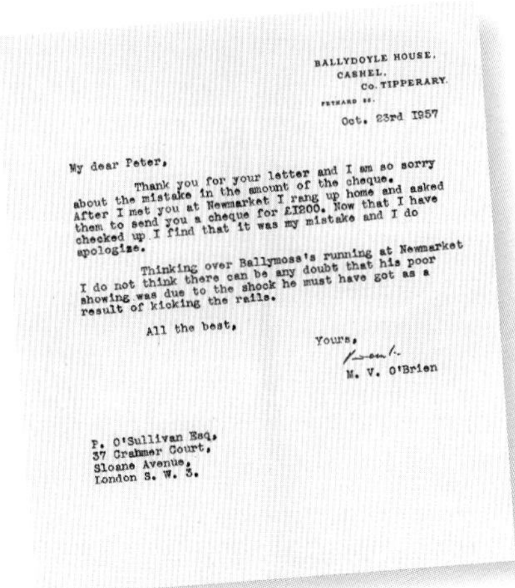

BALLYDOYLE HOUSE,
CASHEL,
Co. TIPPERARY.

Oct. 23rd 1957

My dear Peter,

Thank you for your letter and I am so sorry about the mistake in the amount of the cheque. After I met you at Newmarket I rang up home and asked them to send you a cheque for £1200. Now that I have checked up I find that it was my mistake and I do apologize.

Thinking over Ballymoss's running at Newmarket I do not think there can be any doubt that his poor showing was due to the shock he must have got as a result of kicking the rails.

All the best,

Yours,

M. V. O'Brien

P. O'Sullivan Esq,
37 Cranmer Court,
Sloane Avenue,
London S. W. 3.

He had certainly caught them a right clout when lashing out on leaving the paddock.

Anyone who figured that 10 furlongs might be short for him missed the six lengths winner of the 1958 Eclipse, which was preceded by victory in the Coronation Cup and followed by success in the King George VI and Queen Elizabeth Stakes and the Arc. So this was the one for the nap hand.

My assignment was to file 'copy' on arrival at Idlewild Airport, New York; proceed to the track (the since-defunct Jamaica) and do a piece for 'Features' from there, then fly on to Washington and out to Laurel daily to cover the preliminaries.

As the transatlantic flight made its way west and Vincent and I drank a last nightcap before retiring to our respective sleeping quarters, the maestro articulated his principal concern for next week. The next day's copy read as above.

DAILY EXPRESS

TRAINER REVEALS BALLYMOSS FEAR

From PETER O'SULLEVAN: New York, Wednesday

No amount of ballyhoo disturbs Ballymoss. No opponent was found capable of ruffling the Ballymoss-Breasley partnership in Europe's richest race prizes this year.

Triumph in next Tuesday's Laurel International would establish the John McShain-Vincent O'Brien-trained four-year-old as the top money-earner in European racing history, with a credit of more than £124,000.

These facts you are probably aware of already. But you may be as surprised as I was to learn from 41-year-old ace horse-handler O'Brien what he rates the chief danger to success in the great colt's ultimate objective. Could it be the Russian opposition? The American, Argentinian, Australian, German or fellow traveller Tharp?

Or even the latest addition to the International field – Escribano, recent winner of the Simon Bolivar at Caracas who, ridden by Indian Manuel Camarcaro, will represent Venezuela, the country successful at Laurel in 1955? No!

NOT THE DIET

Could it be the change of diet? For by American laws every oat and every other scrap of imported horse fodder must be burned on arrival.

No. Because the great strength of Ballymoss has been built up for the past 12 months on Canadian oats.

And a consignment awaits him when he is due to touch down at Friendship Airport six miles from the Laurel track at 3pm local time tomorrow afternoon.

We were midway across the Atlantic in the early hours of the morning when my flight companion revealed his one major concern.

'It's the ponies,' said Vincent.

The noise from the aircraft's engines was discreetly muted. But I had obviously not heard properly. 'It's the what?' I asked.

'The ponies,' repeated the wizard, his brow furrowed with anxiety.

'I'm sorry,' I said, 'I thought you said the ponies.'

Which, it turned out, was exactly what he did say.

LOSES POISE

It appears that the otherwise phlegmatic and indisputably aristocratic horse of the European racing year is violently allergic to 'lesser' breeds.

Even an inoffensive hack upsets him. But a pony positively 'sends' him.

'He gets terribly agitated,' explained Vincent, 'and loses all the poise which ordinarily helps him to be the horse he is.'

And the trouble is that hereabouts ponies are widely used at exercise times when horses are 'ponied around' the track. They are even used to conduct some horses to the start in races.

And I don't think Vincent thought a whole lot of my idea of fitting Ballymoss with bifocals.

So, it remains to be seen what happens.

Above:
Aubrey Brabazon wins the first leg of a Cheltenham Gold Cup hat-trick on Vincent O'Brien-trained Cottage Rake, 18 March 1948.

Below:
Dr Vincent O'Brien with old friends Scobie and Lester at the **Racing Post** Racing Greats lunch at the Goring Hotel. London, 5 June 2003.

Nine years earlier (1949) Vincent flew three to the Cheltenham Festival for the first time. They were Cottage Rake, Hatton's Grace and Castledermot. The experience evidently provoked no adverse result since, respectively, they won the Gold Cup, Champion Hurdle and National Hunt Chase.

Even so, flying for racehorses still had an aura of novelty about it. So it was a considerable achievement by the pioneer of international racing, John Schapiro (who died, aged 87, in 2002) to establish the Washington DC International at Laurel as early as 1952, having been appointed chairman of the track only two years before.

In the first year there were three solid home defenders challenged by top horses from Canada and Germany and a duo from Britain, one of whom, Wilwyn, trained by George Colling and ridden by Joe Mercer's elder brother Manny (who was tragically killed at Ascot in 1959) won for Kent farmer, Bob Boucher.

Since then there had been distinguished invaders from many countries, but, until this year, none with quite the credentials of Ballymoss.

Regrettably, although the 'ponies' maintained a discreet profile, the credentials proved inadequate protection against misfortune. In a sensational, drama-packed race the 11-10 favourite ran third. (*See Scobie 'It was bloody rough out there' Breasley, page 53.*)

So Vincent had to wait until 1968, by which time Laurel's former hazards had long since been eliminated, to collect with the breathtakingly talented and marvellously manoeuvrable Sir Ivor.

One of the most priceless stars in the Ballydoyle firmament, Sir Ivor ended a four-race, two-year-old career winning twice over seven furlongs at The Curragh, then at Longchamp in the one-mile Grand Criterium worth £30,108, which was money in those days.

Sir Ivor was taken to Italy for a winter holiday in the hope that a little sunshine would give him an advantage in his second season. A subsequent 2,000 Guineas/Derby double, among other significant triumphs, suggested he'd come to no harm.

However, he did have to be extricated from a roadside ditch outside Pisa one day (that was kept pretty quiet!), so I don't think the experiment was repeated.

Six years earlier Vincent won the first of his six Derbys with Larkspur following a dramatic classic which evoked one of the strangest official reactions in my experience.

In this era more than a quarter of a million thronged Epsom Downs on the first Wednesday in June. Viewed from the stands there was a short blind spot between Tattenham Hill and the descent to the famous corner due to closely packed buses and coaches.

It was in this area, incompletely covered by either film-patrol or television cameras, that the calamity occurred.

I remember calling the order (for television) running into Tattenham Corner and noting, with horror, that several were riderless.

What happened was that Romulus, in the Engelhard colours, struck into the heels of the only grey, Crossen. As the two fell they brought down the favourite, Hethersett, over whom Bobby Elliott's first Derby mount, Pindaric, capsized. Likewise Persian Fantasy, Changing Times and King Canute who, tragically, splintered a leg and had to be destroyed. Larkspur threaded his way through the prostrate Hethersett's legs and Arcor (second) jumped the favourite's head.

Arcor's rider, the stylish Roger Poincelet, who had won on 66-1 outsider Psidium ('If Psidium wins I'll be psurprised,' I had written) the previous year, considered that the chief contributory factor to the pile-up was the poor quality of many who made up the 26-horse field. 'By the time we'd gone seven furlongs most of them were already dead beat,' he insisted.

My selection, Le Cantilien each-way (backed from 100-6 to 8-1) finished a close third after meeting interference which, in the candid opinion of his young partner, Yves Saint-Martin, probably didn't affect the result.

Left, inset and below:
1968 Derby. Sir Ivor and Lester deliver a devastating challenge: they sprint past Connaught and are becomingly led in by Mrs Raymond Guest.

Well before the setback which had threatened Larkspur's participation, Ballydoyle stable jockey, Pat Glennon, had chosen to ride Sebring. As Larkspur sailed by him at Epsom, he reflected: 'Well, Mr O'Brien has won it anyway.' He still thought Sebring to be the better horse and said he'd pick him if they met again. They did, next time out, in the Irish Derby, in which Sebring was third, 2½ lengths ahead of Larkspur, who started favourite, back in fourth place.

Ten days off post time at Epsom, US Ambassador Raymond Guest was at Ballydoyle to see Derby jockey-elect, Neville Sellwood, meet his horse Larkspur for the first time. Imagine the dismay when head lad Maurice O'Callaghan, looking none too happy, turned up at the house to report that the recent, impressive, 12-furlongs winner at Leopardstown had got a nasty lump on his near-hind below the hock. The team's loyal and skilful vet, Bob Griffin, was summoned hastily from Dublin.

Box rest was prescribed. And frequent fomentation. It did not look too good. In fact, non-appearance was a distinct possibility. Vincent felt duty bound to alert the press to the situation.

The colt had been out of action for six days when Bob revisited him and pronounced that he'd come to no harm by travelling to Epsom and taking his chance. Hardly the ideal preparation, but an immense relief to Ambassador Guest who, earlier in the week, having been resigned to owning a non-runner, now decided to push his luck and have a bet – such is the lure of being able to take a price in contrast to wagering on the mutuel only, 'at home'. Not that the owner's optimism had great impact on the market; Larkspur drifted from 20-1 to 22-1 on the day.

And yet, while the unfortunate King Canute was being put down; loose horses were being caught; cuts and bruises were being attended to; the one injured jockey, Harry Carr, was being hurried to hospital; what were the stewards exercised about?

Vincent O'Brien was summoned before them to explain how he accounted for support for a winner who had been reported a doubtful runner?

This remarkable development was to permanently affect the future attitude of a naturally reserved individual towards communication with the press.

It reminded me of a bizarre piece which appeared under my name in the *Express* in April 1954. (*See below, left.*)

This temporary hindrance to a training career of unparalleled twentieth century achievement raised the perennial question – how good at his job can a trainer afford to be?

Vincent, who endured further isolation when Chamour, a son of his first Irish Derby winner, Chamier, was alleged 'positive' after a £200 Curragh maiden – resulting in comprehensive revision of dope testing procedures – was not the only victim of his talent in this era.

The contrastingly ebullient Paddy Prendergast, another whose uncanny instinct in relation to horses served him so brilliantly, displeased the Ascot stewards on Saturday 10 October 1953.

His representative in the one-mile Cornwallis Stakes for two-year-olds, Blue Sail, was bred for stamina and backed to improve on his efforts over a lesser trip in Ireland. He was beaten a neck by a fair filly, Plainsong, trained by Jack Leader.

The stewards reckoned there was a discrepancy in his form and referred the matter to Cavendish Square. The outcome: a *Calendar* notice to the effect that no further entries would be accepted from PJ Prendergast.

The ban imposed by the Stewards of the Jockey Club aroused as much dismay as ill feeling. Especially since the Stewards of the Irish Turf Club held an exhaustive enquiry, interviewing officials, jockeys and owners from three countries, before satisfying themselves that there was no evidence of any unexplained discrepancy in the running of Blue Sail at Ascot.

Another outstanding instinctive horsemaster, Ryan Price, who shared with Paddy unbridled

DAILY EXPRESS

ROYAL TAN TRAINER SUSPENDED THREE MONTHS

Mr Vincent O'Brien, 36-year-old star Irish National Hunt trainer who prepared Royal Tan for his Grand National victory, had his licence suspended yesterday for three months.

The stewards of the Irish National Hunt Committee, after an enquiry, 'were not satisfied' with Mr O'Brien's answers to allegations that the form of four horses in his stable was 'inconsistent'.

Among the 'inconsistent' horses named was Royal Tan. An hour after Mr O'Brien left the meeting of the stewards at their Dublin headquarters a statement typed by his attractive 28-year-old wife Jacqueline said:

'I was asked by the stewards to explain the "inconsistent" running of four horses trained by me, namely Royal Tan, Early Mist, the 1953 National winner, Lucky Dome and Knock Hard.

IN THE DARK

'The stewards said they could not accept my explanations. I am in the dark as to what – if any – offence I have committed.

'No suggestion was made against the manner in which the horses were ridden in any of their races. In fact no specific charge in respect of the running of any horse in any race has been made.'

Mr O'Brien said that the stewards' ban would affect his Flat runners as well as the National Hunt horses in his stable.

It would bar his entries in the Irish Grand National – Royal Tan and Quare Times – and might affect Knock Hard's running in America's International Steeplechase at Belmont Park, New York.

The enquiry was called a fortnight ago and, after a formal meeting, was adjourned until yesterday.

WITNESSES

Officials of the English National Hunt Committee were then invited to give evidence. Two secretaries of the Committee, Admiral HR Jacomb and Colonel JM Monsell, flew to Dublin yesterday. So did Bryan Marshall, who rode Royal Tan and Early Mist to their National victories.

Mr John Woods, of Cork, owner of Lucky Dome, a surprise 100-6 winner at Cheltenham, was another witness ...

Main picture and insets:
The year of Nijinsky, 1970. The Triple Crown hero winning the Derby (top left) and St Leger (top right) and being led in by Vincent after nonchalant victory in the King George VI and Queen Elizabeth Stakes.

Above:
Vincent and Lester standing before Emma McDermott's fine sculpture of Nijinsky at The Curragh.

Below Right:
Golden Fleece (Pat Eddery) shrugs off overnight scare to win 1982 Derby by three lengths – in faster time than it took the caterers to run out of ice.

Opposite Page:
Top:
1984 Derby. Son shocks father, as David O'Brien-trained Secreto (Christy Roche) beats Ballydoyle 'good thing' El Gran Senor (Pat Eddery) by a photographed short head.

Bottom:
The Gran Senor at the Gran Coolmore Stud in Kentucky.

optimism, a passion for his horses and a sometimes dangerous disregard for his fellow mortals, was another victim of his talent. His treatment in respect of dual Schweppes winner, Rosyth, was in my view, a misjudgement. The episode is well covered in my fair-minded and greatly respected late colleague Peter Bromley's biography of Ryan, *The Price of Success*.

Looking back, it is difficult to avoid the reluctant conclusion that there were occasions when conspicuous talent evoked perverse resentment.

Nothing in racing is as simple as it appears to have been prior to the fulfilment of hope. Irrespective of Vincent's single-minded, permanently focussed attention to detail, Larkspur was by no means an isolated example of triumph over potential disaster.

On the morning of Tuesday 2 June 1970 before the next day's Derby, the highly strung superstar Nijinsky, probably Vincent's most inspired yearling purchase, lay in his Epsom racecourse box sweating freely and in acute pain. Diagnosed to be suffering from a sharp attack of colic, the poor favourite could not be given any medical help because of the proximity of the classic, for which he looked more 100-8 than 11-8.

Would the Larkspur stewards have alerted the media?

Vincent decided to delay any announcement which, in the prayed-for event of full recovery could, and probably would, be misinterpreted. In one and a half hours the pain eased, and the horse who was to become the first Triple Crown winner since Bahram (1935) hesitantly accepted a small offering of bicarbonate of soda blended with a little bran and greenery.

While the rest of the entourage left the stable precinct to take breakfast, Vincent, like Nijinsky's lad, could not be prised from his side.

The following afternoon multi-millionaire platinum king Charlie Engelhard's unbeaten champion surged to his eighth victory at the expense of Sea Bird's outstanding son Gyr. It

was a personal delight to have enjoyed the privilege of 'calling' such equine marvels. Not least at Ascot on 25 July, when Nijinsky positively sauntered to devastating success over winners of two Derbys; a Washington International; French Oaks and the current Coronation Cup holder in the King George VI and Queen Elizabeth Stakes.

Another with a touch of the 'Larkspurs' was Nijinsky's strapping and beautifully balanced son Golden Fleece, who would fly to Epsom in June '82, unbeaten in three races from eight to ten furlongs. Because of his Ferrari-like power of acceleration and speed, there existed a slight doubt concerning his stamina. Not that Vincent was worried on this score, assuring Pat Eddery (contracted in '81 after Lester had signed on with green-fingered Newmarket neighbour Henry Cecil): 'The longer you hold him up, the further you'll win.'

The first worry concerned Golden Fleece's apparent antipathy to horsebox travel, a routine trial run revealing severe claustrophobia. The worry whether this might inhibit future travel resulted in lifelong, loyal Ballydoyle employee, Gerry Gallagher, devoting six months to reassuring his 'patient'.

The next anxiety was provoked by an unexplained swollen hock. But the worst was reserved for last.

On the morning of Derby eve Pat Eddery, accompanied by a stable companion, worked 'Himself' around the course – intending to ease up at the stands. But, during the work, Golden Fleece coughed three times. This was seriously alarming.

Pat suggested that they continue an extra furlong to the stables so that he could talk to the 'governor' privately. When they pulled up Golden Fleece coughed again and was led into his box by his lad.

Vincent hurried down the course to confer with his jockey. The colt's temperature was taken and, once again, Ballydoyle vet, Bob Griffin, was urgently contacted.

It could be dehydration owing to the unusually warm weather, he suggested. There was no temperature. No nasal discharge.

But supposing he coughed during the race; had to be pulled up, even? Vincent deliberated anxiously whether to reveal the situation – and risk recrimination if it was a false alarm – or keep quiet, and hope. He stationed a staff member outside the favourite's box. If the cough was renewed he'd *have* to report it.

There was no sound. And on a warm afternoon on Epsom Downs Golden Fleece hacked up, justifying a 3-1 nap by three lengths, slicing through a useful field in faster time (according to my 'copy') than it took the caterers to run out of ice.

Thus did Golden Fleece set up the prospect of a unique family (and Robert Sangster) double in the Prix du Jockey-Club (French Derby) on Sunday.

A double completed in equally emphatic style by 25-year-old David O'Brien-trained three lengths winner Assert, the first Irish-trained winner of the Chantilly classic in the twentieth century.

Like father, like son. For David and his jockey, Christy Roche, flew to France's 'City of the Horse' over 60 hours before the race and spent two days walking the course and studying every gradient before deciding, despite a favourable inside draw, to follow an 'outer' route.

For Christy, who had won all the Irish Classics – and a nap hand in India, come to that: 'This was the greatest thrill of my career. Not just winning, but the fact that David stood by me.'

Two years later David and Christy were to combine even more dramatically, this time at Epsom, where the duo's hope, Secreto, beat O'Brien Sr-trained, odds-on favourite El Gran Senor by a short head in the Derby.

Irrespective of Vincent's unlimited attention to detail ('He was acutely aware of the details that mattered,' was a perceptive comment by horsewise Texan jockey Cash Asmussen) and his 'uncanny knowledge of pedigrees and bloodlines,' to quote his son-in-law and global authority John Magnier, there remains one vital element in racing which none can control. Luck.

1977 was a case in point. It was the second time (1970 was the first) that Vincent had been elected Flat Race Trainer of the Year by the Horserace Writers and Reporters Association.

It was the second time (1966 was the first) that he had achieved the trainers' championship in England, with 13 horses aggregating a record £439,124.70 in 18 races.

Above: Lester and Alleged make it look easy once again when completing the second leg of the Arc double, 1978.

Opposite Page: Top, before the 1977 Irish Sweeps Derby at The Curragh, and below, winning the Larkspur Stakes at Leopardstown. 1976.

The roll-call in that record-breaking year included The Minstrel (Derby, Irish Sweeps Derby, King George VI and Queen Elizabeth Diamond Stakes); Alleged (Voltigeur, Prix de l'Arc de Triomphe); Artaius (Coral Eclipse, Sussex Stakes); Be My Guest (Waterford Crystal Mile); Try My Best (William Hill Dewhurst); etc. ...

So where does 'luck' fit into this redoubtable catalogue?

When The Minstrel went to Epsom for the Derby he had been beaten in the 2,000 Guineas in both England and Ireland, and had not won beyond seven furlongs. The horse Lester wanted to ride was Blushing Groom.

It was only after this covertly debated option had been eliminated that Lester said to Vincent: 'Run The Minstrel and I'll ride him,' adding the almost defiant rider: 'And I'll win too.'

I remember Vincent reflecting wryly: 'Who am I to gainsay the master?'

Ballydoyle was already to be represented by Be My Guest, bidding to become the first since Blue Peter (1939) to complete the Blue Riband Trial-Derby double and ridden by my proposal of 1973 winner, Edward Hide. Jacqueline had a tenner each-way at 33-1 this one. Also Geoff (Mill Reef) Lewis-partnered Valinsky, the only product of a Derby-winning sire and Oaks-winning dam. And well backed to overcome a surprisingly unsuccessful formula.

It was nearly two decades before the ill-conceived decision to abandon custom and run the Derby on a Saturday instead of the traditional first Wednesday in June.

As the 22 runners threaded their way across the Downs, The Minstrel proceeded in what he may have felt to be an eerie silence – insulated against the tumult by cotton wool-plugged ears. Just another O'Brien ploy to ease the pressure on a sensitive Thoroughbred.

And there at the start was Vincent's tall aide, John Gosden, to reach out and restore the colt's hearing.

In the race 34-year-old ex-champion Willie Carson and the relatively modest Hot Grove looked as though they'd nicked it, before the 'old firm' grabbed them by a hard-fought neck.

Apart from his unique talent, Vincent appreciated that a major advantage of having Lester ride for you lay in him not riding against you.

Below:
Belmont Park, 1990. Substituting for injured John Reid, Lester stages a memorable climax to the Breeders' Cup Mile on Royal Academy.

Bottom:
Lester and The Minstrel 'at home' in Ireland

Suppose he had been offered Blushing Groom, who did not appear to stay, would The Minstrel have run? And who else would have won on him?

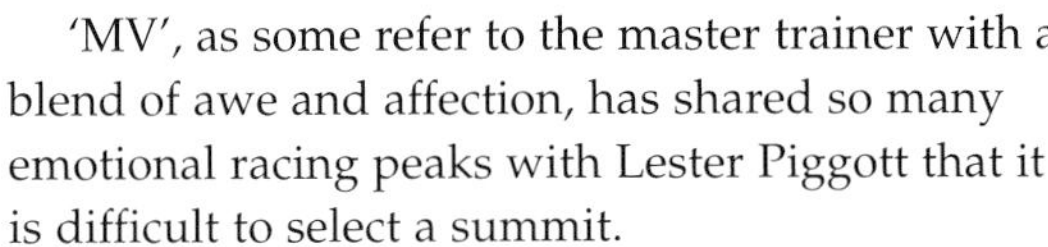

'MV', as some refer to the master trainer with a blend of awe and affection, has shared so many emotional racing peaks with Lester Piggott that it is difficult to select a summit.

There was Ascot 1975 when Vincent won with six of the seven horses he brought to the Royal meeting at which Lester equalled his best eight-winner total.

Fifteen years on and a substitute for injured stable jockey, John Reid, was urgently required to ride Ballydoyle's Royal Academy in the Breeders' Cup Mile at the Belmont Park, New York, world championships.

Five years 'retired', Lester had resumed the profession he loved, on Vincent's advice, a month earlier. But he was now in his 55th year and, at that age, could scarcely be expected to tackle such a daunting international assignment.

Several talented young men had been proposed when family friend and Ladbroke Communications Director, Mike Dillon, enquired diffidently: 'What about the "long fellow"?'

Vincent usually deliberates a while. This time he didn't. 'Lester will do me anytime,' he responded instantly. A neck they won.

Awestruck transatlantic aficionados still talk about the jockey, the horse, and the trainer who prepared him.

In September 1994, the 50th anniversary year of the Drybob/Good Days Irish Cambridgeshire/Cesarewitch double, Vincent trained his last winner, Mysterious Ways (Christy Roche) at the Curragh. Why retire so young, I enquired? On 19 October he wrote:

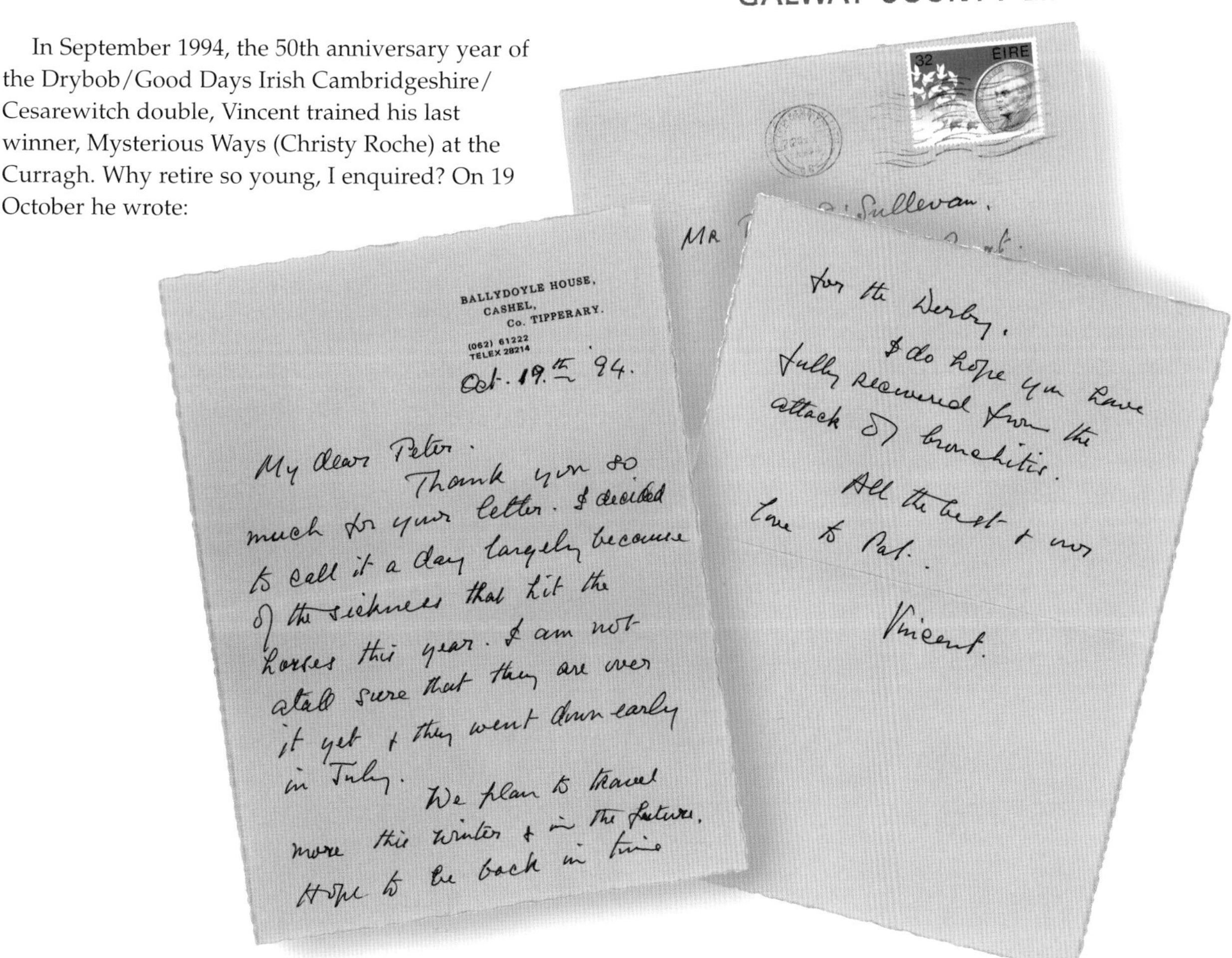

BALLYDOYLE HOUSE,
CASHEL,
Co. TIPPERARY.
(062) 61222
TELEX 28214

Oct. 19th '94.

My dear Peter.

Thank you so much for your letter. I decided to call it a day largely because of the sickness that hit the horses this year. I am not at all sure that they are over it yet & they went down early in July.

We plan to travel more this winter & in the future. Hope to be back in time for the Derby.

I do hope you have fully recovered from the attack of bronchitis.

All the best & our love to Pat.

Vincent.

ALEC HEAD

For connoisseurs of the remarkable dynasty of Anglo-French racehorse trainers based in France, the distinguished *famille Head* is a prime exhibit.

As a reporter for the PA (Press Association) I first met the charming twentieth-century patriarch of the family, Willie, at his Maisons-Laffitte stables in 1946 – the year he won the French Champion Hurdle with Vatelys, ridden by his 22-year-old youngest son, Alec.

Born at St Germain-en-Laye on 21 January 1889, Willie was well established as a successful jockey by the outbreak of World War I when he was enlisted in the Lancashire Fusiliers, later transferring to the 16th Lancers, serving on the Western Front and being decorated for gallantry.

Towards the war's end, while stationed at The Curragh, he won the Irish National (run at Punchestown) on Ballyboggan, finishing second in the Grand National on the same horse in 1919. Winner that year was Poethlyn, ridden by Lester Piggott's grandfather, Ernie Piggott.

Son of a jockey-trainer, also William, Willie married into another wholehearted racing family when Netta Jennings became his bride in 1915. Netta's father, Harry, trained Gladiateur to win the Grand Prix de Paris in 1865. But the great horse, whose life-size sculptured image stands proud at the entrance to Longchamp, was handled by his brother Tom at Newmarket when winning the Triple Crown, also before triumph in the Goodwood Cup the following year.

Like his elder son Peter, who was born four years before Alec, Willie trained with sustained success in France – seldom venturing overseas. In fact, between them, they ran only four horses in England, a winner and three placed.

Willie's first raider was Le Paillon in 1947, the year of the deep freeze in England where racing was abandoned between 22 January and 13 March. Cheltenham's March National Hunt Festival was a casualty.

At this time I was supplementing unextravagant PA remuneration by writing a bi-weekly column for *The Racehorse*, price three pence, under a pseudonym as my principal employer did not permit staff to contribute elsewhere. At £3.50 per week, only my readers may have rated the pay excessive. Anyway, I phoned Maisons-Laffitte to draw Willie's attention to the detail that the Champion Hurdle had been re-opened and was scheduled for Saturday 12 April. So Le Paillon could, and should, be nominated. He was a cracking good hurdler and had lately (at Auteuil) confirmed both his well-being and his talent.

I am sure Willie was well aware of the situation but he was much too polite to say so. Come the day he reported that his cousin, Epsom trainer Vic Smyth, was very bullish about the tall chestnut National Spirit. But *Patrick Moore*'s 'Best Bet of the Week' would take some beating and, if I would kindly handle it, he would like a tenner on him.

From two out the 14-horse field was a match, with the ultimate 2-1 favourite Le Paillon (Alec Head) and 7-1 chance National Spirit (Danny Morgan) jumping the last upsides. The favourite was beaten a fair-and-square length by the horse who won the following year as well. But what a consolation prize, when on 5 October, Le Paillon returned the 1½ lengths winner of none other than the Prix de l'Arc de Triomphe.

Right:
Alec Head's imminent champion jockey son Freddy with grandpa Willie Head, 1966.

Alec Head with father Willie, 1972.

Admittedly it was a depleted 12-horse field this year due to a series of injuries and the proximity of Ascot. However, it was a notable training feat on the part of 'Grandpa' Head (who died on 30 March 1984 at the age of 94) to sustain Le Paillon's zest throughout two years' continual racing on the Flat and over obstacles.

The maintenance of the Head dynasty was in fleeting jeopardy on 14 December 1945, the day that crack Belgian amateur rider Louis Van de Poele's lovely daughter Ghislaine and Jacques Alexandre Head (to give him his full quota of christian names) were married.

Driving away from the reception the happy bride was at the wheel and under instruction from her husband to beware at the roadworks ahead. Regrettably – emphasising that love is blind? – Ghislaine's precautionary measures proved inadequate. The car lodged conclusively, and with an air of finality, in a freshly excavated channel. Long renowned for possessing a very short fuse, Alec refrained from comment. He simply extricated himself from the inert vehicle, slammed the door and strode ahead.

Happily the roadworkers' response was more helpful and, in due course, the abandoned bride caught up with her nomad, and there is evidence that the brief rift was fully repaired.

Reacting to injuries and responding to pleas from his young wife to pursue a less accident-prone profession, Alec retired in 1947, rider of 160 winners (92 Flat; 68 jumps) and took out his first trainer's licence, aged 23.

A Head marking time is a very rare occurrence and, within a very short while of receiving his licence, Alec was up and running with his first winner, Sarabry, owned by Roger Guthman, in an Auteuil hurdle on 1 November 1947. His first year accounted for 13 more winners.

Very soon Alec took over the Pierre Wertheimer team and the blue and white colours were first successful aboard Djebe.

Now in '51 he was ringing to report a problem, which he flew over to discuss. He'd been offered the position of private trainer to the bloodstock mega-rich Aga Khan. It would enable him to handle much-improved stock, quality-wise.

"A Head marking time is a very rare occurrence and, within a very short while of receiving his licence, Alec was up and running with his first winner ..."

I thought it would be madness to abandon a loyal following – even if the reward was potentially exciting.

Soon he rang to say: 'You'd better be first with the news. I've decided to take the Aga's horses.'

In 1952 he won the Coronation Cup and Arc de Triomphe with Nuccio and at the age of 28 topped the list of winning trainers in France (67 winners) for the first time – and still only on the threshold of a great career.

In 1953 – top trainer again – Alec had planned a Lincoln raid with the gifted but enigmatic Nahar. A typical Aly Khan gamble may have succeeded, but the old rogue hit the front too soon and, having done so, pulled up with Sir Gordon Richards.

The now seven-year-old's handler had seen enough to convince himself that redemption was a viable option. As he didn't have Gordon's weight in '54 he allocated the ride to 22-year-old, first-time Lincoln visitor Jean Massard and requested me: 'For goodness sake find the right one for him to follow.' Since the ante-post favourite, Dumbarnie was a confirmed front-runner, carrying the readily identifiable maroon and white colours of Major Lionel Holliday, this wasn't a difficult choice.

In the early hours of 9 March that year I'd driven with Alec to see 'Nigger', as the near jet-black horse was stable named, complete a serious trial with the useful former Marcus Marsh-trained Masai King and others. Breakfast *en route* was country paté, hot baguette, coffee and a generous sized carafe of Calvados. After a couple of glasses I recall reminding myself not to get too carried away by the gallop. It would have been impressive even without the calva.

I'd napped Nahar in '53 but thought it prudent to go each-way after receiving a well-intentioned call from Charlie Smirke. He'd read my abridged report of the work and warned: 'Don't get too carried away by that bastard Masai King. He wouldn't tell you the time if he had ten watches!'

On 'the day', Alec persuaded his father-in-law, Lulu Van de Poele, to accompany him to the wilds of Lincolnshire. They'd started none too promisingly with a puncture on the way to Le Bourget. And Lulu missed the finish. When Nahar

Opposite Page:
Alec and PO'S discuss season's programme at Villa Vimy, Chantilly, late 1960s.

Below:
Lavandin sharing seventh place rounding Tattenham Corner – Rae Johnstone in white cap and sleeves – before winning 1956 Derby.

struck the front inside the last furlong Alec clapped him on the head in his excitement and jammed his pork pie hat down over his eyes. I'd missed the victory too because the BBC truck from which I broadcast the first six furlongs for radio (before handing over to Raymond Glendenning in the grandstand) had to divert behind the enclosures. Nahar started 100-7 and the nap won at 4-1. But my £4,000-£10 spring (and *Daily Express*) double, Nahar with Tudor Line, was beaten a neck!

Alec did *Express* readers another good turn in '55 when Vimy (10-1) won the King George VI and Queen Elizabeth Stakes in which favourite Phil Drake underlined the folly of following Grand Prix de Paris form: at that time the once-famous race was run over an excessively testing 1 mile 7 furlongs.

Vimy's giant half-sister Midget II was another benefactress when dwarfing the Cheveley Park opposition in the paddock and mislaying them in the race at Newmarket on 28 September 1955 under ever-stylish Roger Poincelet.

Alec was infinitely less enchanted with Roger after the 1956 1,000 Guineas when his jockey returned to the unsaddling enclosure, beaming happily in the mistaken belief that he had won. The French filly and Honeylight were racing wide apart on opposite sides of the course and it was the latter, on the stands rails, who was the official winner – by two lengths. Roger began to lose the Derby ride on Lavandin this day, and completed the severance at the weekend when riding an ill-judged race on Pierre Wertheimer's Epsom hope in the Prix Hocquart.

The neck winner of the 1956 Derby, Lavandin probably represented his handler's greatest training performance and jockey Rae Johnstone's most sensitively achieved Classic triumph.

Alec had to handle the same problem as his great friend Sir Noel Murless faced the following year – albeit with a far superior horse – when Crepello had to be given enough work without compromising his delicate frame. Each succeeded brilliantly.

On the day before Derby morning, 5 June 1956, Rae was under firm instruction to 'work' the last seven furlongs of the outer perimeter of the Derby course at a very leisurely pace, only quickening marginally over the last quarter mile.

When they pulled up and Rae slid from Lavandin's back, Reg Perkins, the travelling head lad who had been with the Head family all his working life and who moved on to Alec's daughter Criquette when her father retired, stepped forward, slipped the reins over the Derby favourite's head and let him bend for a pick of rain-freshened grass.

Pierre Wertheimer leads bandaged Lavandin into the rainswept winner's circle after Derby triumph.

It was then, as he redistributed his weight, that the colt appeared to 'prop' – as if feeling a stab of pain in a tendon. Perkins looked up sharply and caught Alec's eye. Rae and I exchanged anxious glances. Lavandin continued to crop unconcernedly. 'Walk him round, Perkins,' said Alec. There wasn't a trace of heat. Maybe we'd misinterpreted the movement. Maybe.

The prospect of him becoming a first Epsom Derby winner for his trainer (there were successive French ones to follow), a first in 46 years' ownership for Pierre Wertheimer, with his first runner, and a 30th classic for Rae Johnstone, had not improved.

Alec, who planned to equip his chief hope (he doubted French Guineas winner Buisson Ardent's stamina) with supportive bandages, decided to stay on at Epsom for a while and see the horse back in the yard. Rae and I returned to London, stopping off for coffee in a joyless Epsom café which our presence did nothing to enliven.

For those of us engaged in tipping for a living it is always important to select winners – doubly so on Derby and Grand National days when the racing pages will be studied by many more of the paper's regular readers, and by new ones too.

Supposing the worst happened and Lavandin's suspect off-fore gave way and he fell lame during the race? Alec would be quoted, saying it was a fear he had had to live with. What was I doing, not only tipping a 'suspect' horse, but failing to warn potential backers of the favourite that there was an additional hazard involved?

I could hark back to my 14 March Stables Tour article in which, while advising 50-1 Derby speculation, I'd stressed that 'this heavy-topped horse, who ran only once, without success as a two-year-old, has a lot of weight to support on legs which it will be hard to keep trouble free.'

And, having done so, I could reveal that the favourite's bandages would not be worn for protective purposes but to support a significant weakness. Hence my rejection of a horse whose cause I had championed for so long.

And then suppose he won? It is far easier to forgive a man for tipping a loser than it is to absolve him from stopping you backing a winner.

I agonised for hours before finally picking up the phone and casting the die. I went for him wholeheartedly, admitting: 'If Johnny (Lavandin's stable name) does not come marching home ahead of his 26 rivals, as I fully expect, I haven't the faintest idea what will.'

In the race Rae gave him every chance to warm up. Running down the hill to Tattenham Corner he was 10 to 12 lengths off the lead but travelling sweetly on ground eased by persistent rain. Quickening readily in the straight he had them covered at the furlong pole, where Alec released months of tension with such a devastating roar that his neighbour, Aly Khan, doubted whether his eardrums would ever be the same again. From this point, thinking of his partner's future, Rae just 'nursed' him home. Although Montaval finished strongly enough to force a photo there was no doubt that 'number 27' had won by a cheeky neck. It was some 'nursing' job.

For Alec, classic success in Britain was reinforced the very next year when, avenging the 1956 defeat of Midget II in the 1,000 Guineas, he turned out the first two in the 20-runner fillies' classic, Rose Royale II (6-1) and Sensualita (33-1).

Aly Khan had asked me to back them both for him ante-post and I quoted him afterwards, saying: 'For the first time in my life I found myself praying that one of my horses would be beaten.' Rose Royale II (happily the selection for *Express* readers) was owned by the Aga Khan, who was not in good health at the time, and Sensualita by his son. 'It is his first ever "1,000" and will have done him the world of good,' exclaimed a jubilant Aly.

It was Alec again, and Aly's colours (and *Express* readers!) when Taboun fulfilled firm expectation in the 1959 2,000 Guineas. In the interim Willie Head and Alec *père et fils* combined to purchase the fine Normandy Chateau du Quesnay and the adjoining stud which was created in 1903. Alec later took over Willie's share and the magnificent Haras du Quesnay, visited and admired by the Queen, has been superbly managed by Alec and Ghislaine's youngest daughter, Martine, since 1988.

Her Majesty Queen Elizabeth II is received by Alec Head at the Haras du Quesnay. Left, Comte Roland de Chambure.

"The neck winner of the 1956 Derby, Lavandin probably represented his handler's greatest training performance and jockey Rae Johnstone's most sensitively achieved Classic triumph."

Come the 1960s and few issues polarised Anglo-French racing opinion to the extent of starting stalls. No sooner had an experimental set been introduced to the Chantilly training grounds on 1 December 1961 than feeling ran as high as the Eiffel Tower.

The following year I reported Alec Head, supported by Miguel Clément and Rae Johnstone, to be a passionate advocate; François Mathet, backed by George Bridgland and others, vehemently opposed.

I quoted Alec: 'First, present starts in France are terrible.' This was one point in respect of which the protagonists were unanimous. 'Second,' continued Alec, 'if you have a photo-finish camera at one end it is absurd to be completely haphazard about the other end.'

He had 'schooled my 60 two-year-olds in the stalls without a single accident. With the tapes start I had three kicked and two loose the other morning. Rubber suction pads make the opening and shutting of the stalls noiseless, and instead of ribbons flicking up in a horse's face the doors just part naturally. So there is nothing to distract him. They quickly get used to walking into the stalls and the lad can just sit quiet and pat them – instead of hauling them about and trying to keep them straight.'

One of the stable's senior lads, an instant convert, asked: 'What is the good of "my" horse having perfect manners if another ignorant one crashes into him at the start, or an ignorant starter lets them go anyhow?'

Trainer, like Alec, of more than 1,000 winners by 1962, François Mathet insisted: 'What we need is a competent starter, not traps.' Others, like 100-horse trainer Max Bonaventure, were strongly opposed until watching Alec's in action.

Willie Head gently recalled 'the outcry when the present system replaced flag starts. The die-hards all thought the horses and riders would get hanged in the tapes.'

On 25 July 1962 Chantilly racecourse – inaugurated in 1834 – was selected for France's first stalls experiment. It was a great success, and appropriately, the system's principal advocate trained the winner for his wife, Ghislaine Head.

As Lester Piggott observed: 'Stall starts are the fairest method of all ... they've got to come sometime, there's no doubt about that.'

It still wasn't until 8 July 1965, three years on, that – despite some powerful local prejudice – Newmarket staged the first stalls start under Jockey Club Rules in England. And I was able to report:

DAILY EXPRESS

Following minimum delay and maximum efficiency at the despatch end, Newmarket's first stalls-started race ended as a lot more events should – with the jolly favourite streaking home a clear three-lengths winner.

It may have been no more than coincidence that four of the five jockeys with previous stalls experience taking part in the contest filled the first four places. But familiarity with the medium must be an advantage – as in any other sphere of activity.

Snap interviews among the 'also-rans', behind Lester Piggott-partnered Track Spare, produced such observations as: 'Super; mine flew out;' 'Absolutely perfect.' And from five-times champion Doug Smith: 'It was a first time for me and I thought they were very good indeed' ... It is doubtful whether many previously prejudiced observers remained unconverted to the view that this is the fairest method for horse, rider and punter.

Alec's enthusiasm for and demonstration of starting stalls was a major factor in their general European introduction.

Because we had both invested in similar bloodlines in 1969 (*see Attivo*) Alec kept me abreast of Pistol Packer's progress via regular bulletins. And what a fine filly the daughter of Gun Bow (whom I saw running against the redoubtable Kelso in 1964) turned out to be – winning seven of her 12 races and never out of the first three.

Winner of the French Oaks, Prix Vermeille, Prix Saint-Alary, Prix Chloe, etc., and runner-up, from the most unfavourable draw, to Mill Reef in the Arc, her record was a tribute to the trainer's remarkable eye for a horse. As Timeform's *Racehorses of 1971* put it: 'How she was bought for so little [$15,000] is a mystery.'

Alec's daughter Criquette, as Christiane has always been identified, had only been training for 18 months – her first success was at Rouen – when represented by Three Troikas, carrying the colours of her mother and ridden by her brother Freddy, in the 1979 Prix de l'Arc de Triomphe.

Criquette had been a bloodstock agent before taking out her trainer's licence and had guided the 41,000 guineas yearling (sent to the sales by Alec's partner, Count Roland de

Alec with youngest daughter Martine.

Chambure's Haras d'Etreham) to Chantilly. Freddy, who was to win six jockeys' championships, had already won three Arcs, the first as a 19-year-old for his grandfather, Willie, on Bon Mot III in 1966.

Three Troikas was opposed by the respective winners of the English and French Derby, Troy and TopVille; the impressive Coronation Cup winner, Ile de Bourbon, and 18 others. She didn't just win, she positively hacked up. It was some family triumph. And an oft-repeated one as the only female to train an Arc hero won her fourth Anglo-French 1,000 Guineas with Matiara (1995) bred by papa (from Criquette-trained 1986 French Derby winner Bering), ridden by Freddy and owned by the family.

The roll of family honour is endless. Few trainers, if any, have matched Alec's achievement as a breeder of racehorses. Nor has he done too badly on the human plane.

The dynasty, sustained by the Cartier awardee and the only European trainer to have been honoured by the Thoroughbred Club of America, is due for a long, long run.

Well done, Alec.

Above:
Three Troikas, trained by Alec's daughter Criquette and ridden by his son Freddy, wins the 1979 Prix de l'Arc de Triomphe in the colours of his wife Ghislaine.

Left:
The Head dynasty: Freddy, Criquette, Criquette's daughter Patricia, Alec and Willie, 1982.

SEA BIRD II

When Sea Bird II set out for England from Chantilly on Monday 31 May 1965 he was one anxious fledgling. He had never before been airborne and the prospect was painfully unnerving. So when the Bristol Freighter's engines started he grabbed his lad Maurice Debreuil's thumb for comfort: and held it in a tight grip until take-off. So tight that medical attention was required on arrival.

The next morning, while endeavouring to conceal the heavily bandaged laceration, former jockey Maurice insisted: 'He didn't mean any harm. In fact he's been ashamed and very apologetic.'

Dan Cupid's naturally playful son Sea Bird was on his very best behaviour when ridden out in the early hours of Tuesday 1 June: as if wishing to atone for his regretted 'in-flight' lapse. The early hour was to conform with the horse's routine.

Among all professions racehorse trainers are probably motivated more by individual attitude towards their task – enabling a horse to fulfil his maximum potential – than most.

The brilliant Etienne Pollet, who started training in 1942 and retired nearly 30 years later, believed in limiting his stable intake to no more than 50; he believed in the beneficent properties of a sweet-smelling hay mixture, *Foine Crau*, which he obtained from the distant region of the Pyrenees; and above all, he believed in exercising the Pollet *pensionnaires* on virgin ground. Hence the exceptionally early morning call at the immaculate, black-and-white gated yard at No. 30, Route Nationale, Chantilly.

Here, one wall of the *Patron*'s neat bureau is decorated by paintings of the stable's heroes collecting such prizes as the local Derby and Oaks, Arc de Triomphe, Grand Prix de Paris, Guineas, etc. ... On another there is a remarkable vertical row of six photographs headed by Tyrone (1956) and concluded by the powerful grey Grey Dawn (1964).

Remarkable because with this sextet, the tall wizard tutor of young horses, the Gallic 'Darkie' Prendergast, won France's richest two-year-old prize, the Grand Critèrium, six times in those nine years – and turned out four seconds as well!

This year, 1965, was the 15th of my annual March visits and positively the first one during which the trainer who won with his first runner in England's 2,000 Guineas (Thunderhead II, 1952); first runner in the '1,000' (Never Too Late, 1960) and first runner in Ireland (Tambourine II, Irish Sweeps Derby, 1962) had suggested that he might have 'serious' three-year-old potential. It was the box containing the chestnut with the white blaze and two hind stockings at which Etienne Pollet lingered.

"It was the box containing the chestnut colt with the white blaze and two hind stockings at which Etienne Pollet lingered."

Owned and bred by his cousin Jean Ternynck, a textile magnate from the north-east town of Lille, Sea Bird was by the American-bred son of Native Dancer, Dan Cupid, an inconsistent performer who was nevertheless good enough to run second in the Middle Park as a youngster. Then, following three-year-old failure in the English Guineas and Derby, and accompanied by grave doubt regarding his stamina, he ran Herbager to a short head in the 1959 French Derby. If Sea Bird and his box neighbours ever got around to discussing their antecedents it is a reasonable assumption that the Derby favourite kept fairly quiet about his distaff side.

Sicalade, his dam, ran twice without success. She had circulatory problems, poor dear, and had a wretched time when foaling her son on 8 March 1962. Her dam, Marmelade, was similarly unsuccessful under any Jockey Club Rules; likewise her granddam, Couleur; great granddam, Colour Bar, and great-great granddam, Lady Disdain. Thought waif-like, Colour Bar, having failed in sellers (like Attivo), did win a race under Pony Turf Club Rules.

Etienne mapped out Sea Bird's 1965 programme in early March and, with the co-operation of the incomparable conductor of a vintage orchestra, fulfilled every engagement. First the 10½ furlongs Prix Greffulhe on 4 April. On target.

Then the 10½ furlongs Prix Lupin, opposed by swift-emerging Rothschild star Diatome as well as impressive French 2,000 Guineas winner Cambremont, the 'conductor' had six lengths to spare over the highly talented Diatome and a further half-length over Cambremont.

Geoff Watson, long-time respected and experienced handler of the notable Rothschild team, instantly pronounced Sea Bird to be in the class of Ribot. To holders of ante-post vouchers in

AE 15421

William Hill PARK LANE Ltd

HILL HOUSE, LONDON, S.E.1.

World's Biggest Bookmakers

DIRECTORS: WILLIAM HILL, LIONEL BARBER, F.C.A., A. H. R. SUTTERLIN, A. C. SCOTT. ESTABLISHED 1922

MEMBERS OF THE N. S. L., B. P. A., T. G. S. AND VICTORIA CLUB

TELEPHONES: WATERLOO 7979 (400 LINES) TELEGRAMS: HILHOUSE, TELEX, LONDON CABLEGRAMS: HILHOUSE, LONDON

May 17th 19 65

Dear Sir,—We confirm having laid you the following at 9-21 AM on

£	s.	d.	TO	£	s.	d.	ENTRY	Price	Win or 1-2-3	EVENT
1,000	–	–		200	–	–	Sea Bird II	5	Win	Derby

To P J O'Sullivan Esq

A/c No. OB108

Amount Invested £200 – 0 – 0

Checked by

E. & O. E.

Britain's Biggest Bookmakers

OVERSEAS CABLES ADHERBAL, LONDON, W.1
INLAND TELEGRAMS ADHERBAL, LONDON, TELEX
TELEPHONES REGENT 6700 (150 LINES)

DIRECTORS: H. STEIN (CHAIRMAN), C. STEIN (MANAGING), H. GREEN, S. RADLEY, A. G. BURNETT, P. HALPERIN, F. R. KAYE, I. STEIN, R. U. GASKELL, G. M. GREEN

LADBROKE & CO. LTD., LONDON, W.1.

Dear Sir,

17th May 1965

9-48 am

According to your instructions we have obtained for you:—

RACE	HORSE	WIN	PLACE 1-2-3
Derby	Sea Bird	1000 – – 250 – –	

O'Sullivan Esq

OR 216

Yours faithfully,

№ 63317

LADBROKE & CO. LTD.

Bankers: WESTMINSTER BANK

Telephones: HULL 36941 (Multi-lines)

Voucher

No. 1748

John Hudson (Turf Accountants) Ltd.

TATTERSALLS RING MEMBER NORTHERN B.P.A. & VICTORIA CLUB

Time 2 – 15 PM

Date 17 5 65

9 - 11 WRIGHT STREET, HULL

Dear Sir, According to your instructions the following commissions have been obtained for you:

Amt. OBTAINED	TO	Amt. INVESTED	NAME OF HORSE	WIN PLACE	NAME OF RACE
£200	To	£50	Sea Bird	Win	Derby

YOU WIN	YOU LOSE

Mr Peter O'Sullivan

Yours faithfully, pp. JOHN HUDSO[N] (Turf Accountan[ts])

NOTE: IN THE EVENT OF ANY ERROR PLEASE RETURN THIS VOUCHER

Telephone: BELL 3711 (all lines)

Thomas Marshall

TURF and FOOTBALL ACCOUNTANT

4-6-8 John St., Glasgow, C.1

Telegrams: "CHIVALROUS GLASGOW"

3657

Time

Dear Sir,—In accordance with your instructions I have booked for you the following (all in, Run or Not)—

To Win £	s.	D.		Investment £	S.	D.	Quoted Price	Description	Win or Place	Event
600	–		to	200			3/1	Seabird	Win	Derby

This Voucher must be returned in support of any Claim.

Mr. P. O'Sullivan

(Nom de-plume)

19 May 1965

Yours faithfully,

E. & O. E.

THOMAS MARSHALL

Although every precaution is taken in executing clients' instructions, this voucher is issued on the distinct understanding that should any clerical error whatsoever arise, through miscalculation, etc., we reserve the right to rectify such errors at any time.

Vouchers from the collection of a persistent Sea Bird supporter.

respect of the Derby and featuring the Pollet-Ternynck star, the new concern became the coughing epidemic which was plaguing European stables. Otherwise Epsom prospects looked very fair for the Sea Bird entourage including, importantly, 38-year-old Melbourne-born Pat Glennon, who joined the Pollet stable in 1963 from Vincent O'Brien.

Pat did not speak French and, although he was married to an American, I never heard Etienne speak English. So when it came to receiving instructions the pilot would request: 'Share shay Madame Polly.'

The formula seemed to work OK because he'd ridden two Grand Critèrium winners as well as a 1,000 Guineas victress for the stable, and handled the potentially volatile Sea Bird with exceptional *sang-froid*.

For more than a quarter of a century Clive Graham and I were partners in both journalism and broadcasting. We lived within a furlong of each other in Chelsea; seldom agreed on racing matters, relished our disagreement, and never conferred regarding selections.

Because of preoccupation with ante-post betting my Derby preference, for what it was worth, was usually signposted well in advance.

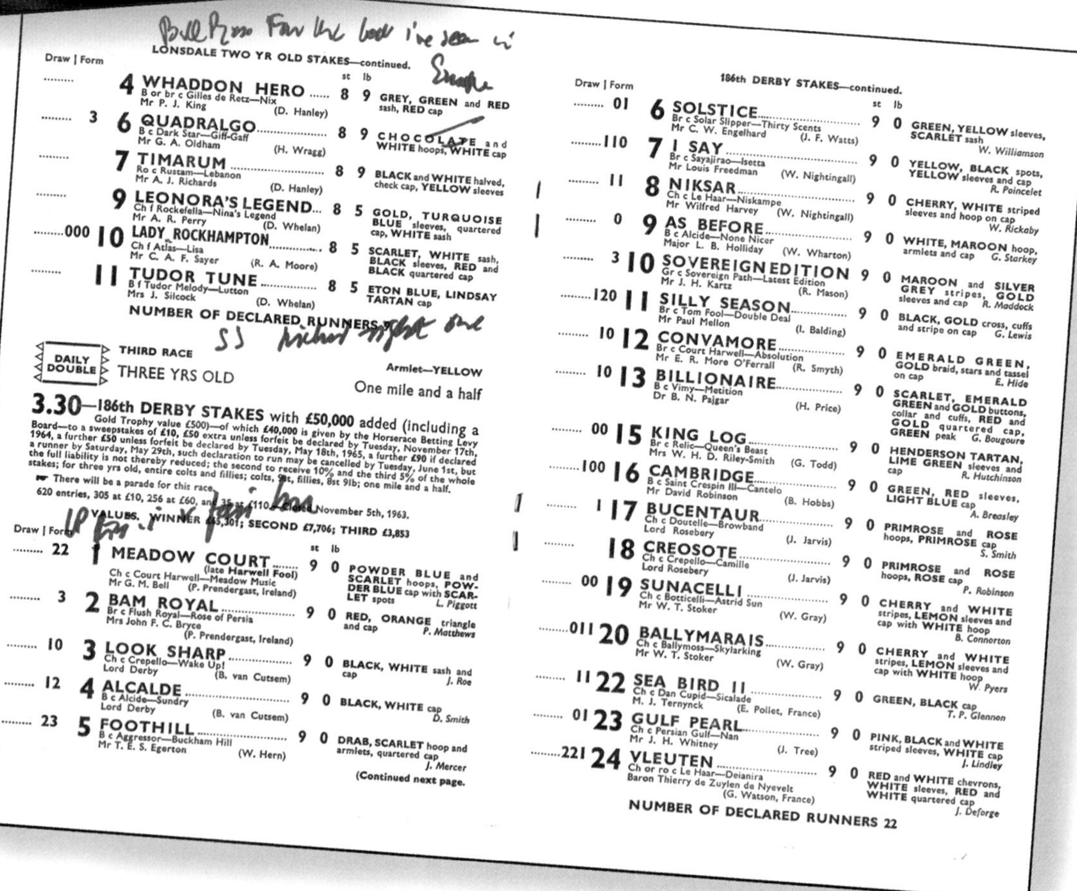

LONSDALE TWO YR OLD STAKES—continued.

Draw | Form — st lb

.... 4 WHADDON HERO ...... 8 9 GREY, GREEN and RED sash, RED cap
B or br c Gilles de Retz—Nix
Mr P. J. King (D. Hanley)

.... 3 6 QUADRALGO .... 8 9 CHOCOLATE and WHITE hoops, WHITE cap
B c Dark Star—Giff-Gaff
Mr G. A. Oldham (H. Wragg)

.... 7 TIMARUM .... 8 9 BLACK and WHITE halved, check cap, YELLOW sleeves
Ro c Rustam—Lebanon
Mr A. J. Richards (D. Hanley)

.... 9 LEONORA'S LEGEND... 8 5 GOLD, TURQUOISE BLUE sleeves, quartered cap, WHITE sash
Ch f Rockefella—Nina's Legend
Mr A. R. Perry (D. Whelan)

.........000 10 LADY ROCKHAMPTON .... 8 5 SCARLET, WHITE sash, BLACK sleeves, RED and BLACK quartered cap
Ch f Atlas—Lisa
Mr C. A. F. Sayer (R. A. Moore)

.... 11 TUDOR TUNE .... 8 5 ETON BLUE, LINDSAY TARTAN cap
B f Tudor Melody—Lutton
Mrs J. Silcock (D. Whelan)

NUMBER OF DECLARED RUNNERS 9

DAILY DOUBLE — THIRD RACE
THREE YRS OLD — Armlet—YELLOW
One mile and a half

3.30—186th DERBY STAKES with £50,000 added (including a Gold Trophy value £500)—of which £40,000 is given by the Horserace Betting Levy Board—to a sweepstakes of £10, £50 extra unless forfeit be declared by Tuesday, November 17th, 1964, a further £50 unless forfeit be declared by Tuesday, May 18th, 1965, a further £90 if declared a runner by Saturday, May 29th, such declaration to run may be cancelled by Tuesday, June 1st, but the full liability is not thereby reduced; the second to receive 10% and the third 5% of the whole stakes; for three yrs old, entire colts and fillies; colts, 9st, fillies, 8st 9lb; one mile and a half.

There will be a parade for this race.

620 entries, 305 at £10, 256 at £60, and 35 at £110.—Closed November 5th, 1963.

VALUES. WINNER £[illegible]5,301; SECOND £7,706; THIRD £3,853

Draw | Form — st lb

.... 22 1 MEADOW COURT .... 9 0 POWDER BLUE and SCARLET hoops, POWDER BLUE cap with SCARLET spots — L. Piggott
(late Harwell Fool)
Ch c Court Harwell—Meadow Music
Mr G. M. Bell (P. Prendergast, Ireland)

.... 3 2 BAM ROYAL .... 9 0 RED, ORANGE triangle and cap — P. Matthews
Br c Flush Royal—Rose of Persia
Mrs John F. C. Bryce (P. Prendergast, Ireland)

.... 10 3 LOOK SHARP .... 9 0 BLACK, WHITE sash and cap — J. Roe
Ch c Crepello—Wake Up!
Lord Derby (B. van Cutsem)

.... 12 4 ALCALDE .... 9 0 BLACK, WHITE cap — D. Smith
B c Alcide—Sundry
Lord Derby (B. van Cutsem)

.... 23 5 FOOTHILL .... 9 0 DRAB, SCARLET hoop and armlets, quartered cap — J. Mercer
B c Aggressor—Buckham Hill
Mr T. E. S. Egerton (W. Hern)

(Continued next page.

186th DERBY STAKES—continued.

Draw | Form — st lb

.... 01 6 SOLSTICE .... 9 0 GREEN, YELLOW sleeves, SCARLET sash — W. Williamson
Br c Solar Slipper—Thirty Scents
Mr C. W. Engelhard (J. F. Watts)

.........110 7 I SAY .... 9 0 YELLOW, BLACK spots, YELLOW sleeves and cap — R. Poincelet
Br c Sayajirao—Isetta
Mr Louis Freedman (W. Nightingall)

.... 11 8 NIKSAR .... 9 0 CHERRY, WHITE striped sleeves and hoop on cap — W. Rickaby
Ch c Le Haar—Niskampe
Mr Wilfred Harvey (W. Nightingall)

.... 0 9 AS BEFORE .... 9 0 WHITE, MAROON hoop, armlets and cap — G. Starkey
B c Alcide—None Nicer
Major L. B. Holliday (W. Wharton)

.... 3 10 SOVEREIGN EDITION 9 0 MAROON and SILVER GREY stripes, GOLD sleeves and cap — R. Maddock
Gr c Sovereign Path—Latest Edition
Mr J. H. Kartz (R. Mason)

.........120 11 SILLY SEASON .... 9 0 BLACK, GOLD cross, cuffs and stripe on cap — G. Lewis
Br c Tom Fool—Double Deal
Mr Paul Mellon (I. Balding)

.... 10 12 CONVAMORE .... 9 0 EMERALD GREEN, GOLD braid, stars and tassel on cap — E. Hide
Br c Court Harwell—Absolution
Mr E. R. More O'Ferrall (R. Smyth)

.... 10 13 BILLIONAIRE .... 9 0 SCARLET, EMERALD GREEN and GOLD buttons, collar and cuffs, RED and GOLD quartered cap, GREEN peak — G. Bougoure
B c Vimy—Metition
Dr B. N. Pajgar (H. Price)

.... 00 15 KING LOG .... 9 0 HENDERSON TARTAN, LIME GREEN sleeves and cap — R. Hutchinson
Br c Relic—Queen's Beast
Mrs W. H. D. Riley-Smith (G. Todd)

.........100 16 CAMBRIDGE .... 9 0 GREEN, RED sleeves, LIGHT BLUE cap — A. Breasley
B c Saint Crespin III—Cantelo
Mr David Robinson (B. Hobbs)

.... 1 17 BUCENTAUR .... 9 0 PRIMROSE and ROSE hoops, PRIMROSE cap — S. Smith
Ch c Doutelle—Browband
Lord Rosebery (J. Jarvis)

.... 18 CREOSOTE .... 9 0 PRIMROSE and ROSE hoops, ROSE cap — P. Robinson
Ch c Crepello—Camille
Lord Rosebery (J. Jarvis)

.... 00 19 SUNACELLI .... 9 0 CHERRY and WHITE stripes, LEMON sleeves and cap with WHITE hoop — B. Connorton
Ch c Botticelli—Astrid Sun
Mr W. T. Stoker (W. Gray)

.........011 20 BALLYMARAIS .... 9 0 CHERRY and WHITE stripes, LEMON sleeves and cap with WHITE hoop — W. Pyers
Ch c Ballymoss—Skylarking
Mr W. T. Stoker (W. Gray)

.... 11 22 SEA BIRD II .... 9 0 GREEN, BLACK cap — T. P. Glennon
Ch c Dan Cupid—Sicalade
M. J. Ternynck (E. Pollet, France)

.... 01 23 GULF PEARL .... 9 0 PINK, BLACK and WHITE striped sleeves, WHITE cap — J. Lindley
Ch c Persian Gulf—Nan
Mr J. H. Whitney (J. Tree)

.........221 24 VLEUTEN .... 9 0 RED and WHITE chevrons, WHITE sleeves, RED and WHITE quartered cap — J. Deforge
Ch or ro c Le Haar—Deianira
Baron Thierry de Zuylen de Nyevelt (G. Watson, France)

NUMBER OF DECLARED RUNNERS 22

Scribbles on my racecard include post-Derby quotes from gifted Australian jock Bill Pyers – 'Far the best I've seen in Europe' – and dry aside from Lester: 'This is a very fair horse'!

Sea Bird and Pat Glennon coast home to win the 1965 Derby in breathtaking style. Respectful pursuers are Meadow Court (Lester Piggott) and I Say (Roger Poincelet).

In contrast, Clive was not satisfied to play his cards close to his chest; he'd effectively hide the whole pack until minutes before copy time.

For the best part of our lives the *Daily Express* was a broadsheet. So it suited the caption writers when we concurred in the big races. Exceptionally we agreed on four Derby winners during the five years 1964-68. Royal Palace ('67) and Sir Ivor ('68) being preceded by 50-year-old Scobie Breasley's 13th Derby ride, Santa Claus, ('We believe in Santa') in '64, and 'SEA BIRD II CAN FLY IT say the big two' (in 1965).

'My verdict,' wrote Clive in his summary, 'is that Sea Bird II will leave his rivals puffin'.'

Remembering that Sea Bird's sire, Dan Cupid, had been almost flattened during a violent knock-about in 1959, Pollet equipped his star with protective leather-strapped gaiters, first tried after he'd suffered several nicks during the Grand Critèrium. The only instruction Madame 'Polly' was required to relay to the rider of No. 22 in the 22-runner field for the 186th Derby was: 'Monsieur Pollet wants you to pull up before reaching the road which crosses the course after the finish line.' Etienne Pollet was already thinking of the future.

What Pat Glennon was thinking about at the start was less certain. Because as the sartorially elegant Alec Marsh released the barrier the favourite (3-1 to 7-4 on the day) was facing towards the far rails. Not that the remarkably relaxed horse and rider appeared at all inconvenienced by forfeiting a few lengths.

The locally (Walter Nightingall) trained pair I Say (five lengths winner of Ascot's White Rose Stakes) and 2,000 Guineas winner, Niksar, made the running. Bing Crosby, who was over from Hollywood with his partners in Meadow Court, and who courteously took the trouble to climb up on to the grandstand roof to be interviewed by me for BBC television earlier, saw his still-progressive colt run a fine race.

Meadow Court would go on to win the Irish Sweeps Derby and the King George VI and Queen Elizabeth Stakes. But on this day, as Sea Bird swooped, like a tern devouring minnows, he had to settle for finishing runner-up to one of the most breathtakingly nonchalant winners in Derby history.

'I was always cocky and confident as a kid,' admitted the 5ft 7½ins tall rider after his official, two lengths victory in the race he had vowed to win 30 years ago – as an eight-year-old.

Sea Bird just never came off the bridle. Returning to weigh in with the runner-up's saddle, Lester Piggott cast an admiring glance at the winner and smiled: 'He daren't let him go in case he couldn't pull him up!'

By way of an encore the assured Racehorse of the Year, 1965, next reaffirmed his immoderate talent with a victory stroll in Saint-Cloud's £41,000-to-the-winner Grand Prix.

Ah, said some knowingly, wait for the Arc de Triomphe: he won't win *that* on the bit.

So we waited.

And the more we thought about it, the more we appreciated the magnitude of the task ahead. Foremost among the opposition in the great, all-aged, 1½ miles prize – inaugurated on 3 October 1920 and won by Newmarket-trained Comrade, who changed hands for 25 guineas as a yearling – was the unbeaten Reliance.

Above:
Sea Bird, led in by owner-breeder M Jean Ternynck, expended no more energy winning the Derby than walking to the unsaddling enclosure.

Right:
Before an admiring assembly, the hero of the hour enters the winner's circle. Etienne Pollet, in grey topper, follows.

Sea Bird hacks up in the 1965 Grand Prix de Saint-Cloud.

It wasn't just the fact that Monsieur François Dupré's Reliance was unbeaten in the five races he had contested – including the French Derby, Grand Prix de Paris (run over an extended one mile seven furlongs at that time) and French St Leger – but that he was trained by one of the all-time masters of his craft, François Mathet.

The former cavalry officer, champion amateur and holder of the Legion d'Honneur set out with two cheaply purchased (£375 the pair) jumpers and shortly became the first 200 horse-power trainer in Europe.

For 30 years he was at the forefront of his profession, turning out more than 3,200 winners, including four 'Arcs', and becoming responsible for producing one of French racing's greatest champion jockeys, Yves Saint-Martin.

As a teenage apprentice the young man quit Chantilly after breaking both wrists in a fall. 'Send him back when they've mended,' Mathet commanded Saint-Martin's Civil Servant parents, 'he'll make a jockey.'

The perennial French champion jockey rode seven Classic winners in England, including 1963 Derby winner Relko, as well as most of the important weight-for-age races at least once.

Relko, Phil Drake (100-8 Derby winner in 1955) and 1958 1,000 Guineas and Oaks heroine Bella Paola were Mathet-trained benefactors to PO'S followers – to employ the plural somewhat loosely.

So when the maestro opined that Relko's half-brother Reliance appeared to be still improving (he didn't run as a two-year-old), a 'walk-over' for Sea Bird became even less foreseeable.

Nor were the 'big two' the only Derby winners in the 20-runner line-up justifiably billed as 'the most representative international horserace ever run.'

The three further Derby winners were Meadow Court (Irish Sweeps Derby) whose connections had just bought the Desmond Stakes winner, Khalife, to ensure a fast gallop; Anilin (Russian Derby, Moscow); and Tom Rolfe (American Derby).

As well as Meadow Court and Khalife, Paddy Prendergast was represented by the Great Voltigeur winner Ragazzo, who had run an excellent race when second to Reliance in the French Leger.

The splendidly consistent Diatome, winner of the Prix Noailles and Prix du Prince d'Orange, and runner-up in the French Derby and Grand Prix, was one of two carrying Baron Guy de Rothschild's blue and yellow colours. The other was one of the top older horses, Free Ride, winner of the Prix Ganay.

Anilin, the first 'Arc' runner from Russia and undefeated in 1964, was now a four-year-old – like the English challengers Oncidium (Coronation Cup) and Soderini (John Porter Stakes and Hardwicke). Demi-Deuil, another excellent senior, was a four-race winner in '65, including the Grosser Preis von Baden.

The only filly in the field was Lavandin's daughter Blabla, winner of the Prix de Diane (French Oaks).

The starting prices – the only domestic odds which are available to French racegoers – were as follows: 6-5 Sea Bird; 9-2 Reliance; 15-2 Diatome and Free Ride (coupled); 7¾-1 Meadow Court and Khalife (coupled); 8-1 Tom Rolfe; 22-1 Anilin; 23-1 Emerald and Ardaban (coupled); 24-1 Blabla; 33-1 Ragazzo; 55-1 Marco Visconti; 60-1 Demi-Deuil; 70-1 Sigebert; 75-1 Oncidium and Timmy Lad; 80-1 Carvin; 90-1 Soderini; 120-1 Francilius.

Above:
Sea Bird on the wing in the '65 Arc. Having galloped into the memory of 75,000 racegoers, he is led in by his owner, right – and, left, probably recovers his breath faster than Messieurs Ternynck, Pollet or faithful lad Maurice Debreuil.

The Pari-Mutuel revealed that the equivalent of £5 million was bet on the race in France. Of this sum, well over £4,500,000 was accounted for by *Tiercé* and *Couplé* bettors.

The former seek to nominate the first three in correct finishing order; the latter to name the first two in order. There is a consolation dividend for *Tiercé* backers who name the first three, but in their incorrect order of finishing.

Sunday 3 October 1965 was a warm, sunlit day in Paris where a crowd of 75,000 gathered in the Bois du Boulogne for the richest-ever (£85,000) running of France's premier horserace, the Prix de l'Arc de Triomphe. I remember lingering in the paddock area to view the horses for as long as I dare before hurrying to the international television commentary point in the Old Stand.

Even allowing for the temperature Sea Bird was clearly overheating; likewise his chief rival Reliance. Ribot's little son Tom Rolfe was finding the unfamiliar set-up very strange. He'd crossed the Atlantic bringing all his own food and an impressively-built ex-sheriff to guard him, but without his running shoes – spikes being locally taboo.

The going was on the soft side of good, with possibly too much 'give' to favour Lester Piggott's partner Meadow Court, whose odds had been dramatically reduced from 18-1 to 7¾-1. Lord Howard de Walden's Oncidium (Scobie Breasley) had failed his stalls test on the Friday and passed (only just) the next morning. Now, at post-time, his antipathy resurfaced momentarily before he agreed entry; and they were off.

Off at a right gallop, too. Marco Visconti, who lost all of 20 lengths at the start of the Italian Derby, was not going for a repeat. The hope of Italy established instant advantage over the filly

Blabla, the Boussac Grand Prix de Marseille winner Ardaban, Anilin and Khalife. The last-named, third in the Irish Leger, vainly trying to fulfil his role as pacemaker for Meadow Court.

By the top of the hill Blabla had had enough; Khalife, under pressure from Irish star Johnny Roe, was in trouble; Marco Visconti led from Anilin, going well, Ardaban and Sea Bird. Little Tom Rolfe and Willie Shoemaker followed; Diatome, running sweetly, was next just ahead of Meadow Court, Reliance and Free Ride.

Approaching the home turn Anilin took over from Marco Visconti; Meadow Court moved closer; Sea Bird was cantering with Reliance and Diatome just behind.

This was going to be a horse race. At least, that's what this commentator was thinking when, in an eye-blink, it was over. You had to see it to believe it.

Pat Glennon might have just remembered he'd carelessly forgotten to release the handbrake and, having done so, Sea Bird fled the cage.

'It's Sea Bird on the wing,' I called. Four lengths; 6 lengths, 8. Then Pat began to ease him down, holding him snug but letting him drift across the course if that's what he wanted to do. No histrionics. No finger wagging. No whip waving. Just leaving the star of the show to gallop into our hearts; into our memory.

We came, some of us, to see Sea Bird confirm his status as Racehorse of the Year, 1965. We saw him affirm entitlement to be considered Racehorse of the Twentieth Century.

The official verdict was: 1 Sea Bird, 2 Reliance, 3 Diatome, 4 Free Ride, 5 Anilin, 6 Tom Rolfe, 7 Demi-Deuil, 8 Carvin, 9 Meadow Court, 10 Marco Visconti, etc. ... Distances: 6 lengths; 5 lengths; short neck; ½-length; 5 lengths; 6 lengths; 1½ lengths; ½-length; etc. ...

Like Etienne Pollet, Pat Glennon deserved great credit for his sensitive handling of the horse he described as 'undoubtedly the greatest horse I've even seen, let alone ridden.'

Endorsement of the merit of 1965 'Arc' form was forthcoming from Diatome and Carvin, who finished first and second in the Washington DC International, beating the best senior American horse, Roman Brother, as well as the Canadian champion, George Royal. Anilin went on to hack up in the Grosser Preis von Europa in Cologne and Demi-Deuil was a six lengths winner of the Premio Roma.

An estimated 75 million television viewers in six countries saw the 41st Longchamp-staged Arc de Triomphe 'live'. Regrettably, the UK was not one of them.

While commentating, along with Clive Graham, on Arc eve at Newmarket (which the corporation was about to lose), I was still lobbying on the 'phone for live coverage the next day. In vain. Three minutes of a recording was slotted in between other recorded programmes, *Cluff*, a police series, and the US sit-com *Our Lucy* on Sunday. Even this concession had not been mentioned in *Radio Times*. Or leaked to newspapers.

It was this ambivalence towards the sport that lost the BBC Arc coverage in the 1980s. A situation which was redressed single-handedly by Channel 4 Racing's egregious John McCririck, whose uncharacteristically restrained disguise as a pantomime onion seller so offended the promoters that *faute de mieux* they returned to 'Auntie' in 1995.

As for our hero whom the urbane, erudite, long-time senior Jockey Club Handicapper, Major David Swannell, rated the best horse he had ever seen – or was ever likely to see – he was leased to an American stud for seven years before returning 'home' in 1972. Sadly, he died of a blocked intestine in 1973, having sired the outstanding mare Allez France and the gifted but wayward 1970 Epsom runner-up Gyr, who would have won seven Derbys out of ten.

Sea Bird was one helluva racehorse.

PO'S presents Etienne Pollet with a commemorative Sea Bird tray on behalf of England's Horserace Writers and Reporters Association.

FRED WINTER

Frederick Thomas Winter CBE realised for National Hunt racing the parallel to Sir Gordon Richards's contribution in respect of the Flat. They were two men whose commitment and talent was matched only by transparent integrity.

Fred was born in 1926, the son of jockey prodigy Frederick Neville Winter, who was 17 when he won the 1911 Oaks on the remarkable Cherimoya. Remarkable in that the filly, trained by Charles Marsh, was by a sire, Cherry Tree (fee 18gns), who never won a race, out of a mare, Svelte, who was similarly without a single racecourse success. Further, the Oaks winner neither ran before or after her 25-1 victory.

Below:
A confident 4½-year-old Fred Winter leads his father's string at Epsom.

Opposite Page top and bottom:
Fred with his father.

Fred senior, who finished fourth in the jockeys' championship that season and later accepted a retainer to ride for the Imperial stable in Germany, was interned there throughout the 1914-18 War.

Despite his outstanding pre-war record, he found it difficult to re-establish his career (though he did win the Irish Derby and other significant races) and, because of increasing weight, applied to train at Newmarket. Rejected, he settled for Epsom and achieved considerable success with modest material until suspending activity on the outbreak of World War II.

It was Kent farmer Percy Bartholomew who then had the foresight to employ the charming and evidently gifted Frederick Neville Winter. The popular handler, who was widely admired for achieving notable results with inexpensive purchases, finally made it to Newmarket in 1963.

He'd won an impressive series of premier races at Royal Ascot, Goodwood and Newmarket before time caught up with him and, in 1965, his Highfield Stable was taken over by his long-time assistant and younger son, John Winter, who was quick to make his mark.

So, with such a background, it was not surprising that when Fred junior turned to training – after the Jockey Club had rejected his application for a starter's job – he showed a fair understanding of what was required. Well, enough to train the winners of 1,557 races and to achieve eight Champion Trainers' titles after kick-starting his career as a horse-handler supreme by winning successive Grand Nationals (Jay Trump and Anglo in 1965 and 1966) in his first two seasons with a licence.

But that was all in the future.

Young Frederick Thomas Winter was 4½ years old when he first rode out with his father's string; not a great deal older when gathering rosettes in the show ring; and 13, in 1940, when obtaining leave from Ewell College to ride in his first race on Tam O'Shanter in the Lambourn Nursery Handicap at Newbury. He finished ninth of 22 and, shortly after, won at Salisbury on the same filly.

It was not the beginning of an avalanche of success. He joined the stable of Newmarket trainer Harry Jelliss but race-riding opportunities were limited and, by 1942, his weight had risen to 8st 7lbs.

He left to re-connect with his father, now training at Southfleet in Kent; joined up in 1944 and, while on demobilisation leave three years later, Lieutenant Winter of the 6th Airborne Division became horse-borne in the Kenton Handicap Chase at Kempton on Saturday 27 December 1947. His partner, the 12-year-old stalwart Carton, 100-8 outsider of seven and trained by his father, was the lieutenant's second ride under National Hunt Rules.

I was reporting for the Press Association at the time and, prompted by reference to the *Form Book*, I remember the old horse jumping very impressively. More positively, I recall how stylish Fred was when scooting away from the last to win by six lengths.

Back in action for the 1948-49 season, he was booked by his father for old Carton once again at Folkestone on 6 September 1948 and, once again a 100-8 chance, the now-13-year-old obliged.

Fred's half-length nearest victim in the 10-runner Westgate Handicap Chase was one of jumping's outstanding jockeys of the era, Bryan Marshall.

Then, disaster. On his third ride of the season, in the £102-to-the-winner Folkestone Novices' Hurdle at Wye, he set out on elderly '20-1 others'

mare, Tugboat Minnie, on 13 September.

In her previous appearance on Boxing Day 1947 at Wolverhampton (also '20-1 others'), she had fallen at the second flight. This time she went at the first and Fred suffered a broken back – and a legacy of apprehension.

His enthusiasm for race-riding under National Hunt Rules had already been tempered by concern over injury. Now Fred's resolve would be critically tested.

On 5 September 1949, almost 12 months on, 14-year-old Carton was called up to fulfil the role of confidence restorer. Backed from 9-2 to 9-4 favourite in the Westgate Handicap Chase at Folkestone, again, the old horse ('never placed to trouble leaders', wrote *Chaseform*) earned a distinction of sorts when running last of five finishers. He was surely the only horse who did not receive a 100 per cent positive ride throughout the long, brilliant and distinguished career of his record-breaking partner.

Above:
Young Fred unsaddling after his first ride.

Below:
Kilmore, ridden by Fred, wins the 1962 Grand National.

Comeback winner Dick The Gee (Plumpton, 14 November 1949), trained by his old friend George Archibald, proved the perfect conduit to Ryan Price who, much impressed by the riding of our Fred, promptly proposed an association that would endure for the remaining 15 years of the Winter saga. They christened one of racing's longest-running, most successful partnerships on Boxing Day 1949 at Newton Abbot, where Smoke Piece became the first of more than 500 winners for the trainer-jockey alliance. Ryan, a hero in his own right, always insisted that Fred's skill was such that he won him at least 100 races 'he shouldn't have won.'

It seemed that in next to no time, without exceeding a steady canter, Frederick Thomas Winter became a role model, a *personnage* – as the French put it so euphoniously. And a very successful one.

He rode 83 winners in the 1951-52 season, finishing second to Tim Molony's 99 winners in the jockeys' title race. I rather hoped he might ride one for me on the opening day of the season, which then ran from 4 August to 2 June.

Diplomatically overlooking my unpromising record as an owner – 12 individual horses had competed during 12 years, on every available circuit, without one achieving a place – he assured me, in his unfailingly disarming manner, that he would be delighted.

I knew that my current dream-horse, The Solid Man, was fit because he had 'schooled' me that very morning at Upavon. And following the

1957 National winner Sundew and Fred Winter led in by Mrs Geoffrey Kohn, beaming bowler-hatted husband following.

excursion over three fences he had decided on an uncomfortably rapid tour of the Wiltshire Downs. I hadn't been so fast since my Morris 8hp's brakes failed approaching Cheltenham from Cleeve Hill.

Fred's hopefully more controlled partnership of The Solid Man was scheduled for the third day of the season at Newton Abbot. That was before his mount, Ocean Gem, fell at the last flight in the first hurdle race on day one, and the rider broke his collarbone.

So another future champion (1954), Dick Francis, accepted the responsibility of handling the 10-1 fifth favourite in the £132 Plymouth Selling Handicap Chase.

They were approaching obstacle number five ('second and going easily', according to *Chaseform*) and I was thinking I should have had more on this one, when the old lad, who scaled the heights of Aintree without brushing a twig in his younger days, just belted the fence about six inches from base. Defying the dictates of gravity, he succeeded in gaining the far side and, finding a 'spare leg', remained vertical.

Unequipped with emergency landing gear, wartime Flying Officer Francis was horizontal.

That Dick blamed himself for severance of the partnership reflected both his charitable disposition and the wealth of imagination which led to his creation of some 40 best-sellers.

I was abroad on holiday when Dick bravely teamed up with The Solid Man over the same course, in similar company, a fortnight later. But *Chaseform* reported of the unplaced 5-2 favourite: 'Jumped badly, never going well.'

Fred was back in action early in September – winning for Ryan Price on Campari at Fontwell on the 12th – and happy to ride The Solid Man in a Towcester 'seller' on the 21st. He'd try 'holding him up' and, when he ran sixth, beaten 30 lengths ('nearest finish'), he characteristically blamed himself and assured: 'We'll get nearer than that.' We didn't (beaten out of sight) at Chepstow on 5 October. But Lingfield in the New Year was a bit of a thrill.

The course was subject to extremes of going at that time. On this day, 11 January, it was pretty desperate. Seriously testing. Most of the 'connections' I'd spoken to were very unsure about ability to handle the surface.

Well practised in self-delusion, I figured 10-1 was 'value' and helped to back The Solid Man down to 13-2. 'Look after each other,' I proposed expendably as the duo left the soggy paddock.

There was no doubt that some were finding the ground very arduous. But the solid old man, at 14, one year senior to 8-1 rival Duharra and three years older than favourite Cavaliero, was skimming through it in good rhythm.

Running down the steep hill into the home turn the duo were five lengths clear with, it appeared, nothing going well behind. Three plain fences ahead in the level home straight. When Ted Binns, the last bookmaker to enliven the course by betting in running, called: 'I'll take 5-4 The Solid Man don't win,' he was instantly under siege.

£100-£80 was bet on; £50-£40; £100-£80 again and again, as well as £25-£20 etc. ... But old Ted (Fred Sturman) didn't make too many mistakes.

As the leader jumped the third-last clear, it sure looked as though they'd take some beating. Unless you were the man on top and could feel the weariness draining into the 14-year-old legs beneath you. At the second-last a horse less than half his age, receiving 12lbs, had got him.

Fred, sensitive horseman that he was, knew his partner was 'dead' and, properly, spared him further effort. It was the sort of ground on which, if you took your foot off the pedal, you stopped. Sixth and last they finished. 'He did everything he could,' said Fred, acknowledging his muddy partner with a friendly slap.

This was the season (1951-52) that Bill Wightman, a cracking all-round trainer, first asked Fred to ride that brilliant hunter chaser, Halloween. Ridden by his owner Dick Smalley and trained by Bill, Halloween had won all his five races under Rules the previous season, culminating in the Cheltenham Foxhunters'.

He'd since been bought for a robust sum by another patron of the stable, the Contessa di Sant Elia. After that there had been an embarrassing hiccup. Two, in fact. Taken over by a professional jockey for Hurst Park's Grand Sefton Trial, Halloween made a series of mistakes before falling at the fifth. The jockey was changed for his next venture at Newbury, where he fell at the first.

So the former owner/rider, who was to become a Jockey Club Starter, was invited back into the saddle for another event at Newbury, where he won neatly. And, after a little break, to Newbury again on 22 February 1952. He won by 6 lengths. No sweat.

It is unusual for a professional jockey to seek the advice of an amateur. To Fred it made common sense, for whatever Dick Smalley was doing, it certainly seemed to work.

The answer was: 'Nothing really. I just leave it to him.'

So that was it. Accustomed to making his own arrangements, in the manner of many rigorously loose-schooled French jumpers, Halloween became confused with requests that conflicted with his instincts.

Above:
50-1 National winner Anglo led into winner's enclosure in 1966.

Opposite Page:
Following the memorable 1965 National triumph of Jay Trump, owner Mary Stephenson and trainer Fred Winter seek a smile for the camera – with only partial success.

"'In all the time he rode for us,' recalls Ivor, 'he never hit a horse. Never.'"

Henceforth, when partnered by Fred, if he seemed to be errant in his approach to an obstacle, he was left to adjust as well as he could. From a rider's standpoint, easier said than done.

Both the approach and the solution were typical Fred.

This was probably the first really good horse that he rode and he played a sure part in shaping Halloween's notable career. Together they won the King George VI Chase in 1952 and 1954. They finished runner-up in both the 1953 and '55 Cheltenham Gold Cup, and third in 1956; and they won nine races together. The durability of Halloween owed much to Fred Winter's sympathetic handling – as well as to that of Dick Smalley.

Fred was never a 'stick' jockey. Like his fine contemporary, Stan Mellor, he used the impulse of his own body and his sensitive hands to induce optimum effort.

Fred and Diana's wedding, 1956

His advancement was dramatically swift:

1950-51 season, 38 winners from 219 mounts; fifth in jockeys' list

1951-52 season, 85 winners from 402 mounts; second in jockeys' list

1952-53 season, 121 winners from 471 mounts; champion jockey

The 1952-53 season total was a record at the time and remained so until Josh Gifford, who also kicked off on the Flat, beat it by one in 1966-67. Ron Barry (125) bettered that in 1972-73; then Jonjo O'Neill weighed in with 149 in 1977-78.

At each punctuation point those of us associated with the sport tended to predict that the latest total would never be surpassed. Then along came Tony McCoy with a staggering 289 (2001-02) in the now non-stop jumping curriculum.

Come the 1953-54 season Fred may have questioned whether day one of a new term was ideally suited to personal involvement. Once again he crashed out on the opening afternoon at Newton Abbot – this time suffering multiple left-leg fractures through which he was sidelined for 12 months.

His August first partner, Cent Francs, had fallen in the first race at the first fence in his first novices' chase on his first outing for Ryan Price. Those were his only firsts in a 10-race, place-free season during which he fell twice more. A record similar to most still-nevertheless cherished O'Sullevan horses until Pretty Fair (sixteenth to carry my colours in 15 years) won a selling hurdle at Windsor in March 1954. And dear Fred was first among those who thoughtfully despatched a much-appreciated telegram.

Despite complications to his leg injuries the 1952-53 champion was back reclaiming his title in 1955-56, and winning four in a row aboard Halloween, who'd had a lean season in his absence. More crucially, as a man noted for prize gathering, there was none to match his fulfilment in 1956, when Diana Pearson became his wife. I recollect both a smart wedding in Spanish Place and, more hazily, a lively reception which could in no wise have been mistaken for a temperance celebration.

During a career punctuated by significant landmarks he had won his first Champion Hurdle the year before (Clair Soleil) and his first Grand National (Sundew) the year after.

In the interim Fred accepted a second retainer for the small, *distingué* team of Ivor Herbert; the licence being held by Charlie Mallon at a time

Fred Winter and Mandarin at Saxon House.

when a newspaper writer was not eligible for such authority.

At the 1959 Cheltenham Festival, where he won an unsurpassed five races, Fred rode three horses for the Herbert stable; Gallery Goddess (won Cathcart), Flame Gun (won Cotswold Chase) and Linwell (second in the Gold Cup, a race the horse had won in '57).

'In all the time he rode for us,' recalls Ivor, 'he never hit a horse. Never.'

It is a measure of Fred Winter's achievement in the saddle that, despite riding winners of three Champion Hurdles; two Cheltenham Gold Cups; two Grand Nationals; three King George VI Chases; as well as realising four jockeys' titles, he will still be most vividly remembered for his heroic performance on the afternoon of 17 June 1962, in France's principal jumps racing theatre, Auteuil, while competing for both the premier French steeplechasing prize, the Grand Steeplechase de Paris, and the championship for young hurdlers, the Grande Course de Haies des 4 Ans.

Three-figure odds would not have tempted a man standing in Fred's shoes – even had the tenant been a betting man. For, truth to tell, Di Winter's resolute husband was not really fit to ride.

He'd been wasting severely after the family had taken an end-of-season break in Cornwall. Then, incautiously, the couple had enjoyed an

Look, no steering! Fred and Mandarin land third over the daunting Rivière des Tribunes during 1962 Grand Steeplechase de Paris, Auteuil.

excellent, rich, restorative dinner on the eve of their Paris flight.

The consequent sleepless night and acute discomfort turned aspiration into ordeal. After boarding, which a lesser man would have forsworn, Fred, in a spirit more of desperation than indulgence, requested half a bottle of champagne.

For a few strides he was back 'on the bit'. But not for long. The white hope of England had the pallor of a well-laundered number-cloth.

Having to wait for the big one until after 4 o'clock was no help. He and ace handler Fulke Walwyn walked the tortuous obstacle course together. Fred and Mandarin had already combined that year to win the Cheltenham Gold Cup. This was a contrasting scenario.

From a personal perspective one of the disadvantages of undertaking two full-time jobs, journalism and broadcasting, involving a seven-day week for close on half a century, was the difficulty of incorporating them.

While one of my equine heroes, Be Friendly, was making his racecourse debut at Lingfield on 14 May 1966, I needed to be broadcasting at Ayr. When he ran for the first time as a three-year-old in Kempton's 2,000 Guineas Trial on 25 March 1967, I was commentating at Teesside; and while little old Attivo was racing to exultant victory in the 1974 Northumberland Plate at Newcastle, I was calling the horses for BBC television in the Irish Derby at The Curragh.

Even worse? While Fred Winter and Mandarin were performing the equivalent of racing through

Fred and Mandarin (breast girth) on the run-in.

the Hampton Court maze blindfold, I had to be – perish the thought – in the offices of the *Daily Express*.

Thanks to my great colleague and great friend, John Oaksey, and his imperishable report in *Horse and Hound*, I 'saw' the epic better than had I been on site.

Briefly: when Mandarin's bit snapped clean in the middle, inside the horse's mouth, approaching the fourth obstacle, 5ft 11in of privet, on the serpentine circuit, Fred was left without steering or brakes. To quote John:

> *To visualise the full impossibility of the situation you must remember first that when a racehorse, particularly a hard-pulling chaser, is galloping on the bit, much of the jockey's weight is normally balanced, through the reins, against that of the horse's head and forehand.*
>
> *Now, for both Winter and Mandarin, this vital counterbalance was gone completely. The man, with no means of steering but his weight, had to rely entirely on grip and balance; the horse, used to a steady pressure on his mouth, had to jump 21 strange and formidable obstacles with his head completely free – a natural state, admittedly, but one to which Mandarin is wholly unaccustomed.*

The 'Grand Steeple' course is virtually two figures of eight, running both clockwise and anti-clock, with one circuit round them both. Further, as John pointed out:

Below:
Fred Winter and Beaver II, 1962 Grande Course de Haies des 4 Ans.

Bottom:
Shattered. Fred holds on by an ear after Beaver II's triumph. Trainer Ryan Price looks nearly as drained.

There are at least four bends through 180 degrees and to negotiate them all as Winter and Mandarin did, without bit or bridle was, quite literally, miraculous.

Until the No. 1 went up in the frame (Mandarin by a head) the issue was in doubt. And it was no good asking Fred. He couldn't speak.

John gave due credit to the French jockeys who, rather than riding their adversary off the course, as could easily have been done, actually went out of their way to help. 'Proving gloriously,' wrote Lord Oaksey, 'that the comradeship of dangers shared can, in some sports at least, count for more than international rivalry.'

Forty minutes later Fred was due to line up in the French Triumph Hurdle (Grande Course de Haies des 4 Ans) on the little, Ryan Price-trained Beaver II. This horse had already proved a source of acute embarrassment to Ryan.

While buying a horse from the powerful Strassburger Stable in Chantilly a local agent, Sid Walker, had been given this very small son of Fast Fox as a 'makeweight' by the American Ralph Beaver Strassburger. Sid passed him on, *gratis*, to Ryan, who had paid a lot of money for a potential Triumph Hurdle horse on behalf of Enid Chanelle.

This was Catapult II who, ridden by Fred, went off a good favourite for the Triumph in which he appeared to be hacking up – until along comes Josh Gifford on Beaver II, both of them wearing a wide grin. There were some glum faces around the unsaddling enclosure at Hurst Park, where the big four-year-old prize was still run, and some angry voices. For, naturally, the 'Master of Findon' was credited with having brought off another 'stroke'.

Talking of which, Catapult II ran a very similar race in the following year's Schweppes, setting off at a brisk pace before fading dramatically. Later the poor lad dropped dead in his box after a heart attack.

Fred Winter was in such a state of total exhaustion after the 'Grand Steeple' ('He was virtually unconscious,' said Fulke) that there was, apparently, no chance of him riding either in the next race or next few days. It would be akin to sending back into the ring a boxer who's been knocked out.

Yet his friend and colleague Stan Mellor (thrice champion; first to ride 1,000 winners) dressed him, led him to the paddock, and then, partnering Beaudeer, rode against him.

Fred won by a length. 'Rode an absolutely perfect race,' related Stan afterwards.

CARRY ON, WINTER – HE DID!

By Peter O'Sullevan

Another chapter in the immortal Fred Winter's tale was written in the race that so nearly wasn't at Leicester yesterday.

The race that took 13 incident-packed minutes to run.

And ended in triumph for Fred after his even-money Quorn Chase partner Carry On had fallen twice and 'retired' once.

Four set out on the three-mile journey over 18 fences, at the first of which 6-4 second favourite Norwegian overlooked take-off and fell heavily.

'That one's out of the way,' reflected Fred, noting happily that horse and rider seemed unscathed.

But four fences later he was exclaiming: 'Blimey – now we're in trouble.' For at this point Kilvemnon fell and brought down King Fin.

So that Carry On was left to carry on on his own. 'And I knew he wouldn't fancy that,' said his rider later.

Passing the winning post on the first circuit with 10 fences left to jump, Carry On was preceded by the riderless trio Norwegian, King Fin and Kilvemnon – in that order and evidently in high spirits.

ALL HAPPY

Though less high, maybe, than the favourite's backers who, unaware of Fred Winter's misgivings, were busy lighting cigars, slapping each other on the back and agreeing that this was how all races should be run – all 'on the floor' bar the jolly favourite.

One astute investor laid £100 to £3 ON Carry On at this stage, knowing that if none 'completed', the race would be declared void – and, likewise, all bets on it.

So, he figured, he could win £3, but not lose his 'ton'.

As the riderless trio pulled up at the paddock Carry On glanced over to watch them enviously – and ... splash! jumped straight into the water.

Fred, pitched on to the bank, was first up and quickly retrieved his dripping partner.

Cheered on by their temporarily dismayed supporters, the pair then made for the open ditch (No. 10), at which Carry On adamantly applied all four brakes.

Fred turned the six-year-old, patted him, whispered encouragement, and aimed for another go. But no refusal could have been more complete.

Carry On slithered up to the guard rail, belted it hard, and turned over straight into the ditch.

Fred helped him up and was leading him back to the paddock when David Nicholson, having retrieved Norwegian, set off for fence No. 2 (they had earlier landed on the far side of the first), jumped it very sketchily, 'climbed' over the third and then pulled up.

Meanwhile Kilvemnon's owner-trainer Maurice Bailey had caught his mare and was riding her down the course in search of Clive Chapman.

And Phil Harvey's jockey pal Tim Ryan had captured King Fin and was returning him to the point of original departure.

TACTICIAN

Quick-thinking Ryan Price, showing himself to be as fit as any horse in the Findon string, immediately sprinted off the stand and across the course to mud-plastered Fred Winter, whose greeting was: 'What do you want me to do now?'

'Wait till the other two get round here and take a "lead" off them,' he was instructed – the trainer adding: 'Just shut your eyes and keep driving!'

Gratefully accepting the 'lead' when it materialised Carry On (whose £100 to £3 ON supporter was a near-hospital case by now) nimbly negotiated the open ditch behind the other two.

He moved up at the second-last fence, quickened on the flat, and to tumultuous roars drew away to win.

A very cold judge, Malcolm Hancock ('I thought of bringing you a cup of coffee and sandwiches,' said a sympathetic trainer), placed Carry On three-quarters of a length winner from King Fin, with Kilvemnon four lengths away third.

There were six other races at Leicester, and in one of them Arthur Freeman achieved his first National Hunt training success with Pipe Down.

But there was no other race quite like the 2.30.

Fred and Friendly Again on their way to post for Cheltenham's Clive Graham Handicap Hurdle on 11 April 1964.

Meanwhile Sid Walker sent Ryan a telegram: 'You can't kill a beaver with a catapult.'

Wherever Fred was in action – whatever the weather, the quality of performer or reward – he gave it whatever was required. Like Leicester, on 26 November 1963. (*See cutting on previous page.*)

This was the year (1963) in which Fred Winter became the first jump jockey to be awarded the CBE, and in which the latest of his injuries – three cracked ribs and a punctured lung – caused him to ponder the future.

He had no fervent wish to become a trainer ('All those bandages,' he grimaced one day when visiting Ivor Herbert's yard, 'I couldn't bear it') and Di had no *penchant* for the life of a trainer's wife. Little wonder that he called into the Jockey Club's London offices, one day after medical treatment, to make the aforementioned unsuccessful enquiry.

In any event he would retire in 1964, agreeing that Beaverbrook Newspapers-sponsored raceday at Cheltenham in April would be good timing. The event was enthusiastically endorsed by Max Aitken to assist the sport after programmes had been decimated by a 'foot and mouth' outbreak, as well as unfavourable weather.

I hoped very much that my grey four-year-old Friendly Again, elder half-sister to Be Friendly,

Left:
Beaverbrook Newspapers Meeting, Cheltenham 1964. Fred is placed for the last time after Friendly Again (owned by PO'S, trained by Cyril Mitchell) finishes second in Clive Graham Hurdle.

Below:
Fred receives the trophy on behalf of owner Juan Ceballos from PO'S after Rodman's victory in the Finale Junior Hurdle at Chepstow, 21 December 1977.

might be the means of a last-day televised winner for the great man. Not that her trainer, Cyril Mitchell, was exactly brimming with confidence. 'If he can win the Clive Graham Hurdle on your mare,' opined Cyril, 'he'll prove he's a magician as well as a wizard.'

They came by the trainload (£3 return, Paddington to the racecourse station first class; £2 second class) to cheer him as a jockey for the last time.

He was on two favourites, Kirriemuir and Sunbeat, and the 100-9 outsider Friendly Again in the 16-runner second race.

I was as apprehensive commentating the grey girl as at any time. But she ran a lovely race, leading until jumping the last where one outran her. The other two were out of the money, so Fred Winter's last placed ride had been in my colours. Last of his British jumping winners (923 of them) was Vultrix on 25 March 1964.

And so began the remarkable training saga which, together with his career as a jockey, reaffirmed his eminence in jumping history. Fred not only trained horses superlatively well; he trained trainers and jockeys with the same sensitive and dramatically effective touch. And, above all, he earned the respect, admiration and affection of just about everyone with whom he came in contact. Some man.

LESTER PIGGOTT

Ernest Keith Piggott had the profile of a pugilist, the pedigree of an assured horsemaster and a charming, easy-going disposition.

Before taking up training in 1944 and establishing a successful Flat and jumping stable the 500 winners he partnered, on the level and as a fearless National Hunt jockey, included the Champion Hurdle, Welsh National and Grand Sefton Chase.

His father, Ernie, thrice champion jumps jockey, rode three Grand National winners and he, Keith, was to train one himself (Ayala) in 1963.

Fifteen years earlier the success of a filly whom he trained to win the contrastingly modest Wigan Lane Selling Handicap over one mile at Haydock may have given him as much, if not more, satisfaction as his triumph in the world's most renowned steeplechase.

The Chase, as she was named, carried 6st 9lbs on 18 August 1948, including Keith and Iris Piggott's 12-year-old son, Lester.

It was the deceptively angelic looking young man's first visit to the winner's circle.

In this era the Flat racing season opened traditionally on Lincoln's Carholme, a bleak tract of flatland which was invariably host to a March wind of numbing intensity.

After three days, culminating in the Lincolnshire Handicap, first leg of the Spring Double, the racing circus moved west, by way of the oft-snowbound Derbyshire Peak District, to Liverpool.

Here the three-day programme featured 12 Flat races and seven over hurdles and fences, climaxed, of course, by the Grand National.

Come the 1950s and Keith enquired one day: 'Can you look after "the boy" and give him a lift to Aintree?'

'The Boy', who had virtually by-passed childhood, was already streetwise and saddlewise.

At an age when many of his contemporaries were collecting cigarette cards, 14-year-old Lester Piggott was the unwilling recipient of four or five plain yellow ones.

Provided he did not have a ride in the last race on day three at Lincoln we'd leave after the fifth and drive straight to a hotel in Chesterfield or Macclesfield – depending on progress – where my passenger would drink a cup of sugarless tea while I phoned copy to the *Express*.

He was an ideal travelling companion. Instinctively aware that my thoughts would be focussed on the next day's column until it had been transmitted, he'd quietly study Thursday's 'probable runners' – there were no overnight declarations then – until we resumed our journey.

Driving over the Cat and Fiddle Pass down into Cheshire we'd dine at the George Hotel, Knutsford. Then on to the Adelphi, Liverpool. A formula repeated for several years.

Lester's precocious skills were fostered by Brandy, a firebrand of a New Forest pony, and honed by two of the most qualified and committed mentors imaginable in the persons of Keith and Iris Piggott.

His mother's instruction in the basic skills of horsemanship could not have been articulated by a more accomplished authority.

The former Iris Rickaby was a member of an immensely successful and respected racing family, being the daughter of three times Classic-winning rider Fred; great-granddaughter of a Derby-winning trainer; and sister of Frederick Lester Rickaby, who rode five Classic winners and was the father of Bill and another Fred, who

Above:
Lester Piggott, 12, rarely sat on the fence in later years.

Right:
Twelve-year-old Lester already favoured the company of horses.

Tête à tête: PO'S and LP at Kempton.

distinguished themselves both in the saddle and in the Second World War before the latter became a champion trainer in South Africa.

Not surprisingly, Iris herself was a very polished horsewoman – twice winner of the famed 4½-miles Newmarket Town Plate, the only race available to lady riders at that time.

She was the restraining influence in her son's career, insisting on him remaining in school at least until aged 14.

By then, 1950, 'The Boy' was a star. Champion apprentice, with 52 winners that season, he left school with speed and without regret, adjudging any activity which separated him from horses to be 'a waste of time'.

Iris, who had witnessed sad examples of successful jockeys reaching the end of their professional life virtually 'skint', constantly encouraged thrift.

Keith, in contrast, shied away from offering any counsel which might cool the fire which fuelled 'the Boy's' intense ambition.

Racing had been restricted during the war and opportunity for the development of apprentices severely limited. So home-grown Lester had few contemporaries. Even fewer following victory in the Brighton Autumn Cup, on 20 May 1950, aboard Zina. For this success meant that he was no longer eligible to claim any weight allowance against his seniors, whom he met on equal terms the next day.

The outcome was triumph on his first Ascot winner, Tancred, in the Buckingham Palace Stakes, in which he opposed jockeys such as Gordon Richards, Charlie Elliott, Harry Carr, Willie Nevett, Frankie Durr , Tommy Lowrey etc. ... as equals.

There had been four or five yellow cards lately; notably at Hurst Park, Worcester, Lincoln and Kempton. But worse was to come. On 10 October at Newbury he was riding Barnacle, a four-year-old with 7st 7lbs in the 14-runner two miles Manton Handicap, when clearly tightening up Scobie Breasely's partner, Royal Oak IV, well inside the last quarter of a mile. Barnacle finished ¾ length ahead of Royal Oak IV with the nearest of the rest 4 lengths away.

According to my report Scobie rode in with a torn left boot; his mount with rails paint along his flank.

An objection for 'crossing and boring' followed; Royal Oak IV's trainer, Vic Smyth, apologising to Keith Piggott for the protest, 'for which there was no alternative'.

The objection was promptly upheld, with Lester being reported to the Stewards of the Jockey Club.

"By then, 1950, 'The Boy' was a star. Champion apprentice, with 52 winners that season, he left school with speed and without regret ... "

Hartley Lass who, with pipe-smoking Bert Packham substituting, won on the Saturday at Sandown at 100-7!

I hoped they didn't receive the Sunday papers in Arosa, where Keith and Iris had taken Lester for his first experience of speed on snow.

Soon after returning to Britain Lester fell in with a right villain, one whose antecedents provided a clue to his frequently unacceptable behaviour.

This was Zucchero, who was not only sired by the talented but temperamentally flawed Nasrullah, but had a liberal quota of neurosis on his dam's side as well.

After exhausting the patience of both his owner and several professional handlers, the original 3,100 guineas yearling was passed on without reluctance to Berkshire bookmaker and occasional National Hunt owner, George Rolls, for a relative trifle.

George was among the early believers in the genius of the 'Wonder Boy' who was now riding frequently for Ken Cundell. Hence the decision to

Above:
Lester at Epsom, June 1954 – the year he won his first Derby. In background, journalists Jimmy Park (**Evening Standard**) and, right, Claude Harrison (**Sporting Chronicle**)

Right:
The 'Wonder Boy' and the wayward lad, Zucchero.

Outcome of the Newmarket hearing, which took place on Cambridgeshire day (Wednesday 25 October 1950), was suspension for the remainder of the season – just over three weeks.

Magnanimously the stewards still allowed him to ride on that afternoon which was not improved, from 'The Boy's' perspective, by photographed neck defeat on Zina in the 31-runner big handicap – one of the only events of consequence in the *Racing Calendar* which he was never to win.

'The stewards told me they were punishing me for my own good, though I might not think so now,' he related a little wistfully.

The wistfulness promoted by the thought of the rides that had been booked in the near future. And which, he was convinced, included a winner or two. So I named four of them for any PO'S reader who might be interested and included

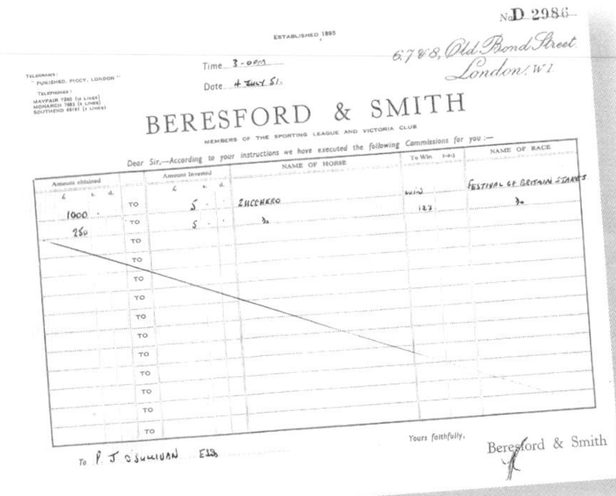
No D 2986

ESTABLISHED 1895

TELEGRAMS: "PUNISHED, PICCY, LONDON"
TELEPHONES: MAYFAIR 7260 (9 LINES) MONARCH 7683 (4 LINES) SOUTHEND 65181 (4 LINES)

Time 3-0pm
Date 4 July 51.

6, 7 & 8, Old Bond Street
London, W1.

BERESFORD & SMITH

MEMBERS OF THE SPORTING LEAGUE AND VICTORIA CLUB

Dear Sir,—According to your instructions we have executed the following Commissions for you:—

Amount obtained £ s. d.		Amount Invested £ s. d.	NAME OF HORSE	To Win 1-2-3	NAME OF RACE
1000 .	TO	5 - .	ZUCCHERO	win	FESTIVAL OF BRITAIN STAKES
250	TO	5 - .	do	123	do
	TO				
	TO				
	TO				
	TO				
	TO				
	TO				
	TO				
	TO				
	TO				
	TO				
	TO				

To P. J. O'Sullivan Esq.

Yours faithfully,
Beresford & Smith

Beresford & Smith voucher. One of an optimistic collection held by PO'S in favour of Zucchero's 'King George' prospects.

place his enigmatic acquisition with the Compton trainer.

Zucchero clearly had difficulty determining whether or not he wished to compete. All he knew for certain was that no one but himself was going to resolve the question.

Lester spent hours at the Compton stable, seeking to gain 'Sugar's' confidence. All concerned were immensely heartened when he won Epsom's Blue Riband Trial after consenting to jump off on equal terms with his adversaries.

Now, granted the inclination, he just could be 15-year-old Lester Piggott's first Derby winner. On the day Ken Cundell made his way across the colourfully encumbered infield to the distant Derby start. Here, at the appropriate moment, he took gentle hold of Zucchero's bridle and led him into the tapes at a trot.

The barrier flew skywards and Nasrullah's wayward son applied the brakes with resolute finality. And that was the unpromising end to our hero's initial bid for Epsom glory.

Britain's all-aged showpiece, initiated in 1951 as the King George VI and Queen Elizabeth Festival of Britain Stakes, was to be the duo's next ambitious target. It was widely considered to be an absurdly optimistic objective.

A while ahead of the contest the odds against success were reckoned to be all of 200-1. Personally, I had a fair little collection of vouchers like the one above, and I hope the commentary was reasonably unbiased.

In a high-class field Charlie Elliott and Supreme Court only got the better of Lester and Zucchero by ¾ length in the closing stages of a tense encounter.

The following year, by which time the enigmatic one had been moved to Bill Payne at Lambourn, Lester avenged defeat by Charlie when Zucchero upset the odds laid on Marcel Boussac's Dynamiter in the Rose of York Stakes. The Lambourn partnership having earlier floored another odds-on chance (Le Sage; Gordon Richards) when creating a 20-1 surprise in Newmarket's Princess of Wales's Stakes.

It was a season embracing extremes of racing fortune, beginning with a broken collarbone in March and ending, prematurely, with a repeat fracture as well as a broken leg in August. In between there was a second apprentice championship; Zucchero, and one of the luckiest riding engagements of his career – resulting in a 15-year-old winning the prestigious Eclipse Stakes with breathtaking nonchalance.

Chantilly trainer Percy Carter's stable jockey Freddy Palmer, the charming, locally-born son of an English father and French mother, had to forgo the ride on Mystery IX through weight problems. So Edgar Britt was approached. He much regretted having to ride at Manchester and proposed Scobie Breasely. Scobie had no sooner accepted than he was sidelined with a virus.

'I didn't know I was riding until I reached the course,' said Lester after one of his most accomplished and significant performances to date.

Meanwhile, harbingers of Zucchero's quasi reform at previously mentioned York and Newmarket resulted in an invitation to Laurel Park for the inaugural running of the Washington International on 18 October 1952.

Zucchero's previous handler Ken Cundell had second claim on Lester at this time and (there was a bit of 'needle' here) he refused to release him for the venture.

The four-year-old's regular partner was not too happy about that, but somewhat mollified by winning the Solario Stakes for Ken, on March Past, the same day.

Charlie Smirke deputised in Maryland and Zucchero ran third to follow English traveller, George Colling-trained Wilwyn.

The latter was the closest of Zucchero's victims the next year when the reunited team achieved their most eminent triumph in the 10-runner Coronation Cup. The now five-year-old seemed to be in a grumpy mood in the paddock. Lester

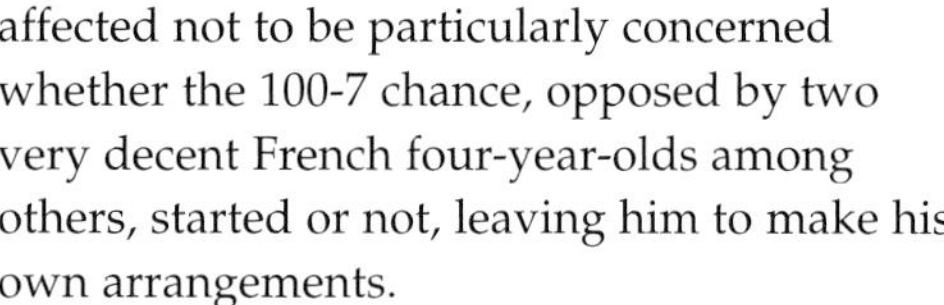

affected not to be particularly concerned whether the 100-7 chance, opposed by two very decent French four-year-olds among others, started or not, leaving him to make his own arrangements.

Zucchero jumped straight into his bit at the 'off', then dropped himself off the pace. At the start of the descent to Tattenham Corner, his interest and pace quickened.

Once into the straight, while Lester kept him perfectly balanced, he began, unasked, to pick off rivals with nonchalant efficiency. Approaching the winning post he had a clear uninterrupted view of the pub, The Rubbing House, directly ahead.

This was top class form, raising high hopes for the 'King George VI'.

Unfortunately he'd been kicked at the start by an unruly Frenchman, Mat de Cocagne, the previous year. His memory of the incident ruled out any question of renewing participation.

And yet, next time out, there were the tandem, exercising their familiar favourite-toppling role by thwarting Gordon Richards on Paddy Prendergast-trained Thirteen of Diamonds in a second Rose of York Stakes victory.

Now for the jackpot, the Prix de l'Arc de Triomphe, run by tradition on the first Sunday in October; just as the English Derby was once, and still should be, decided on the first Wednesday in June.

Because of the absurd (in my view) practice of coupling for betting purposes all horses representing like interests, effectively constraining punter initiative, four of the 25 runners were coupled as 3¼-1 favourite; three more were linked as 5¾-1 second favourite. And so on.

Although the useful Worden II had been beaten by Zucchero in the Coronation Cup he was a 16-1 chance, whereas Lester's less dependable conveyance figured at 27-1. English visitors who chanced the wayward one taking to Sunday racing in the Bois de Boulogne must have been heartened by his faultless start. Less enchanted when, before the second furlong, he pulled up to a walk.

Above Right:
Lester receives the Sir Peter O'Sullevan Charitable Trust Annual Award from PO'S at the Savoy Hotel, 2000.

Below:
Lester's dedication to sustaining minimum weight had no limit.

Even then, having changed his mind and decided to pursue his distant rivals, he still beat five home.

At the time he was the highest class horse to have received the unwelcome *Timeform* Squiggle – 'somewhat ungenerous, fainthearted, or a bit of a coward' – from Phil Bull himself.

I first met Phil Bull during the World War II years, when he was operating a Greyhound Ratings service under the pseudonym of 'William K Temple', before he had conceived the idea of *Timeform*.

I have since seen *Timeform* grow from a one-man band in the 1940s into an international organisation with a matchless reputation for service and integrity.

This is what Phil himself wrote of Zucchero:

> *He was one of the most exasperatingly unpredictable racehorses of recent times, prepared to race only when he felt so inclined, and absolutely immovable in his determination not to race when he didn't feel like it. On his day he was a brilliant racehorse; on his off-days he was impossible.*

There was, forgive me Lester, a degree of affinity between Zucchero and his partner. Not that the young man who was to gain 11 champion jockey titles and the adulation of his peers – despite a cavalier tendency to purloin a desired mount from beneath a still-warm bottom – was often less than brilliant in the saddle. The affinity was social.

In November 1973 the sponsors of the Bull Brand International invited four jockeys from the

UK, Willie Carson, Joe Mercer, Tony Murray and Lester Piggott, to ride in the £25,000 three-year-old prize over one mile at Pietermaritzburg, Natal, where I was invited to commentate.

We flew out together with South African Airways. Lester was already more than 10 years into the regimen which would enable him to exercise his unique talent (for four decades) at 21lbs below his normal bodily weight. At mealtime we all sat with our respective colourfully presented trays of varied dishes which tasted remarkably similar to each other. All except Lester. He had spoken with the pretty stewardess while declining a cocktail and there he sat with the most identifiable, unadulterated nourishment aboard – a boiled egg.

A day later I was reporting:

Lester had ridden several bits of 'work', astonishing connections of a renowned tearaway who reacted to him like an old sheep, and champion Willie Carson was already demolishing eggs, bacon, sausages, tomatoes, toast etc. ... with all the restless energy of a pigmy shrew when, softly, like a cheetah, the ex-champion stalked into the ranch house to order his morning meal – black coffee.

'What's the matter Lester, you look pale,' says Willie in a tone which is a blend of challenge and concern.

'That,' says the maestro quietly, 'is because I am *pale.'*

In fact Lester was in good form throughout the trip, riding the opening winner for his trainer cousin, Fred Rickaby, who (again) trained the big winner, ridden by subsequent British champion 'Muice' Roberts.

But Willie, an underrated champion, with an armoury of guile, was right when he said: 'Lester either feels like chatting and he's great. Or he doesn't and you may as well forget it. If he's not talking, he's not. And that's it.'

I always used to make allowance for the austere dietary regime. That and imperfect hearing, a handicap which I became more acutely aware of, through personal experience, in later life. Lester learned to lip-read, saying once: 'I watch people's faces: they're more expressive than horses's, but not so reliable.'

Meditating in 2004 on the longest running commitment to athletic perfection in sporting history (well, name me another!), it is remarkable to reflect that it is 50 years since, once again, we drove out of the Lincoln car park, bound for Liverpool, with Lester commenting 'I suppose you'll be able to retire now' because I'd tipped and backed the Lincoln winner, Nahar.

Back at The George, Knutsford, for dinner – with Lester unobtrusively, but scrupulously, self-monitoring his intake – we discussed the colt who he was riding in tomorrow's Classic trial, the one-mile Union Jack Stakes, Never Say Die.

Lester's first Derby win, 1954: 33-1 outsider Never Say Die obliges like an odds-on chance.

Right:
The desperate finish to the 1977 Derby. The Minstrel narrowly makes it no. 8 for Lester with a hard-fought neck victory over Hot Grove and Willie Carson.

Below Right:
Lester shows off his ninth and last Derby winner Teenoso (1983) to the Ebor Meeting crowd at York.

Below:
Lester and Susan after their wedding, 1960.

By Nasrullah, like Zucchero, his two-year-old form in six runs (one success) had been nothing special. Lester, who had never sat on him, said: 'They think a lot of him, you know.'

'They' were Gerald McElligott, manager to the colt's 77-year-old American owner-breeder, Robert Sterling Clark, and 73-year-old trainer of ten Classic winners Joe Lawson.

In the Free Handicap Never Say Die was given 8st 3lbs, which was 18lbs below unbeaten Paddy Prendergast-trained top weight The Pie King. In tomorrow's race he would receive 5lbs from Jack Jarvis-trained Tudor Honey who was rated 8st 6lbs in the official assessment of merit.

We agreed that Never Say Die would need to have improved – considerably.

In the event a relatively portly Piggott partner was beaten a length by race-fit Tudor Honey who carried no more 'spare' than a towel-less towel horse.

Joe Lawson, who had been deliberately easy on the son of Nasrullah (because of the sire) to date, figured that the race would put him spot on for the Free Handicap, in which he was a well backed 9-2 favourite.

He looked fitter but clearly found the seven furlongs trip too sharp. Lester agreed with 'connections' that the thick-set chestnut would be better suited by 1¼ miles plus; but when I, tiresomely, interrupted his progress to the weighing room seeking an opinion, he gave one of his trademark shoulder shrugs, accompanied by a low-key grunt, which translated, at best: 'He's no world beater.'

And when the veteran trainer asked Lester, who had no commitment to the stable, if he would ride the current 100-1 Derby outsider in the forthcoming 1¼ miles Newmarket Stakes (which Pinza had won the year before) he said he'd prefer to go to Bath where he could have five rides.

So Manny Mercer, who had ridden Never Say Die to his only success as a two-year-old, took over.

A brilliant, instinctive jockey, Manny probably didn't ride a handful of bad races during his too short life, but this appeared to be one of them.

Making up his ground very quickly in the 10 furlongs trial, he hit the front in the Newmarket 'dip', became unbalanced and was run out of it close to home.

The colt had a marked tendency to hang right and Gerald was strongly opposed to running him at Epsom. Joe was contrastingly in favour. He emphasised that the horse was improving hourly, needed the trip and would be representing an owner and trainer who were imminent patrons of the last chance saloon.

OK, they could not reasonably encourage RS Clark to make the trip (they didn't and he didn't) but, what the hell? They should run. 'The Boy' clearly had no faith in the horse, so Joe Lawson telephoned Charlie Smirke who reacted: 'I'm sorry governor, I would have been pleased to accept, but I've just taken the ride on Elopement.'

It was back to the 'The Boy' and when ringing me, thoughtfully, on 23 May to say 'I'm going to ride that horse,' he added that he couldn't see that he had a big chance.

When reporting in the *Express* on 24 May: 'Never Say Die will no longer be 100-1 after this evening's call-over. Lester Piggott rides the American-owned and foaled colt,' I did not appreciate how limited would be future opportunity to obtain three-figure odds about L Piggott riding the winner of the world's premier Classic.

Already the firm housewives' choice, 18-year-old Lester Piggott's swiftly-developed ability to reach the Derby flashpoint, the top of Tattenham Hill, with minimal interruption – as a skilled footballer creates his own room to manoeuvre – meant that Never Say Die enjoyed a seemingly effortless route to 33-1 victory.

Because of both the gradients and the camber, Epsom is essentially a 'jockey's course', placing the highest premium on the most vital ingredient in a jockey's armoury, the ability to 'balance' a horse. It is this gift which separates the rare superstars from accomplished performers more than any other.

So what does this entail?

In mid-June 1970, by which time Lester had added another four Derby winners towards his all-time record nine, my friend Kenneth Harris asked if I could persuade Lester to be interviewed by him.

Encouraged by his delightful wife Susan, an indispensable power in the operation of LK Piggott Ltd, Lester received the renowned *Observer* inquisitor on the morning of a Newmarket raceday.

At the outset the world's premier reinsman gave a clear impression of being 'not off'.

In his most resolute oyster mode he reacted to initial questions in terse, one-word responses.

'Mr Piggott,' said Kenneth, who had an engagingly dry manner, 'you remind me of the late Lord Attlee: you answer questions as if you were filling in an application for a driving licence.'

Lester liked that.

So when Kenneth asked him: 'When people say that you are a tremendously "strong" jockey, what does "strength" mean? Is it the kind of strength that bends iron bars?', the reply, in part, was:

Well, you need muscular strength to hold a horse that's pulling for his head ... but when you talk about a jockey being 'strong', or being able to ride a strong finish, it's a bit different.

It's like this: a lot depends on the horse's balance. If he loses balance he loses speed and direction, and that might cost him the race ... the horse has his own centre of gravity just behind his shoulders. The jockey has a centre of gravity. But the jockey can shift his and the horse can't. At every stride the horse's centre of gravity is shifting in relation to the jockey's. Getting a horse balanced means keeping your balance, every stride, every second, to suit his.

Where strength comes in is that to keep doing this all the time without throwing yourself about in the saddle needs a lot of muscle control – you've got to be holding yourself as still as you can while you're making the right movements. The more control you have of your body, the fewer movements you have to make – but the more muscular effort you need: You need more strength to stand still on one leg than to walk down the street.

No, I don't say it's the strength that bends iron bars. It's the strength of an acrobat on a tightrope. Or of a juggler.

In the finish of a race as well as keeping your horse balanced you've got to be doing things with him. You've got to be encouraging the horse – moving your hands forward when his head goes forward, squeezing him with your knees, urging him on with your heels, flourishing your whip, maybe giving him a crack, and all this without throwing him off balance, which means doing all these things and not letting yourself be thrown about in the saddle.

In a tight finish a strong jockey may seem to be doing nothing in the saddle except throwing his hands forward – that's all you'll see, but the horse is going flat out and still going straight.

In the same finish a 'weaker' jockey will be throwing himself about in the saddle, and his horse will be rolling about off balance. Keeping the horse balanced in that last 100 yards, and making him put it all in, can take a lot out of a jockey.

It's got to be there to start with.

It was 'there' alright. 'There' from the time he rode the first of his 4,493 domestic winners on the

Lester and Alleged coast home in the 1977 Arc, initiating a magic double completed the following year.

Lester beats another outstanding twentieth-century rider, Joe Mercer, as Dahlia wins the 1974 King George VI and Queen Elizabeth Stakes from the Queen's Highclere.

Flat at Haydock in 1948 to the last, at Haydock again, in 1994 on his 59th birthday.

The only way to keep him out of the winner's circle for 47 years was to suspend him or lock him up.

There was an element of rough justice about the six months ban imposed following his Ascot ride on Never Say Die a fortnight after the Derby.

The King Edward VII Stakes in which Arabian Night (13-8) met Never Say Die (7-4) 8lbs better for two lengths beating at Epsom featured eight runners, half of whom were involved in a serious rough house on the home turn.

The difficulty of apportioning blame was highlighted by the Ascot Stewards originally registering an objection to the first past the post, Gordon Richards-ridden Rashleigh (5-1), and then withdrawing their own complaint. From a commentary viewpoint, the origin of the mêleé – which resulted in *Raceform* recording 'bumped' or 'swerved' against four horses – was far from clear.

The opinion of the favourite's rider, Tommy Gosling, was: 'We were all getting in each other's way ... and it was very much six of one and half a dozen of the other.'

After a little over three months Lester's sentence was unexpectedly commuted and a crash diet needed to be swiftly imposed on his marginally relaxed regime. He made the weight and, before an 8,000 Newmarket crowd on 29 September 1954, his comeback ride, Cardington King, beat 35 rivals when landing a public gamble. Even the teenage idol was nonplussed by the wild enthusiasm of his reception which would have done justice to a winner at Cheltenham National Hunt Festival where, incidentally, he rode the opening winner over hurdles for his father on 2 March that year.

Throughout a mercurial career the regular high peaks repeatedly superseded the infrequent low troughs.

It was no coincidence that the most significant heights were scaled on three of the most difficult courses to ride in Britain and France: Ascot, Epsom and Longchamp.

Ascot because of the relatively short run in; Epsom because of the configuration of the course, sharp turning gradient and camber; Longchamp because, irrespective of skills, for an inexplicable reason, it placed those unfamiliar with its topography at a clear disadvantage.

After Lester had ridden at Longchamp, sporadically, for a few years the acerbic French racing journalist Jean Trarieux wrote: *'Grand homme chez lui, ce Piggott m'épate pas.'* Roughly: 'Highly regarded domestically, he doesn't impress me.'

Yet, within several seasons he was writing, following a virtuoso performance in the Bois de Boulogne: 'This Piggott ... it is the first time I have ever considered the jockey to be more important than the horse.'

For the record ...

Ascot included 116 winners at the Royal Meeting, where Cajun (1981) was his 100th winner (including 11 Gold Cups) since Malka's Boy in 1952. Twice (1965 and 1975) he rode eight winners at the meeting. Epsom included nine Derbys; nine Coronation Cups; six Oaks etc. ... Longchamp three Arc de Triomphes; thirty Classics etc. ...

On Wednesday 1 June 1960, shortly after 5.15pm, Lester and I were driving from Epsom to a BBC London studio where I was to interview him.

He'd been winning the Derby for Sir Victor Sassoon on St Paddy. I'd been commentating on the first full-scale television transmission of the premier Classic horserace.

Lester had just won the last on Dairialatan for his father-in-law of three months, Sam Armstrong. It had been a good day.

'I bet you I'm getting more for this interview than you are,' he volunteered.

'I bet you wouldn't be sitting in that passenger seat if you weren't!' I replied.

It was the second time, following Crepello in 1957, that Lester had won the Derby for Sir Victor,

Two legends. Lester wins the 1981 Irish Sweeps Derby on Shergar.

a particularly kind man who was concerned for his jockey's future.

Wheelchair-bound since receiving injuries while serving with the RFC, Sir Victor's family originated in Baghdad before moving to Bombay.

Now he lived in the Bahamas and was one of the few in the Piggott circle able to give sound, friendly advice. Insisting: 'You will be a rich young man one day,' he suggested that, among other financial provisions, Lester should set up a Trust in the Bahamas on behalf of his family, fortifying it according to opportunity.

However, both fiscal rules and attitudes are subject to change; and as the authorities began to shuffle the goalposts and question the validity of 'presents', what was once legitimate became a grey area.

To all who knew him, and a far greater number who felt that they did, the proceedings at Ipswich Crown Court on 23 October 1987, however legally justified, were a doleful exercise.

In a letter dated 1 July 1987, Lester's solicitor, Jeremy Richardson, wrote: 'Do you feel able to write to me with a character reference?'

To which I responded forthwith as follows:

I have known Lester Piggott since he was an introverted 12-year-old who communicated more readily with animals than humans.

Experience has inclined him towards a pragmatic view of the Racing World. In his very early teens I was instrumental in him being booked for a winning ride by an Irish trainer with whom he later formed a highly successful association.

The following week, at Newbury races, he slipped into my hand a neatly folded square of white paper which, in those days, was a £5 note.

When I politely rejected the gift on the grounds that, as a journalist, I was fully recompensed by being first with the news he clearly regarded my reaction as indicative of possibly dangerous imbalance.

I have always maintained that in representing one of the all time Greats of Sport as a dour curmudgeon (the public perception for so much of his career) those responsible were not only inaccurate but unmindful of the strain of sustaining athletic brilliance while operating for over thirty years at 21lbs below his bodily norm on a diet only a calorie or two above subsistence level.

I find it doubtful whether he is the financial expert of popular portrayal; barely believable that these reflections are evoked by the knowledge that Lester Piggott is before the court on criminal charges.

In his single-minded pursuit of athletic excellence and success his attention has been focussed intently on his own sphere of activity.

Just as he used to communicate more readily with animals than humans, so has he remained a better judge of horses than men.

The *Daily Mail* front page on 24 October 1987 read: 'Lester Piggott jailed for three years after tax fraud' above a banner headline 'DOWNFALL OF A LEGEND'.

On page 17, emphasising how attitudes are subject to relatively swift change, the headline was: 'Give burglars a wallop'; the sub-heading: 'We should be armed and ready for them Judge tells Court.'

Judge Brian Watling, QC, praised the bravery of a 73-year-old farmer who laid into two intruders with an iron bar. He told Chelmsford Crown Court: 'It is very much to be hoped that householders will arm themselves and, if young men go into their premises, wallop them hard.

Opposite Page:
Queen Elizabeth congratulating Lester after The Minstrel's victory in the 1977 'King George'.

Below:
Newmarket, 1992. The old magic is still there as Lester wins his thirtieth Classic in England on Rodrigo de Triano.

Perhaps then we shall have fewer burglaries to contend with.' Because of their injuries the burglars were caught and jailed for three years and the farmer awarded £250.

In 2004 the farmer would have been jailed and the burglars generously compensated for an 'accident at work'.

Lester's capacity to handle adversity with courage and humour was frequently demonstrated after a series of horrific accidents.

I remember towards the end of the '61 season, during a fluctuating championship battle with Scobie Breasley, he crashed at Lingfield – virtually ending the contest.

As an ambulance man crouched beside his prostrate form, a solicitous friend enquired if there was anything he could do for him. Lester raised his sore head from the turf. 'Not unless you can get me a bit of evens Breasley for the title,' he responded.

Similarly, aged 54, having effected the most dramatic comeback in sporting history, winning the richest prize of his career on Royal Academy in New York, two years after release from prison, he went on, aged 56, to win his 30th English Classic – and 16th Irish – on Rodrigo de Triano.

Then, within a week of his 57th birthday, he was stretchered to intensive care in Miami's Hollywood Memorial Hospital following a horrific-looking crash at Gulfstream Park, where his poor partner, Mr Brooks, was fatally injured. 'A tragic loss of a fine horse,' as he put it.

Lester, who has more 'bottle' than a cargo of Jeroboams, was the focus of the media spotlight having been knocked unconscious by a gash in the head and enduring upper and middle body fractures as well as a collapsed lung.

He had, he maintained, suffered worse falls tumbling out of bed; but was nevertheless flattered and delighted to receive a thoughtful message from the Queen. Which reminds me ... During a Buckingham Palace reception in the 1970s he and I were chatting about a recent Royal winner he had partnered when The Queen came over and mentioned that she hoped he would be able to ride the filly again in next season's staying races. Lester responded with one of his beguiling little smiles and muttered noncommittally. 'Well,' I remonstrated when The Queen had moved on, 'you might have shown a little more enthusiasm.'

The filly was Example, an impressive winner of the 14 furlongs Park Hill Stakes. Two days later he'd won the St Leger (his sixth winner of the Classic he won eight times) on Athens Wood. He considered my remark thoughtfully before commenting: 'You know, that Athens Wood might be the better ride next year.'

Above: The Queen leading in Carrozza and Lester after her first Classic success in the 1957 Oaks.

Opposite Page: An immensely popular duo, Lester and Park Top, gallop to glory in the 1969 King George VI and Queen Elizabeth Stakes at Ascot.

Below: One of my heroes depicts another. John Skeaping's **'Hommage à Lester'**.

Nobody could accuse Lester of currying favour with anyone.

Nor, incidentally, was he into the self-destructive pursuit of nursing grievances. He could be irritable all right, but that would pass like a fleeting cloud. In fact, the only times I've known him seriously upset (apart, obviously, from when Susan suffered a grim accident while he was incarcerated) was when he felt he'd ridden below his best: and when, following conviction for nourishing the Treasury below the level of requirement, he was stripped of his OBE which had been awarded him in 1975. He considered that an unacceptable and unwarrantably hurtful act. So do I.

Clearly unaffected by this sad manoeuvre was the most scintillating of the maestro's nine Derby winning partners, the Piggott Pegasus, Sir Ivor.

Vincent O'Brien always insisted that the outstanding son of Sir Gaylord instantly recognised and appreciated his partner in glory when he visited Ballydoyle. Later this was made abundantly clear to all at Claiborne Farm who witnessed the welcome which greeted Lester when he looked in on one of his very favourite equine stars in Kentucky.

Vincent O'Brien once said of LK Piggott: 'It was my good fortune that I trained at a time when Lester was riding. God gave him a great gift and he exploited it to the full.'

It was a privilege for this one-time commentator to 'call' many of the landmark events (Classics apart) during a spectacular career; like the first and last Royal Ascot winners (Malka's Boy 1952; College Chapel 1993) and the first Royal Ascot training triumph with his first runner there, Cutting Blade, in the 1986 Coventry; seven King

"An instinctive loner, the eleven times Champion made his own decisions and employed an often breathtaking range and variety of skills to win nine Derbys. An iconoclast who became an icon."

Above:
Two stars. Lester Piggott by the wonderfully gifted Sue Crawford.

Opposite Page:
Above:
Himself standing beside the commemorative Lester Piggott Gates at Epsom.

Below:
Lester 'shot' in the weighing room.

George VI and Queen Elizabeth Stakes; eleven Ascot Gold Cups; five Goodwood Cups; nine King Georges (Goodwood, 5 furlongs); the 4,000th British winner (Ardross in colours of long-time friend Charles St George) in 1982; the liaison between two stars, LP and Petite Etoile, the grey filly who was one of his six Sussex Stakes winners.

Apropos the ten-race winner's controversial half-length defeat by Jimmy Lindley-ridden Aggressor in the 1960 King George VI and Queen Elizabeth Stakes, Lester had uncharacteristic misgivings about the race beforehand. Despite four previous successes over 1½ miles he always felt that the filly's optimum trip was 10 furlongs.

This would be her first experience of 'dead' ground and, due to a slight cough, she'd missed an intended prep race.

Scobie Breasley 'owed' Lester one in respect of a past misdemeanour and claimed in a book with that outstanding racing journalist, Chris Poole, to have held Lester in a pocket. He added: 'To give him [Lester] his due, he didn't complain.'

Well, one reason he didn't complain was that he did not know it had occurred. He always held up Petite Etoile and he was just where he wanted to be at the home turn.

It was here that he made an unsuccessful bid for the rails and became obliged to challenge wider than intended. This placed him on a strip of grass mown towards the runners in contrast to Aggressor's section on the 'inner'. Hence Lester's response when asked whether there was any excuse for the 5-2 on loser: 'They cut the grass the wrong way.'

As excuses go, this was thought to be a good one to put in a double with British Rail's 'Wrong kind of snow on the line.' However, make of it what you will, since 16 July 1960 Ascot has been mown one way only, the grass flowing with the action.

In 2004, while reflecting on my heroes, I put the same question to Scobie and Lester independently. 'If you were to take part in a match between two horses of identical ability, over their favoured distance, and your life depended on the outcome, who would you least like to be opposed by?'

Aware of Scobie's admiration for Gordon Richards' unique skills, as well as his experience of the top riders in Australia and America – where he'd trained for a spell – I thought he'd find it difficult.

Similarly, given Lester's appreciation of Yves Saint-Martin in France, and others in 26 more countries in which he'd ridden winners, he might want notice of that one.

Scobie, on a clear line from Melbourne, took two seconds. 'Lester,' he said.

Lester, after lip-reading my question in the high decibel count of Annabel's Bar, ran a dead-heat. 'Scobie,' he said.

Finally, to borrow and paraphrase a few of the inadequate words I penned to accompany the Lester Piggott Gates at Epsom, 'An instinctive loner, the eleven times Champion made his own decisions and employed an often breathtaking range and variety of skills to win nine Derbys. An iconoclast who became an icon.'

ATTIVO

It isn't easy to choose a bride for somebody else. Especially in the cold light of a December morning.

It was 9.45am on 3 December 1969. A while ago, yet I still recall vividly the mould of her figure, the supple swing of her gait and the bold, bright eye of a Thoroughbred.

'Five thousand I am bid,' intoned the auctioneer, 'and I am selling.' So she was on the market.

My great equine friend and benefactor, Be Friendly, had just retired to stud. He was to hold court in the verdant region of lilting Irish poet Lord Dunsany, Co Meath. Naturally I wanted the best for him, within the limits of my financial resources.

'At seven thousand for this very well-turned mare from a very successful family. Believed in foal to the Italian Derby winner, Appiani II. For the last time is there any advance on seven thousand guineas?'

El Galgo was her name and, although favourably connected pedigree-wise, it could not be claimed that her racecourse performance – one success in a modest Edinburgh maiden – was exceptional.

At £7,350 she had long since passed the sum represented by my annual earnings from the *Daily Express*.

Steeling myself for one more nod, I heard the polished tones of the Tattersalls sales ring auctioneer, Peter Nugent, pronounce: 'Sold to Mr Peter O'Sullevan – seven thousand one hundred guineas.'

"Steeling myself for one more nod, I heard the polished tones of the Tattersalls sales ring auctioneer, Peter Nugent, pronounce: 'Sold to Mr Peter O'Sullevan - seven thousand one hundred guineas.'"

'Limited' would be a flattering description of my expertise in the Thoroughbred breeding department. So, since El Galgo was my first prospective broodmare purchase, it was a little unnerving when, within seconds of the hammerfall, that global authority and longtime friend, Alec Head, enquired with an air of incredulity: 'Have you bought that mare for yourself?'

I had – and what was wrong with her?

'Nothing that I can see,' replied Alec. 'She's a very, very nice mare. The incredible thing is I've just bought a yearling filly in Saratoga who is almost as close to her in blood as you can get. So if mine is any good, I'll be putting value on your mare.'

The yearling, who cost £15,000, turned out to be none other than the illustrious Pistol Packer, described by *Timeform* as 'one of the best fillies to race in Europe since the war.' Never unplaced, she won seven of her 10 races, including the Prix de Diane (French Oaks), Vermeille etc. ... and was beaten only by Mill Reef after drawing the outside in the 18-runner 1971 Arc de Triomphe.

Meanwhile on 26 March 1970 El Galgo had foaled her first-born at 02.30 hours. A colt foal, he was conservatively described as 'not a big one'.

In fact, a friend who visited the stud before I was able to get over to Ireland reported back: 'If only he grows a bit you could have another to run at the White City.'

I used to own a greyhound at this former excellent stadium, which was later taken over by another organisation.

He did grow – but not entirely in the right direction. His feet turned outwards, Charlie Chaplin-like, and his upper jaw exceeded the development of the lower, giving him what is known in the trade as a 'parrot mouth'.

Otherwise, apart from being as narrow as an arrow, he was a perfect physical specimen with a bold, bright and restlessly inquisitive eye.

In the sympathetic hands of stud owner, Robert Elwes, his personality, if not his physique, developed conspicuously.

Right up until the time he was due to leave the quiet countryside around the village of Kilmessan, bound for Epsom to be groomed for stardom by Cyril Mitchell, he had never put a misshapen foot wrong.

The name Amigo had been reserved for him by way of both maintaining the 'Friendly' tradition and incorporating El Galgo but, owing to a bureaucratic failure, it became unavailable.

My wife, Pat, suggested Attivo (active, busy etc. ... in Italian) to take account of his Latin father and lively temperament.

Young stock are usually the most amenable air travellers. Attivo was a near fatal exception. He became so agitated that, in the interest of the safety of fellow passengers, he received a series of tranquillising shots. Although groggy with drugs on landing, he came to sufficiently in the horsebox transporting him from Heathrow to Downs House

"So, when the poor little lad tottered down the ramp into the yard, he looked as if he'd been attacked by a maniac with a knife."

Stables to set about the full-scale demolition of the vehicle.

So, when the poor little lad tottered down the ramp into the yard, he looked as if he'd been attacked by a maniac with a knife.

It was late evening. In response to Cyril's call I reached Epsom in faster time that it used to take on my bike when riding 'work' for long-departed Charlie Bell.

He was a sorry sight but, wounds dressed, he began to perk up. It is virtually unheard of for a horse who has undergone such a traumatic experience to tackle a meal. Attivo didn't know that.

On a thousand to one off-chance, he was given a light snack. In less time that it takes to say 'hot mash', he licked out his manger and made it abundantly clear that he was unaccustomed to a starvation diet.

An admiring audience watched 'Percy', as he was nicknamed for no reason that anyone can account for, wade into a substantial evening feed.

Generously described by *Raceform*'s expert commentators as 'unfurnished', Attivo made an unspectacular debut at Windsor's evening meeting of 19 June 1972. Returning to the same circuit the following month, he at least beat four of his 11 opponents before running fourth of 13 a fortnight later in a Goodwood 'seller'.

He had been running on so strongly in the sixth and final furlong that it looked as though he'd appreciate a mile.

Early one morning he went to Kempton for a trial over that trip with a fairly useful stable companion; two from Brian Swift's and a couple from the yard of that great perfectionist, Staff Ingham.

After the 'work', Staff gave it as his invariably worth noting opinion: 'There is no one mile selling race for two-year-olds in the *Calendar* that Attivo wouldn't win.' Adding that, whatever the selected target, he would like to be included in the stable commission 'for the maximum'.

We aimed for the eight-furlong Barrow Selling Plate at Newmarket on 26 October. On all public evidence, his four opponents appeared to be exceptionally mediocre.

Both this selector's *Daily Express* readers were alerted and a substantial four-figure commission was organised.

While the cash was being 'invested' at all rates from 5-2 down to 10-11, the object of feverish market activity was shuffling round the freezing paddock, clearly discomfited by the chill for which the region is renowned, and showing alarming lack of concern for his imminent responsibilities.

In the event Attivo and his partner Brian Jago opted for conflicting tactics. 'Percy' felt he

Above: Owner and hero-in-waiting.

"'It's only fun,' insisted black-and-blue Derek, lightly dismissing the handiwork of his equine tattooist."

should jump off and go from the outset. Brian favoured conserving energy until the vital stages of the contest. By the time they had settled their differences the gamble of the day had either forfeited his vitality or interest – or both.

The two o'clock favourite finished third, 5 long-looking lengths behind the winner. My friend Bert, at the garage, was not best pleased.

Another friend, Tony Murray – one of a collection of top riders from the 'Frenchie' Nicholson jockeys' academy – had observed the conflict at close quarters. 'You can forget that running, Peter,' he offered consolingly. Unfortunately the bookmakers wouldn't.

He 'ran' once more that year when, allowed to stride on from the start, he showed ahead for five of the seven furlongs of Haydock's Vernons Finance Nursery before beating a hasty retreat into ninth place. And into what were platitudinously referred to as 'winter quarters'.

The outlook was not promising. Nor was it brightened in March the following year, when that renowned raconteur, Geoff Lewis, who also happened to be Mill Reef's jockey, took over the reins in the Waterdale Selling Handicap at Doncaster.

We sold ourselves the proposition that Attivo had strengthened immeasurably during the months when frost gripped the Downs, and backed him from 7-1 to 3-1 favourite to support the illusion.

He beat quite a few home, but there were still four ahead of him at the place that matters. It was the same story when he returned to Newmarket for another 'seller' on 10 April.

So that, notwithstanding capability of deceptively encouraging homework, it was becoming increasingly clear that El Galgo's first born would be difficult to place to advantage in public.

Where did we go from here? It was like this ... a new series was introduced in '73 on similar lines to the French *Tiercé*, which had proved such a boon to the Gallic racing set-up. I had proposed its creation in a speech at the Gimcrack Dinner, after detailed discussions with ever-helpful Pools expert, Robert Sangster, and was anxious to support it in any way possible – like supplying a runner.

The Tote Roll-Up was to be based on a 16-runner handicap – runners declared four days in advance – every Saturday.

Punters were required to name the first six home and, in the event of general failure, the pool would be carried forward to the following week – excepting a percentage set aside for consolation dividends – and prize-money down to sixth.

There was £100 appearance money for runners and, ironically, Attivo was balloted out of the inaugural contest on 7 April '73.

With better luck on 5 May at Newmarket, a six-furlong handicap, his burden reduced to 6½ stone by apprentice Chris Leonard's 7lb claim, he came home well to run sixth and collect £30 prize-money.

A week later the Lingfield Roll-Up was over 1¼ miles. First and second were Willie Carson and Lester Piggott respectively; not far behind in third, little old Attivo collected £180. If he kept this up we'd *both* be able to eat. Returning to a shorter distance (seven furlongs) but a longer trip from his Epsom base to Thirsk on 2 June, he slipped back to fourth.

After journeying home for such rest as he could ever be persuaded to take, the Italian Derby winner Appiani II's slimmest son had only to stroll across the famous Downs from his stable, adjacent to the Derby start, to compete in his fourth Roll-Up on 9 June.

He finished out of the first 10. And a subsequent 'run' over the course in April 1976, when he was last of four, confirmed Chris Leonard's impression that 'he just seems to look

Attivo and Roger Wernham – the first to complete the Chester Cup-Northumberland Plate double for 64 years.

upon this as his playground and doesn't want to know about racing over it.'

On 30 June at Lingfield, horse and lad came within a length of ending up in the winner's circle; took third spot at Newmarket on 21 July. And then it happened.

While his owner was lying beside an Algarve pool, dreaming of Attivo and his turned-out Charlie Chaplin feet nipping round Chester's tight circuit and sprinting clear to win the 1½-mile £1,600 Tote Roll-Up on 1 September 1973, he was doing just that.

In fact, he did not negotiate those turns without difficulty and was repeatedly checked in his stride. 'I've never seen a horse act so badly round Chester and still win,' observed Beckhampton trainer, Jeremy Tree, to me the following week. But he had responded eagerly to the challenge.

Finding daylight at the crucial moment approaching the short home stretch, he went for it to such effect that on this, his fourteenth public appearance, Attivo at last finished without a horse ahead of him. And with his nearest pursuer a distant five lengths behind.

If ever a stable lad deserved to have the object of his care and devotion come good it was Derek Wilmot. In the hands of a less tolerant stableman Percy may well have turned 'nasty'.

For, in between employing his teeth for their principal purpose, his chief pleasure was

Attivo (Chris Leonard) wins his first race, Chester, 1 September 1973. Who could foretell that he'd become the only horse ever to be named 'Best Horse Ridden' by three jockeys – Chris Leonard, Robert Hughes and Roger Wernham – in the **Directory of the Turf**?

Attivo leads the 1974 Daily Express Triumph Hurdle field.

striking, thumping and nipping his faithful attendant.

'It's only fun,' insisted black-and-blue Derek, lightly dismissing the handiwork of his equine tattooist.

They set off together again in three weeks, this time Sandown-bound for a step up in distance, to 1 mile 6 furlongs, and the valuable Sportsman Club Handicap, in which he was only one of two three-year-olds opposing 11 seniors.

The ratings of that highly valued aid in the punters' armoury, *Timeform*, indicated that 20-1 outsider Attivo had a very good chance – of finishing tenth!

Chris Leonard, who had got on so well with him, could now claim only 5lbs, so diminutive 7lb claimer Harry Ballantine was called in to ease the burden on one of the narrowest backs in the business. I watched the race from the press stand parapet to which one of racing's heroes, Bob Champion – the man who conquered cancer and subsequently won the 1981 Grand National on another ex-invalid, Aldaniti – was a temporary visitor.

I stood between Bob and my long-time colleague Len Thomas, of the *Sporting Life*.

Six furlongs out the featherweight duo eased to the front. At the quarter-mile pole they were still going strong, no one was sitting in behind with a double handful and Bob was nudging my already shaky binoculars, saying: 'You'll win, you'll win.'

By the furlong marker Harry and Percy had beaten off three successive challenges and Len, loyally abandoning his own selection, was bellowing for Attivo. He looked to have it until the last three strides, when the talented lightweight, Tommy Carter, drove the four-year-old Pamroy to the line to make it a photo-finish.

They were racing well apart and the judge took quite a while to confirm my fears that Pamroy, meeting us on 9lbs better than weight-for-age terms and trained by my old ally, Scobie Breasley, had just got up. By this time the Tote Roll-Up was foundering.

Unimaginatively launched, imperfectly understood, the innovation which could have been a simultaneous source of pleasure and revenue was beginning to increase turnover when the Tote – under feeble management at this time – decided to terminate the pool.

In any event we had resolved that, whether he liked it or not, and he wouldn't, Attivo must have a break. Thereafter, maybe, a pop over a hurdle or two at home to give him a new interest and help to sustain his zest.

This is a ploy more widely practised in France than in England. As a former successful jump jockey, Cyril Mitchell had wide experience of both

The last flight in the Triumph, and the Attivo-Robert Hughes partnership is perilously close to severance.

riding and training some very useful winter performers.

Experience had taught him to exercise caution in his judgement. But there was no trace of reservation in his enthusiastic tone when he telephoned to report: 'This little fellow's brilliant; come down and watch him "school".'

I did, and promptly informed Bert at the garage that he would shortly have no further need to soil his hands with toil. It was a story that he had heard before.

Unfavourable weather, causing loss of programmes, resulted in any immediate hope of separating the bookmakers from their money having to be deferred until the dawn of the following year.

Attivo had a choice of engagements on the 1974 New Year programme at Cheltenham.

He could either tackle the well-established Evesham Hurdle for four-year-olds, featuring the impressive Newbury and Chepstow winner Fighting Kate, as well as hat-trick seeker Park Lawn. Or he could take on fellow novices the following afternoon.

Cyril outlined the options as he saw them. 'If he runs in the novices' you can have a bet, and if he does it half as well "out" as he does at home you'll be unlucky to leave it behind. Or you can avoid the greater risk of injury in a big field and see how he goes against the best.'

It was tempting to start the New Year with a potentially successful punt and winning nap, but the risk of buffeting in a big field was increased by his slender stature. The Evesham Hurdle it was.

At least the already notable achievements of the principals meant that they would have to concede Attivo 10lbs.

There were two defectors, leaving seven runners. So my each-way selection (10-1 to 8-1) would need to beat one of the big two to save the place money.

As the riders of Fighting Kate (3-1) and Park Lawn (1-2) played 'cat and mouse' with each other, Robert Hughes, claiming the 5lb allowance to which inexperience entitled him, let Attivo bowl along. He loved it. At half way, a mile from home, Cyril Mitchell, standing beside me in the BBC television commentary box, whispered: 'They'll have a job to catch him now.' Soon I heard myself

Proud proprietor congratulates horse and jockey after the 1974 Triumph.

1974 Triumph. Derek Wilmot leads in Attivo – followed by dazed owner.

tempting fate over the air with, 'Attivo looking as if he just has to jump the last ...'

The judge posted the official winning margin as 'a distance' – which is to say more than 30 lengths.

A widespread professional verdict was that it had to be a fluke. 'As far as I am concerned,' 'Percy' seemed to be saying as he returned with an unmistakeable swagger, 'they can think what they like.'

Back home he resumed two of his favourite pastimes, colouring Derek's arms and seeking to stretch them way beyond normal length through his exuberant morning 'work'.

Robert Hughes was due for his share of the arm-stretching treatment five weeks after Cheltenham in Newbury's Stroud Green Hurdle – another traditional four-year-old test.

Betting on the nine-runner race reflected a high degree of support for the 'fluke' theory advanced on New Year's Day.

Attivo drifted in the market from 2-1 to 7-2 so that he was replaced as favourite by another recent winner in Bird's Nest. Even Fighting Kate had her supporters to reverse previous placings. While rotund Ron Smyth – who as a spare-framed young man, rode the first of his three Champion Hurdle winners in 1941 – touted the view that Supreme Halo, whom he trained within tic-tac distance of Attivo's Epsom stable, would both emerge as the brightest local hope for the *Daily Express* Triumph Hurdle and make the Cheltenham result look silly.

The little fellow re-adopted his catch-me-if-you-can tactics and by the second of eight flights he was already presenting the opposition with a swift-diminishing view of wafer-wide quarters.

The judge's ultimate posting: first Attivo, second Supreme Halo, third Bird's Nest. The distances: 20 lengths, 1 length.

The next stepping-stone to the championship would be the £5,000 Yellow Pages Hurdle at Kempton on 23 February. However, anyone who spends a lifetime in the game inevitably develops certain 'hang-ups'.

I had long since promised myself that, in the highly unlikely event of ever becoming so lucky as to own a horse good enough to run at the incomparable National Hunt Festival at Cheltenham, I would ensure that he went there 'fresh'.

I appreciated that 'Percy' had positively 'hacked-up' twice, seemingly without any effort, but if the owner was any criterion, a deal of nervous energy had been involved.

A less magnanimous trainer might have protested vigorously when I indicated a firm preference for giving Kempton a miss and keeping the lad fresh for the big date.

All Cyril said was: 'The race is worth five grand and it would only be an exercise canter for him,' adding gently, 'but if you can afford to act the millionaire it's OK by me.'

I couldn't, but did. And Attivo's 20-length Newbury victim won the Yellow Pages.

Instead of the 'exercise canter' we took 'Himself' to Sandown Park one Sunday morning, where he jumped three flights down the backstretch quite brilliantly and almost wrenched poor Robert's arms from their sockets before he could be pulled up.

For all save the principal, who was a bundle of muscle and mischief, the build-up to 'the day' was fraught with anxiety. To begin with, there was the spectre of the ballot coming into operation.

At that time (the 'system' has since been changed) in order to comply with the safety

factor – a maximum 30-horse field in the Triumph – horses were balloted out at random if the number declared overnight exceeded the permitted level.

Meanwhile, first snow and then flooding threatened the whole meeting. The opening day's programme was abandoned except for two sponsored races, which were carried over to the following day.

In view of travelling conditions, Cyril was concerned whether to risk sending Attivo on the morning of his Thursday date.

On the only previous occasion he'd despatched him overnight 'Percy' had been exhaustingly restless and failed to eat up.

Cyril opted finally for a night in a strange box, saying: 'I only hope to God he sleeps better than his owner is likely to.'

He did. And with 21 declared, the ballot was avoided. It was hard for this television commentator to believe, as the horses circled at the start for the 3.05 at Cheltenham on Thursday 14 March 1974, that the hottest favourite on record (4-5) for the *Daily Express* Triumph – the richest juvenile hurdle in Britain – was the same little travel-scarred youngster, with his turned out Charlie Chaplin feet and parrot mouth, who had tottered into the Mitchell yard just over two years earlier.

I wasn't thinking of him winning now, just praying he'd return unscathed. Clive Graham's voice came over the intercom: 'Good luck, Pedro.'

Julian Wilson gave the thumbs up across the commentary box.

And they were off!

There was unlikely to be any running away from this field at the outset. Young Robert Hughes was unable to claim the weight allowance, to which he was normally entitled, owing to the value (£9,000 to winner) of the race. He was out there now competing on level terms with the best jump jockeys in the world.

Attivo home by the shortest of short heads from Kambalda (Philip Waldron) in the '74 Chester Cup.

His instructions from Cyril had been uncomplicated. 'Ride your own race as you find him but, whatever you do, *never* take your finger out of the neck strap.' 'Percy' had a launch mechanism to match anything at Cape Canaveral.

The duo set off in front, without overdoing the pace, and flew the first three of the nine flights before I remember commenting: 'A mistake at the fourth by Attivo.' Others were crowding him soon after halfway, and I thought he wasn't going that well – though John Hislop, champion amateur on the Flat from 1946 to 1956 and a top racing writer, who had been watching him closely, assured me afterwards that the clever little monkey had just been giving himself a 'breather'.

Running down to the second last, the redoubtable Tommy Carberry, on the impressive grey Leopardstown winner, Gleaming Silver, was almost upsides and going ominously well. Then, all of a sudden, as the field swept round the home turn, Attivo simply detached himself from the remainder as if roused by the recollection of his previous visit here. Two lengths clear, 4, 6, 8. One leap between himself and triumph. The crowds were already roaring for him. Now he would really show them what he could do.

The excitement, communicated through Attivo's muscles to young Robert, momentarily overcame him. All instructions were forgotten; out came his finger. Into the hurdle went the odds-on favourite. Into it – and through it, coming to a virtual standstill in the process.

Robert soared skywards. My heart plummeted. More by luck than judgement Robert came down where Attivo was. Meanwhile 'Big Ron' Barry and burly Banlieu, achieving a contrastingly fluent leap, were almost on terms.

It looked 'dodgy' for an instant but, regaining their composure, Robert and 'Percy' fairly scooted up the hill, as if ashamed of their joint lapse, earning a 4-length verdict over Banlieu, with the consistent Supreme Halo a further 3 lengths away third.

Temporary microphone 'cover' was swiftly organised – no one had thought of that beforehand – so that I could hasten to the car park, through which the horses were led at that time, to greet my heroes.

Derek made to pass me the leading rein. I couldn't think of anything more inappropriate. The lad grooms him, sponges his eyes, wipes his nose, feeds him, rides him ... he is the one to lead 'his' horse into the winner's circle, as he did, to an emotional reception.

As I walked in behind them, local trainer and longtime friend 'Frenchie' Nicholson grabbed my hand and said: 'That should put him just right for Chester.'

'Frenchie', so nicknamed because he was apprenticed in 1925 to Charles Clout in France for three years before joining Stanley Wootton, had ridden for me – typical O'Sullevan no-hopers – back in 1940. A champion NH jockey turned successful trainer, he was particularly renowned for his highly productive school of apprentices. Pat Eddery, Tony Murray, Paul Cook, Ian Johnson, Kevin Whyte, Walter Wharton, Richard Fox, Walter Swinburn who joined in 1977, etc. ... the list was endless.

Before racing on Triumph day I had told him that, whatever happened today, I wanted to have a crack at the Chester Cup and would very much like one of his 7lb claimers. 'Have you a particular one in mind?' he asked. I'd been impressed by a red-haired lad who'd come over from Seamus McGrath. 'Fox,' said Frenchie, adding: 'That's a good pick but at the moment, I've got one who may suit you better at this stage of their development. His name is Wernham, Roger Wernham. If Cyril would like him to pop over to Epsom for a sit on your little fellow, Di [his wife] will bring him anytime.'

The young duo got on fine and it was the featherweight's 7lb claim and skill that landed Attivo the last stride, short-head, winner of the long famed handicap on the Roodeye from a regrettably small seven-horse field.

I say 'regrettably' because, exactly a month before the race, Heathorns laid me an ante-post bet £2,000-£160, with the proviso: 'Less than twelve runners, no bet!'

The new partnership's next assignment was to be a bid for the Chester Cup-Northumberland Plate double, last achieved by Elizabetta in 1910. As I was involved in the televising of the Irish Sweeps Derby at the Curragh on Pitmen's Derby Day on 29 June, my wife, Pat, went to Newcastle in case our little hero should inspire presentation of a further sponsor's prize.

Irish television thoughtfully installed a little black-and-white monitor at the commentary point on the grandstand rooftop from which I might follow ITV's relay. The picture wasn't too good, but I thought he had just about won, after a desperately determined effort, when the set blew up.

The London studio confirmed down the line that Attivo was first past the post, but there had been an objection.

My colleague, Michael O'Hehir, leaned across from his broadcasting pitch and enquired quietly:

'Did you hear that announcement?'

It was the Gardai requesting the public to clear the stands as quickly as possible. A bomb may have been planted.

There was no question of us quitting the site, since our respective television links were continuing. 'Nice thing,' I said. 'I may go without ever knowing whether he's won the Plate.'

We were a motley crew along the rooftop gantry watching the crowds below shuffling, reluctantly, on to the course. I offered 33-1 against any of us being blown up. For a few moments I thought Ted Walsh, ace trainer and volatile television pundit, was going to take it (remember, Ted?), but he didn't.

Pity. The bomb was a hoax. Attivo had won. The objection concerned second and third, whose placings were transposed.

Attivo and his handler took a well deserved break, the former for six months, the latter for good.

Cyril Mitchell retired to Majorca and handed over to his son Philip. Attivo, by now acutely aware of his star status, and even more difficult to handle, didn't do his new trainer any favours when undergoing a series of setbacks before returning to action over hurdles at Newcastle with a below par effort behind the talented Comedy of Errors; after which the winner's trainer, Fred Rimell, told Philip a little unkindly: 'You've lost him, boy.'

Meanwhile, 'Percy' had earned his owner the Horserace Writers and Reporters Association's Owner of the Year award – prompting the great Brigadier Gerard's breeder, John Hislop to cable:

An honour well deserved, it's clear
That you are owner of the year.
This glory shone on the Express
Deserves a bonus – nothing less.

To which he received the reply:

An accolade from such a source
Would turn the head of any horse
(For of course, I realise
It was Attivo won the prize.)
He hopes we'll plan his whole career
Just like you did the Brigadier,
Tackling any competition
As long as he's in top condition.
(But keeping a little in reserve
To benefit the girls he'll serve!)

Unhappily, he was never to serve those girls after all.

Following two more uncharacteristically feeble showings, which seemed to leave him rather dispirited, the veterinary diagnosis was that, during effort, a testicle was becoming withdrawn – causing him discomfort – so that he would have to be gelded.

No sooner had he recovered from an op that is taken in its stride nowadays than a fit of exuberance landed him with a self-inflicted disability.

Restored by painstaking treatment, he showed a glimmer of revival when running fourth, and appearing to enjoy himself, in the Coombe Handicap at Sandown on 19 October 1976.

Twelve days later the star of 1974 returned to Sandown for a private Sunday workout. Everything pointed to imminent form recovery when, while being led round the Sandown stable area to cool off, he slipped, lost his footing and – with a look of horror which I will never forget – fell on the tarmac and broke his hip.

The object of treatment, which meant months of boring inactivity for the poor lad, was to give him a chance to recover sufficient mobility to enjoy life without racing. He made several trips to Newmarket's excellent Equine Research Station ('Never had a patient with such high tolerance of anaesthetic,' they declared) and took to swimming at an equine pool in Leatherhead with such enthusiasm that his gait on dry land became increasingly normal.

Strengthened by daily quarts of Guinness, he finally passed his 'medical' to the extent of being declared fit for competition.

Fourteen months after the fracture, Attivo was back at Newbury running third in the L'Oreal Handicap Hurdle.

Lester and 'Percy' go to post at Lingfield.

There followed five unsuccessful runs in five months, during which I felt that 'Himself' was taking the mickey out of his apprentice riders.

I suggested that Lester Piggott have a spin round on him at Lingfield. The now eight-year-old's weight cloth was no longer padded with feathers, as in former times. He had 8st 10lbs in the two-mile Ferrendons Handicap on 13 June 1978.

As we drove from Chelsea, I reminded the maestro not to forget that this horse had a fractured hip and to be very careful of him. I wasn't sure that he had heard. So I said it again.

I always remember him putting his paper down and asking: 'What do you think I am, some sort of butcher?'

I could see that Attivo wasn't doing a lot for him and, inside the last furlong, with the result in the balance, Lester gave him a crack.

It looked as though the favourite's eyes were going to pop out of his head. In his previous 39 races he'd been partnered mostly by apprentices from whom he probably never noticed a smack. You could see him querying: 'What the hell was that?'

Anyway he stuck his head out and that's what he won by.

'He's a bit of a monkey,' said Lester as he gave his partner a pat, and adding, with grudging admiration: 'He doesn't do any more than he wants to.'

The next time, and only other occasion, they teamed up was back at Lingfield on Irish Derby eve a fortnight later – effortlessly concluding a harmonious partnership by making all the running to win by three lengths, conceding 10lbs to the second.

Then, you wouldn't believe it, turned out for his summer holidays, he put his foot in a hole and is back in hospital. Pronounced 'finished' once again, he nevertheless came back, to Philip's great credit, after six months to defy 12st 1lb, under a fine ride from Brian Reilly, at Fakenham. It was some performance but the price of victory was high.

Attivo (Robert Hughes) and Banlieu (Ron Barry) appraise the first flight before finishing 1-2 in the 1974 Triumph.

'Percy' comes to terms with retirement.

The legacy of therapy included a lengthy operation under massive anaesthetic; creation of a surgical shoe by his faithful physician, Michael Symons; homoeopathic treatment; convalescence at the lovely Frant farm of Mike and Angela Pelly; being ridden daily for months in Eridge Park (on a long rein, too) by former *Daily Express* racing secretary and onetime Newmarket 'lass' with Cecil Boyd-Rochfort, Valerie Frost; and exercise in the sea at Worthing to strengthen his dodgy pins. The more therapeutic, the more his spirits soared. And the more he made it abundantly clear to those who lavished tender care on his slender person that action was what he craved.

Action over fences which he clearly regarded as an exciting challenge to his athleticism. So I weakened.

On 2 May 1983, 13 years old, he set off for Fontwell, accompanied by a daunting medical record and preceded by a reputation for taking a fierce hold.

This combination doubtless accounted for his experienced jockey, Robert Earnshaw, placing him under early restraint – a tactic which palpably displeased Attivo, who forfeited all interest in pique. 'Next time I would ride him from the front,' said Robert afterwards. But there was to be no 'next time'.

'Percy' would not agree, but for his apprehensive owner there were clear signs that the battle-scarred limbs could no longer be expected to sustain his ambitions.

So he returned 'home' to Downs House, Epsom; not to be turned out among the flies he detested; to occupy a box, from which he could view the most famous racecourse in the world, and be treated like a racehorse – albeit now an uncompetitive one.

He lived happily on his dreams, polo mints from visitors, and relished star status on 'Open' Days. Until Philip rang me in the early hours of 13 December 1992. He had summoned the vet who was already kneeling beside his prostrate patient when I arrived, trousers and coat over pyjamas.

The agony of a twisted gut had caused him to bang his head in pain, concluded his physician, as 'Percy' lay battered and bleeding. It would not be right, he said, to put him through an operation of dubious benefit.

Even after receiving the life terminating injection, he still struggled valiantly to rise, before falling back inert.

A right little hero.

Philip and I clutched each other and the tears rolled.

"He lived happily on his dreams, polo mints from visitors, and relished star status on 'Open' Days."

Index

References to illustrations are shown in italics.

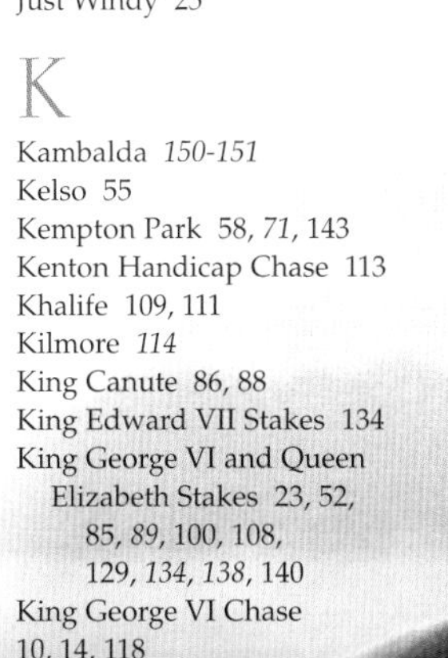

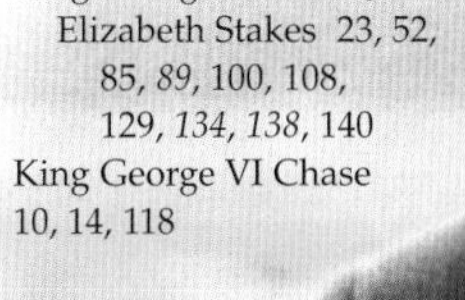

Acknowledgements

PUBLISHERS' ACKNOWLEDGEMENTS

The publishers would like to thank:

- Julian Muscat for his research in relation to the text.
- Seán Magee for his invaluable contribution to checking facts and writing captions.
- Sara Waterson for her enthusiastic and meticulous picture research.

PHOTO CREDITS

The author, publishers and picture researcher would like to thank all those who kindly provided photos and advice at the busiest time of the racing year: in Lambourn, David Arbuthnot, Peter Walwyn, Charlie Brooks, Stan Moore, and especially Mrs Diana Winter and her daughters Jo and Denise; in Newmarket, Hilary Bracegirdle at the National Horseracing Museum; in Ireland, Jacqueline and Vincent O'Brien and their staff, Michael Clower, Guy Williams, and Eugene Donovan; and in France, Mme Criquette Head-Maarek.

- **Express Newspapers** have kindly allowed us to reproduce the following cuttings: 9 btm, 11 btm, 29 btm, 30, 46 top lt & rt, 48 btm, 53, 80, 81, 85, 88, 102 btm, 123.
- **APRH /Bertrand, Chantilly**: 76 top, 93, 96 btm, 97, 98, 103 btm, 109, 110 top & both inserts, 111, 120, 121, 122 top.
- **Associated Newspapers**: 77 (*Evening Standard*).
- **Australian Racing Museum and Hall of Fame**: 51
- **Ballydoyle Archives**: 82 top (Healy Racing Photos), 82 btm (photo Caroline Norris), 84 top (photo Gerry Cranham), 92 top (photo Ruth Rogers), 92 btm (photo J Cashman), 94 btm, 95 (Healy Racing Photos)
- **EMPICS**: 6-7, 8 top, 11 top, 12-13, 15 top, 49, 54 btm, 56, 57, 60, 71 top, 86 top, 87 centre, 89 top, 89 btm, 104, 107, 108 btm, 114 btm, 117126 centre, 132 btm, 139 top.
- **Getty Images**: 7 top, 14 btm, 15 top, 16, 17 top, 17 btm, 19, 23, 29, 31, 36, 48, 53 top, 54 top, 58, 67, 68, 73, 74 btm, 131 centre, 141 top, 147, 148.
- **MGN Syndication**: 8 btm, 12 top, 14, 16 top, 16 centre, 17 btm, 20, 22 top & btm, 32, 35, 36, 39 top, 47 top rt, 50 btm, 50 top, 52, 55, 84 btm lt & rt, 86 btm, 87 top & btm, 90 top & btm, 91 top, 91 btm, 94 top, 96, 99, 100 top & btm, 102 top, 103, 108, 126 top, 126 btm, 128, 130 top, 130 btm, 131 top & btm, 132 top, 133, 134, 135, 136 top, 136 btm, 137, 139 top, 142, 143.
- **National Horseracing Museum, Newmarket**: 15 btm.
- **Guy St John Williams, Racing Historian**: 40 top & btm, 41 top, 42 all, 43 btm, 44 top, 44 centre (photo Caroline Norris), 44 btm (photo J Cashman), 45 top, 45 btm (photo J Cashman), 47 top lt.
- **Mrs Diana Winter and Denise and Jo Winter**: 13, 112 top & btm, 113 btm, 114, 115, 118 (Rex Coleman), 122 btm (Recoupé).
- **Author's collection**: The following photos have been reproduced from the author's archives; every effort has been made to find and to credit the copyright holder and we apologise for any omissions: 2, 5, 23, 24, 27, 29 top, 34, 39 btm, 46 btm, 47 btm, 59 (Photo Alan Raymond), 61 (photo Alan Raymond), 62 top (photo Jeffrey Gilbey), 62 btm (photo Ken Geffin), 66 (photo Alec Russell), 69 (photo Planar Press), 70, 71 btm (photo Rough & Co), 72 (photo Rough & Co), 74 top, 75, 76 btm, 78 (photo RPS Thirsk), 79 (photo RPS Thirsk), 81 btm (photo Alan Wright for Haydock Park), 83, 101 (Tony Leonard Incorporated), 105, 106, 124, 125 top, 125 btm (Chepstow Racecourse), 127, 129, 139 btm (from the collection of RJ McCreery) 140 (photo Rosenthiel Fine Art), 141 btm, 144, 145 (Provincial Press), 146, 149 (Wallis Photos, Doncaster), 150-151, 153 (Gerry Cranham), 154, 155.

THE MARTELL GRAND NATIONAL STEEPLE CHASE (HANDICAP) (CLASS
GARRISON SAVANNAH
COOL GROUND
TINRYLAND
32 Mark Perrett
24 Warren Marston
29 Paul Holley 3rd
IRISH DERBY 1½ m
Going "Good"
£120,000; £60,000; £24,000; £18,000; £12,000;
APPEALING BUBBLES
BOLOARDO
CONTESTED BID
DIVE FOR COVER
Dr DEVIOUS
EZZOUD
LANDOWNER
MARIGNAN
MINING TYCOON
ORMSBY
St JOVITE
Rises 150' in 1st mile
3.35 THE 200th DERBY STAKES
£100,000 added to stakes
w. £119,109 Second: £48,696 Third £23,719; Fourth £10,907
Penalty value £153,980
1 - ACCOMPLICE (USA) (R.E. SANGSTER)
2 - CHETINKAYA (PALL MALL)
3 - CRACAVAL
4 - DICKENS HILL
5 - ELA - MANA - MOU
6 - HALYUDH (USA)
7 - HARDGREEN (USA)
8 - LAKE CITY (USA)
9 - LASKA FLOKO
11 - LEODEGRANCE (USA)
12 - LYPHARD'S WISH (FR)
13 - MAN OF VISION
14 - MILFORD (H.M. The QUEEN)
15 - MORVETTA
16 - NEW BERRY
17 - NINISKI (USA) (LADY BEAVERBROOK)
18 - NOELINO
19 - NORTHERN BABY (CAN)
20 - SARACEN PRINCE
22 - SON OF LOVE (FR) (M. ALEXIS ROLLAND)
23 - TAP ON WOOD (A. SHEAD)
24 - TROY (SIR M SOBELL)
25 - TWO OF DIAMONDS (A SHEAD)